Terence de Vere White is [...]
Academy of Letters and [...] Royal Society
of Literature. The youngest graduate of his
generation in Trinity College, Dublin, he left the law
in 1961 to become Literary Editor of the *Irish Times*.
In Ireland he was a member of the Arts Council,
Trustee of the National Library, and a director of the
Gate Theatre. He is Vice-Chairman of the National
Gallery of Ireland. He lives in London and is married
to the biographer and critic Victoria Glendinning. He
has written twenty-six books including thirteen
novels.

Kevin O'Higgins, the only biography of an
outstanding Irish figure, was prepared with the help
of the stateman's widow and his family and
colleagues. Sources included the diaries of Patrick
Hogan, Minister for Agriculture in the Free State
government, and probably O'Higgins best friend;
Lord Baldwin who was Prime Minister in Britain
when the Boundary Settlement was negotiated in
1925; Leopold Amery, whose notes are in the
appendix; and the widow and son of Lord Birkenhead.

'Answers the requirements of the perfect biography'

– *Harold Nicholson*

TERENCE DE VERE WHITE

KEVIN O'HIGGINS

ANVIL BOOKS

Published in 1986 by Anvil Books Limited
90 Lower Baggot Street, Dublin 2

First published in 1948 by Methuen, London
Paperback edition Anvil Books 1966

ISBN 0 947962 11 5

Printed in Great Britain by
Richard Clay, Bungay, Suffolk

TO HIS WIDOW AND CHILDREN

We thought this age of violence had found
One man whose will had wrought a nation's peace,
And given to men that passion he had crowned
With all the fearless intellect of Greece.

Did we forget that Athens had not room,
Even under Pericles, for those who best
Had loved her, that we thought, short of the tomb,
A mind like his could rest?

R. N. D. WILSON

A figure from the antique cast in bronze

WINSTON CHURCHILL

PREFACE

"WHEN the Historian of this troubled reign turns to Ireland, his task becomes peculiarly difficult and delicate. His steps—to borrow a fine image used on a similar occasion by a Roman poet —are on the thin crust of ashes beneath which the lava is still flowing."

Macaulay wrote that passage with reference to the reign of James the Second; it is equally appropriate to the task which confronts a biographer of Kevin O'Higgins; a task which some have warned me is now prematurely attempted. It does not seem so to me.

Four of the colleagues of Kevin O'Higgins have died since his murder: Patrick Hogan, who was admirably equipped to write the life of his friend, in 1936, Eoin MacNeill, Desmond Fitz Gerald and John Marcus O'Sullivan while this book was in preparation. It seems a pity, instead of collecting material from contemporaries, to leave the historian of the future only documents from which to recreate the dead. In any event, I ignored the warning of the wise and embarked on the task of writing the life of the man who seems to many outstanding among those who have taken part in the public life of Ireland since the creation of the Irish Free State.

I have been particularly fortunate in the assistance I have been given by many of his colleagues, particularly by those who worked with him at the Imperial Conference of 1926. The late Desmond Fitz Gerald, although a sick man, was unstinting in his help, and his memory was phenomenal.

Of those alive, Professor James Hogan is probably best equipped to do what I have done; he was most generous in giving me his assistance. The first Lord Birkenhead was on friendly terms with O'Higgins, and his son has been good enough to supply me with many incidents which would otherwise have been unknown to me. Lord Baldwin wrote me his recollections of the Boundary Settlement. The last letter I received from him was written within a few weeks of his death.

I owe a special debt to Mr. L. S. Amery, who read the chapters of the book which came within his own personal knowledge, and gave me the benefit of his expert advice, and to Miss MacDermott, who voluntarily undertook the dull task of typing my manuscript.

Above all, I must thank the family of Kevin O'Higgins, who made my task very easy. They gave me all the information I asked for, and never embarrassed me with suggestions as to how I should use it.

To avoid confusion, I have called Kevin O'Higgins by that name throughout, although in the early part of his life he was known as Higgins. I have also used no prefixes to proper names. They look incongruous before the dead. I intend no disrespect to the living. *Mister* does not belong in Heaven or in history.

In all, I must have talked with, or had letters from, over forty people who knew O'Higgins at school or university, in time of revolution, or as a Cabinet Minister. Some were his ministerial colleagues, some are now civil servants ; many spoke to me on the clear understanding that in doing so they would not be involved in controversy. May they and others who helped me, and whose help I do not acknowledge here, believe that I am not insensible of my debt to them.

Instead of footnotes, I have numerals in each chapter : these correspond to notes and a bibliography at the end of the book.

Senator George O'Brien very kindly read my proofs.

TERENCE DE VERE WHITE

ST. ALBANS, MONKSTOWN
November, 1946– May, 1948

CONTENTS

CHAPTER I

BACKGROUND

THE murder of Kevin O'Higgins is still, after twenty years,
unsolved, and no one has ever been brought to justice for his
killing. It may be that some day the truth will be disclosed, for
there must be many who know it. He was not shot dead that
Sunday morning in any chance encounter, for the men who met
him unarmed and alone, and who poured their bullets into his
body, had carefully planned their crime. His murder was not
inexplicable. He represented everything that evilly-disposed
people find inconvenient. A civil war breeds unnatural hatreds,
and when O'Higgins died, only four years had passed since the
Irish Civil War had ended. It had been put down with one
instance, at least, of horrifying severity, and the legendary strength
of O'Higgins attracted to him the principal share of hatred.

Even if the mystery of his death is cleared away, there remains
a question which can never be answered : what part would
O'Higgins have played in the life of Ireland had he lived ? There
was not, in the opinion of one writer, " room for a genius so
Napoleonic " in the Ireland of to-day. He was but thirty-five
years old. What were his true dimensions ? To arrive at a just
estimate of his worth, to explain the fierce hatred which he
inspired in some and the deep respect in so many others, is the
purpose of this book.

Kevin Christopher O'Higgins was the fourth son in a family
of sixteen children. His father, Thomas Higgins,* was a doctor in
Queen's County (now Leix), who had married Annie, daughter
of T. D. Sullivan, then Lord Mayor of Dublin. When Kevin
was born on the 7th June, 1892, his father was living at Stradbally,
a small town, in which he kept the dispensary as well as doing
private practice in the neighbourhood. It was not a large house.
When the pressure on its accommodation became alarming
with the steady increase in the number of the family Doctor
Higgins, to provide a supplementary method of supporting them,

*See introduction.

acquired a neighbouring farm with a hundred acres of land, on which stood a house which with care could be converted into a comfortable home. At first Woodlands was used as a summer residence, but after a few years the family gave up the house in town.

Kevin was remarkable in his family for the serenity of his disposition and his fortitude. Fourth in a line of brothers, he acted as a bulwark between his sisters and the teasing of the older boys. Between him and his sister, Kathleen, afterwards a nun, there grew a bond of affection which was lifelong. As children they went to the convent school together ; afterwards when he was at Clongowes he rarely let a week go by without sending her translations of the Greek texts which he was studying. In the grim days when Kevin was " on the run," this sister was at Rathfarnham in the suburbs of Dublin ; he never missed a Sunday visit to the convent, although he was always liable to capture by the Black and Tans.

The local schoolmaster said that Kevin had a head like Daniel O'Connell, and would be a great man some day ; when he met the brother and sister walking hand-in-hand to school, he would say, " Well, how's Daniel O'Connell ? "

O'Higgins did not achieve a reputation for gentleness as a public man. To his intimate friends and his family, gentleness was of his essence, as a child and as a man. Serenity marked the beginning as it graced the end of his life ; on one occasion a large dog, a family pet, picked up the cot in which he slept as a baby and carried it downstairs to the drawing-room, laying it at his mother's feet. He showed no alarm, uttered no cry and never stirred. On another occasion he was found, white with pain, a pony standing on his foot. " Don't excite, don't excite," he was repeating to himself, and he neither shed tears nor called for help. He was conscious of his large head, and when he was taken to the barber for the first time with his elder brothers, he inquired anxiously whether his mother would have to pay double for his hair cut.

At first his age cut him off from his brothers, but when he grew older he worked on the farm with them, went shooting and riding, and, like them, was reckless, self-reliant, argumentative and intensely loyal.

As soon as he became too old to remain at a convent school, he was sent to the Christian Brothers' School at Maryborough. He used to go in a pony trap, and, in later years, still shivered at the recollection of the early drive on winter mornings along that bleak road. Having spent a few years with the Christian Brothers, Kevin, like his elder brothers, was sent to Clongowes Wood, the Jesuit College in Co. Kildare. He made no particular impression at school (one contemporary could only recall untidy hair and a stocking that appeared always half-way up or half-way down), but he was given free access to the library, where he read avidly in French and English—a privilege which he remembered afterwards with gratitude. Without ever appearing to exert himself, he was always able to keep up with the class, but he appeared to have no competitive instinct. A natural irony, sometimes whimsical, sometimes sardonic, made him a more mature companion than the average boy of his age, but he was incorrigibly addicted to practical joking of a rather complicated kind. He learned how to take wax impressions of locks, from which, with the help of a fellow-student, now a respectable Dublin surgeon, he would manufacture keys, and with these the two boys would make their way into the sanctums of the priests.

His talents were for the classics and literature—mathematics he had no head for—and despite his rather easy-going approach to his work, he was awarded a medal in Greek. His career at Clongowes was cut short when he was fifteen, and he was sent instead to Knockbeg College in Co. Carlow, where from the first he was outstanding. He was the best classical student there, and in his final year he got the highest marks in English that had ever been attained by a pupil in the Senior Grade Intermediate Examinations, but mathematics were always his bane, and on this occasion he failed in geometry.

His ironic turn of speech not only gave him a supremacy over his companions, who found that in the use of repartee he always came off best, but it showed itself in his school essays, which had a spare and sophisticated style quite beyond his years. Vigorous and strong, he managed to get a place on the school teams, but this tall, rather heavily-built boy, walking with a stoop and a somewhat waddling gait, for which he was nicknamed " The Duck," was obviously not an athlete. At home in holiday time he went shooting with his elder brothers, or worked with the men on the farm. He was essentially a country boy ; the land had for him always an almost emotional significance. " A man is only half a man," he would say, " if he has never lived or worked on a farm."

To the surprise of his family, at the age of fifteen, Kevin announced his intention of going to Maynooth and becoming a priest. His companions at school had not noticed any indications of a religious vocation ; he had looked for friends among the "characters" rather than the pious ; and his ironical, sometimes biting, tongue was not suggestive of a deeply spiritual nature. But he was reserved and sometimes gloomy—"Like a Rembrandt portrait, all shadows and depth," so one friend has described him —and it was not in keeping with his character to make any display of feeling or to give his confidence easily. That again was partly the result of belonging to a large family living in a quiet part of the country. Brothers do not as a rule give themselves away to one another.

Maynooth is attached to the National University of Ireland, and O'Higgins began immediately to read for his degree, passing the first examination with first-class honours in English and French, in Latin, Greek and Logic. His literary style was so outstanding that his English teacher, more than thirty years afterwards, can still recall the relief it was to encounter his essays among the compositions of his college contemporaries. It was his style, "in the direct line of Burke," that attracted Yeats to him in after-years.

The change in Kevin's plan of life was not accompanied by any outward change. There was an old priest at the College who acted as spiritual director to the students. He was a simple, saintly character, who in all his lectures laid stress on the importance of meditation in the spiritual life. "Ordination makes the priest, but meditation make the good priest" was a favourite saying of his and one which his pupils came to know very well. It was the practice at Maynooth for students who wanted to sell books to advertise the fact on the notice board. One day a notice appeared in the following terms :—

NOTICE
"Ordination makes the priest
Meditation makes the good priest."
Two Meditation Books for Sale,

K. C. HIGGINS

At this time there was a very strict ban on smoking at Maynooth ; the prohibition applied to the staff as well as to the pupils. This rule was insisted upon by the late Cardinal Logue, who brooked no argument, as they discovered who approached him to relax the rule when in a snuff-stained cassock he visited the College. O'Higgins would not observe the ban ; he was warned but with no effect. The practice of the College was to issue two warnings or " cats," as they were called, to an offender before the third, which meant dismissal One evening O'Higgins was standing with other students in a blue haze of tobacco smoke behind a garden hedge when they were caught by a priest who was passing by. O'Higgins, having had his *caveats*, knew that he was almost certain to be expelled.

It is possible that for so trivial an offence he would not have been, had he undertaken to give up smoking ; but he protested that the habit was inveterate and could not be overcome. Meanwhile, the results of the examination had come in and his English Professor hurried off to find and congratulate him. They met on the terrace as O'Higgins was returning from an interview with the President, who had asked him to leave the College.

The Professor, who used to read O'Higgins' essay on " Lady Macbeth " to all his classes as a model of good writing, came to the rescue of his pupil. When the Bishops assembled in Maynooth he invited the Bishop who had sponsored O'Higgins to his room and placed his examination papers in his hands. Was such a student to be lost to the priesthood for so trivial an offence as smoking cigarettes ? The Bishop admitted that it would be a pity, and agreed to let him come to the seminary at Carlow as an external student for London University.

In the autumn of 1911 Kevin O'Higgins entered his sixth educational establishment. The smoking rule applied to Carlow, but two friendly priests told him when he wanted to smoke he could come to their rooms and do it there so as not to give bad example to other students.

At Carlow he studied very little ; an appearance of concentrated industry was explained by the fact that under the table-cloth was an improvised draught-board which came into use as soon as the supervisor of studies had passed by. And when he went to London to sit for his first examination at the University, he failed to wake up in time for the first paper, and returned ingloriously.

The College published an annual magazine to which O'Higgins made some contributions ; in one number appeared a paper which he had read at a debating society, and it was probably more symptomatic of his state of mind than he realized himself. He had, he said, decided to write upon " NOTHING," because it was the only subject about which he knew something. "My subject, gentlemen, is venerable were it only because of its advanced age ; nothing existed before the creation of the world ; it is inspiring and ennobling, for how often have we heard the statement ' Nothing is absolute perfection ' ? And it is a subject which I am qualified to discuss and you to comprehend, for we are often told that we can have here below a perfect knowledge of Nothing. For some time past I have thought seriously of Nothing, worked hard at Nothing, have read Nothing. Therefore, who will deny that I am qualified to discussing Nothing intelligently and intelligibly ? The value of Nothing being so high, it is an important matter to know where it is found. Two gentlemen recently raced towards the North Pole and found Nothing there. Nothing is often found by gold-prospectors. Nothing is often in the pockets of individuals and in the heads of politicians. Nothing is practically ubiquitous." " In conclusion," says the report, " Mr. Higgins put in an eloquent plea for those misunderstood philosophers who do Nothing, think of Nothing, and say Nothing, because he who does Nothing does no wrong ; he who thinks of Nothing planneth no evil, and he who says Nothing offends not with his tongue."

The smoking difficulty had been solved by the help of friends on the College staff, but O'Higgins had not conquered his weakness for burglarious jokes. There was an attractive cake which was a standing dish for the staff, but which the students were not invited to share ; more than once, passing the door of the priests' refectory, he removed one from the side-board. Suspicions were aroused, and the Deans lay in wait. One day, when O'Higgins had helped himself, he heard footsteps on the stairs behind him as he ran to his room carrying the evidence of his crime. Over his doorway there was a deep recess or platform, and as he ran in he hurled the cake on to this ledge. There was a dreadful moment of suspense for the culprit. If the cake made its journey, all was well ; if it fell . . . When the Deans rushed breathless into the room they found O'Higgins sitting quietly at his desk. "Where is the cake ? " they demanded, sniffing hard. "The cake ? " O'Higgins inquired with well-feigned surprise. "The cake ? " A thorough search of the room revealed nothing, and at last, still sniffing suspiciously, the priests left the room.

This narrow escape did not serve as a warning, and on another occasion O'Higgins suggested to some of his friends that they should break into the rooms of the President of the College and have a party at his expense. Keys were counterfeited ; and one night when he was out, his room was entered and his cupboards searched for whiskey and cigars. With counterfeited nonchalance the burglars sat round the table, each anxious to end the joke before it was too late, each afraid to be the first to show his fear. O'Higgins, with his Maynooth record, was well aware that discovery would be fatal for him, but he shared the disinclination to be the first to leave. Instead, he picked out one who looked to him to be the most apprehensive of his companions, and, sitting down beside him, began to play upon his fears. For himself, he explained, it did not matter ; he was bound to be expelled, but what a pity for anyone who had a blameless past. When he saw that he made the impression desired, he passed on to another. By degrees this undermining of morale had the desired effect. One by one the roysterers felt the first flush of excitement wear away, and their hearts went cold at the thought of the reckoning on the morrow. Suddenly footsteps were heard, and O'Higgins told his companions to make off. He stayed himself to confront the President, apoplectic with rage, who ordered him to leave the college. It was the last day of term, and the President never told anyone of this escapade or that he had expelled O'Higgins.

This was not merely an expulsion from school ; it meant an end to his prospects of becoming a priest. What his state of mind was, one can only surmise ; a contemporary at Carlow held the view that he was unhappy there, disliked the atmosphere of a seminary, and had begun to doubt his vocation for the priesthood. To his English Professor at Maynooth he had affirmed that his dearest wish was to become a priest. That seemed out of the question now, but the Jesuits, thinking that their Society might suit his temperament, invited him to enter their Order. He refused the offer. He had come to the conclusion that he had no vocation for the priesthood.

Father and son had to encounter one another, one feeling indignant, the other embarrassed. " What will I do with you ? " said the doctor. " You are only fit for the Canadian police." In those days, Canada was still regarded as an asylum for the unsuccessful. An alternative to Canada presented itself when Maurice Healy, whose celebrated brother, Tim, had married a sister of Mrs. Higgins, and who had a flourishing practice as a solicitor in Cork, offered to take Kevin as an apprentice. But there is little doubt that the prospect of an attorney's office never had any fascination for O'Higgins : in later life he was wont to refer to lawyers in somewhat irreverent language. Once in the Dáil, he remarked : " Deputy Gavan Duffy is a lawyer. I only escaped that fate myself by the intervention of the police," and on other occasions he made the same jest in almost identical words. When the question of appointing the first District Justices was being considered during the Civil War, he observed, " Solicitors and barristers are, as a class, a nervous body unsuited to the robust times in which we live." [1]

Before entering the Cork office, Kevin decided to resume his Arts course at University College, Dublin, His eldest brother, Jack, had passed first out of the Medical School in Trinity after a brilliant career ; Tom, the second, was in the College of Surgeons, and now Kevin entered University College. A fellow-student from Clongowes days, with whom he shared lodgings at this time, was shocked to find what a change had come over him since his schooldays. The humour and whimsicality which tempered his irony had gone, and he had become gloomy and sardonic. For hours on end he used to sit staring out of the window of his lodgings. He did very little work, dressed untidily, and seemed to have lost all zest for life. That was the impression he made on one observer.

Lennox Robinson, in his *Life* of Bryan Cooper, refers to him as " a dissipated student." Other contemporaries recall the impression that his speeches at the College Debating Society made on the hearers. He was, according to Professor James Hogan, considered one of the wittiest speakers in the Society, and his appearance was always greeted with applause. Professor Tierney, now President of University College, has vivid recollections of O'Higgins as a speaker. And yet the brilliant student of Maynooth days, who had taken First Class Honours in five subjects, should have done better than a Pass B.A., even though it was in the Honours grade and in the Law School in which his heart never was.

The truth is that O'Higgins, depressed by his seminarial experiences, and realizing that he had misled himself over his priestly vocation, felt that the life of a law student did not satisfy his imagination. He was indifferent to small success. Without material ambition, and having given up a career which would have been devoted to the service of God, he did not find law lectures a satisfactory alternative. He was bored by the life in the

University and found it callow. He was bored by the competitive enthusiasm of his fellow-students and their anxieties about their careers. He was not looking forward to a future of dusty documents or wrangles over property. A solicitor's life was not his idea of a full one ; and so instead of preparing for it, he preferred to go to Mooney's pub in Harry Street where the talk was sometimes good, where racing was discussed with knowledge and enthusiasm, and politics were washed down by porter. With his coat wrapped round him, he sat on the high stool, sometimes from the hour of opening until the close at night. " The R.M." he was called. He was always prone to fits of gloomy silence, but when these moods passed, he talked away on politics, literature or philosophy to anyone who cared to listen. Sometimes in the summer, he went on circuit and took up his duties at the " Dropping Well Inn," which has a verandah overhanging the river Dodder at Milltown. When supplies ran out, he took pieces of tea-paper and wrote verses or articles on them. These a friend would take to the *Independent* newspaper and bicycle back with ten shillings and sometimes a few guineas, which, with stout at twopence a pint, solved the immediate difficulty. Mooney's he described as the best university. " Every man ought to drink his quota " was a favourite saying of his. A theory which he liked to propound was that there is a certain quantity of drink which every man ought to take. Most men spread it out over their lifetime. He got through his in a few years. " Dissipation " is a word that conjures up more than porter, but that is all it meant in O'Higgins's case. " I was bored," he said ; " drink never got me. I was marking time : I did not know for what."

He disliked any form of sham to such an extent that he could make no pretence, and he was merciless with himself as he would have been with another. With a tongue sharp rather than quick, he had a great capacity for phrase-making, and indulged it sometimes at the expense of kindness. Unhappy are the phrase-makers, they earn a reputation for malice in a second while a man with a dull tongue can spend a lifetime, like woodworm in a rafter, eating away the reputation of his neighbours without anyone realizing what destruction is in progress.

There was at Woodlands a man of a type which is not uncommon. He is to be met with in the country and in city offices ; taking up work as a boy, from laziness rather than lack of ability, he maintains the status of a boy long after he has qualified to be a grandfather, thereby missing some of the rewards of age by avoiding all the responsibilities. The "boy" at Woodlands had been christened "Mother's little messenger-boy" by reason of the fact that whenever his value to the establishment was questioned, his invariable reply was, "You can't dismiss me. I'm the mistress's little messenger-boy." Once when Kevin was at home he encountered "the boy" arriving to work when the sun was at the zenith. "That *was* a nice day," said Kevin. "*Was* a nice day, Mister. Now 'tis you have the bither tongue, and be Gor you'll swing for it yet."

Another difficulty for the phrase-maker is this : he can only be himself among his friends or his peers ; at the approach of a fool, Dr. Johnson exclaimed : "Now we will have to be serious." The dullard, the pedant, the crank and the humbug recognized in Kevin O'Higgins their natural enemy.

He had always been silent rather than communicative, having no small talk. He only dropped his reserve for intimate friends, or in certain expansive moods when the conversation, or the person he was talking to, interested him, but with those in his confidence he had no reserve and delighted to open out his full mind to them. If anything pleased him, a thought or something he had read, he could not wait until he had communicated the experience. But even to his family, whom he always deeply loved, he gave no indication of his state of mind at this period. Later, writing to his future wife, on one of the few occasions that he discussed himself, he confessed, "I am naturally taciturn and inclined to live a good deal within my shell. This natural bent was aggravated by the conditions of my youth, country surroundings and the consequent social isolation, solitude in the fields, thinking all the time to myself, and finding neither the need nor the opportunity of giving out much. Then, I suppose, two years under a pretty constant rule of silence may be taken as another factor in the case. Net result—a brooding old ruffian with no small change of conversation such as characterizes the dwellers in town. A character in literature I think I understand is Charles Lamb."

His kind of life at this time kept him out of the highest company, if not necessarily the best, and it is no wonder that some of the most earnest of his student contemporaries were not aware of his existence. But it would be wrong to assume that none of his time was given to study ; during this period he read avidly anything he could find on the history and politics of his country.

He had still a weakness for practical jokes. In Noblett's, the sweet shop at the top of Grafton Street, there were—there may still be—enormous glass cylinders full of sweets. One day, O'Higgins went into the shop and pointing at a box of chocolates on the top shelf, asked the assistant to get it down. When she climbed on a ladder to do so, he grasped two of the glass pillars, one under each arm, and ran down the street with the shop-girl pursuing him, to the amazement of the passing crowd, for it was the busiest time of the day. There were other adventures with tram-drivers and policemen. It was clear that life in seminaries had not damped his spirits. There was then as always a curious contradiction in his make-up ; his writing or speeches, whether serious or light, were always mature and developed ; he never had ideas that were vague, wild or anarchic, but his behaviour often suggested childishness or irresponsibility. Kevin was at first more countrified in manner and appearance than his eldest brother, Jack, whose social instincts, according to his father, were over-developed. But all the brothers had in common, courage and independence of mind to the point of recklessness. These are qualities which are bred in the bone and cannot be instilled, but they can be developed or stunted ; no parents could have been less repressive to their children than Doctor Higgins and his wife. There was a strongly religious atmosphere in the home without any taint of bigotry, and a firm nationalism was the political creed of the family. T. D. Sullivan, Kevin's grandfather, had been a prominent figure in the political life of the country as editor of *The Nation*, and later as a member of the Irish Party in the House of Commons. Without taking so prominent a part in politics as his brother, Alexander, who in his short Parliamentary career proved himself to be one of the ablest debaters at Westminster, T. D. Sullivan had perhaps won a warmer place in the public affection by his song, "God Save Ireland," composed at the time of the trial of the "Manchester Martyrs," which became for practical purposes the anthem of suppressed Irish nationalism. Doctor Higgins was an admirer of Tim Healy, who, some time after the death of Parnell, cut himself adrift from the Irish Party in the House of Commons. With this Sullivan-Healy background, it was but to be expected that the Higgins children should be brought up politically-conscious. They learnt all the patriotic ballads by heart, and when the family was gathered together, these were the songs they sang. It was a Nationalist house but not a revolutionary one. The Sullivans had never countenanced violence, and Alexander Sullivan had aroused deep antipathy in Fenian circles by his alleged unmasking of an armed conspiracy in Cork so early as 1857.

Kevin O'Higgins, if interested in politics, showed no tendency to involve himself in any political activities. He was in Dublin in 1913 when the organization known as the Irish Volunteers was formed at a meeting in the Rotunda, but he did not, like his elder brother, Tom, enlist, although he was probably an onlooker at the inauguration of the corps.

In the North, Edward Carson, a Dublin man of Italian stock, formed the Ulster Volunteers to oppose by force the inclusion of Ulster in a self-governing Ireland : taking the hint, Eoin MacNeill, a northerner, at the instigation of the Irish Republican Brotherhood, organized the Volunteers in Dublin as a counter-blast. John Redmond was at that time the leader of the Irish Nationalists in Parliament ; he was suspicious of extremism, and endeavoured to swamp the Volunteers with his own supporters. When war came in 1914, Redmond offered unconditional support to the British Government, even agreeing that the Home Rule Bill, which had been entered on the Statute Book, should be suspended until the war was over.[2]

As a result the Volunteers split in two ; MacNeill headed the section who refused to regard the war as Ireland's quarrel ; Redmond those who made common cause with England.

Kevin O'Higgins was in the middle of his University course when war broke out in August, 1914. Many Nationalists, Tom Kettle for one, joined the army at once. But Kettle was a poet with European sympathies ; there were others who regarded the Carson gun-running in the North of Ireland in the previous year, to resist the Home Rule Bill, as a deliberate attack on the Irish nation, connived at by the British Government and the military authorities. These Nationalists believed that there was a more real danger to their own country from certain elements in England than from Germany. They were convinced that the mutiny of the British Army at the Curragh, at the prospect of having to " march against the North," did not come as an unpleasant surprise to the harder-crusted Tories or the military authorities in London. The diaries of Sir Henry Wilson reveal this rather plainly. The fact that Carson could defy the Government unpunished, and the postponement of the Home Rule Bill in 1914, indicated the prevailing wind in British politics, and some Irishmen who were quite prepared to die in battle, as they afterwards proved, preferred to join the Irish Volunteers under Eoin MacNeill than to enlist in Kitchener's Army. "We saw," said O'Higgins, "the law flouted openly, and the Government, with a Parliamentary majority, cowering before the challenge. We saw arms imported into the North of Ireland, and the whole administration held up, so that the measure could never become operative law. Those who had watched the beginning of that situation with interest, with tense interest, were losing, day by day, their faith in the efficacy of constitutional action, and, day by day, a lesson was being burned into their brain by British statesmen, by the Conservative Party of Great Britain and their adherents in Ireland, that direct action was the winning card."[3]

Among the Volunteers there were, no doubt, some who pretended that their principles kept them from going to France when in fact they had decided that the chances of an early death were greater there than in Dublin. There have always been such men everywhere. The eldest of the Higgins family was Surgeon-Commander on Beatty's flagship ; Tom, the second, had joined the Irish Volunteers. He was from early youth an enthusiastic Nationalist. Michael went to Flanders to die. Kevin took the view that the war was not one in which an Irish Nationalist should take part. Although he did not join the Volunteers at their inception, his political attitude at the time can be gathered from the fact that he and another student were arrested for tearing down recruiting posters. This was not an act of hooliganism. He had thought out his position very carefully. His natural impulse was, like his brothers and cousins, to go to the war, but the more he thought about the matter the more he was convinced that England was not at war for Belgium, but for her own self-preservation. He was not at all convinced that England's success would benefit Ireland, or that the fight to save small nations shewed any change of heart on England's part towards the small nation at her doorstep. He argued the matter out with his brother, Michael, who had answered Redmond's call for volunteers ; he was satisfied that England, not Germany, was Ireland's immediate problem. He was impressed by the difference between the attitude adopted by the British towards the gun-running at Larne by Carson's henchmen, who were unopposed, and towards that at Howth by the Volunteers, which was met by armed resistance and involved bloodshed. The shelving of the Home Rule Bill convinced him that he was right in his attitude.

Some time in those early years of the first world war he was sitting in a railway carriage opposite a young soldier returning to the front, and, looking at him, going with apparent unconcern to death, O'Higgins reflected on his own position. It was all very well to refuse to fight in England's war, it was another thing to stay in safety while so many of one's countrymen were dead or about to die. He could not retain his self-respect by clinging to so convenient a principle. It was not enough to keep out of the war ; one were better in it unless there was higher employment. It was not enough to refuse to serve the purposes of the British Empire ; one must serve one's own country. A neutral attitude was untenable for a man.

There were other young men with the same thought. There were older men who had been planning to do something for Ireland for years and to whom the war seemed to provide the opportunity predicated in the revolutionists' handbook. When O'Higgins returned to Dublin, he joined the Volunteers.

CHAPTER II

THE VOLUNTEER

THE Irish Republican Brotherhood was a secret society which originated in America between the unsuccessful revolt led by Smith O'Brien in 1848 and the Fenian [1] outbreak of 1867. Between those years, James Stephens, who had been wounded in the first revolt and escaped to America, returned to Ireland and swore in members to this oath-bound secret society. The Fenians were arrested, imprisoned and dispersed, but the I.R.B. continued, if not to grow, at least to live. It was probably a small group, and therefore more intense than a popular and inevitably looser organization. To constitutional Nationalists—and these were the great majority—the I.R.B. was repugnant. It was in order to keep out revolutionary influence that Redmond had attempted to fill the command of the Volunteers with his followers. MacNeill was not a member of the I.R.B., but the driving force of the Volunteers who seceded with him in 1914, when Redmond lent his support to the British, was the I.R.B. cell in their midst. More than probably, MacNeill was quite unaware of this. He was a learned and an upright man whose head was in the clouds. His failure as a leader was due to his inability to keep an ear to the ground.

The Irish Republican Brotherhood had, since the failure of the Fenian rebellion, awaited the opportunity of a war, in which England was engaged, to make another attempt. In 1914 such an opportunity arose. They were single-minded and sincere, brave and disinterested, but to those who did not share their fanatical enthusiasm, and who were not prepared to put the independence of Ireland above every other consideration, the very opportunity for which the I.R.B. were waiting seemed the most inappropriate time to strike at England. England's enemy was Ireland's ally to the extremists ; to most, Germany was the common enemy and a rebellion during the war was a stab in the back to England.

Many years before, a public funeral had kindled the flames of revolution, when the body of Terence Bellew MacManus, a survivor of '48, was brought back to Dublin from San Francisco. So grave was the apprehension of a rising then that Doctor, afterwards Cardinal, Cullen, the Archbishop of Dublin, refused to allow any lying-in-state or religious ceremony in the churches in his diocese. Despite ecclesiastical disapproval, the procession that November day in 1861, and the enthusiasm it evoked, was the launching of Fenianism as a national movement.

In 1915 an almost identical set of circumstances arose ; for some years the I.R.B. had been planning a revolt. Their spokesman was Patrick Pearse, the son of an English monument maker, who had settled in Dublin and married an Irish woman. Pearse was well known in the Gaelic movement, but he had no wide celebrity in the country. Even the Volunteers, who were formed on a broad basis in comparison with the secret society in their midst, were not generally supported by the people. Beaslai, the biographer of Michael Collins, described in his book how "a parade of Dublin Volunteers in Limerick on Whit Monday, 1915, was attacked by a howling mob. In other places Volunteers were hooted, jeered at, called ' pro-Germans.' However, the persecutions of the English authorities helped to bring a certain amount of sympathy to their side." Then came the death of O'Donovan Rossa in America and the decision to bring his body to Dublin and bury him in Glasnevin Cemetery. Rossa, or Jeremiah O'Donovan as he was then known, one of the first Irishmen to come under the influence of Stephens, had been sentenced to penal servitude in 1858 for his part in the " Phoenix Conspiracy " in Co. Cork, but released on giving security for his good behaviour. Seven years later he was arrested in connection with the Fenian plot and sentenced to penal servitude for life.

This grim sentence was not served in full, but throughout his captivity Rossa made life difficult for his gaolers, and in retirement in America he became the type of fiery patriotism. His appearance was magnificent and patriarchal, well fitting the part which he had now to play as the symbol of his country's unconquerable hostility to English domination. The streets were lined with people to see the funeral go by ; the coffin was followed by Redmond's supporters as well as by MacNeill's Volunteers.

At the graveside, Pearse spoke those words which were to the young men who heard them an incitement to revolt. It was the speech of a mystic, a man to whom the resurrection of a free Gaelic

Ireland was a task of the deepest religious significance, a man who had dedicated himself to the idea of martyrdom. Of the men of the Irish National Revival, Pearse is by far the most interesting. His English blood gave him the enthusiasm of a convert ; for his father had been bewitched by Ireland, and became a Catholic and a zealous separatist. Patrick Pearse was a poet, but a poet in action. He lived his dreams and died in the way he had chosen. But I anticipate. His speech at the graveside has often been written down ; it was the inspiration of the rising which has come to be known as " Easter Week." After a high tribute to Rossa, he ended his speech with the words : " We pledge to Ireland our life, and we pledge to English rule in Ireland our hate. This is a place of peace, sacred to the dead, where men should speak with all charity and with all restraint : but I hold it a Christian thing, as O'Donovan Rossa did, to hate evil, to hate untruth, to hate oppression, and hating them, to strive to overthrow them. Our foes are strong and wise and wary : but strong and wise and wary as they are, they cannot undo the miracles of God, who ripens in the hearts of young men the seeds sown by the young men of a former genera-tion. And the seeds sown by the young men of '65 and '67 are coming to their miraculous ripening to-day.

" Rulers and defenders of realms had need to be wary if they would guard against such processes. Life springs from death, and from the graves of patriot men and women spring living nations. The defenders of this realm have worked well in secret and in the open. They think that they have pacified Ireland. They think that they have purchased half of us and intimidated the other half. They think that they have foreseen everything, think that they have provided against everything : but the fools, the fools, the fools !—they have left us our Fenian dead, and while Ireland holds these graves, Ireland unfree shall never be at peace."

Among those who felt their pulse quicken as these lines were declaimed by Pearse, in his strong, solemn voice, was Kevin O'Higgins. He, like many others, heard the words as a call to service. Henceforth, life was a preparation for a struggle and, if necessary, a sacrifice. The enthusiasm which Pearse aroused in these young breasts may have been dangerous, ill-advised, wrong even ; but if it was, it was nobly wrong. Sincerity is irresistible, and no one can prove his sincerity better than by dying for his beliefs.

This speech by Pearse was delivered in August, 1915. The

rising took place in the following Easter week. In the meantime, O'Higgins had joined the Volunteers. He was at home on holiday when news of the rising came to Stradbally ; he left immediately for Dublin, but had only reached Athy when his progress was halted. Young men were not allowed to enter the Capital, and in a few days the whole affair was ended. It had been greeted with some derision and widespread anger. Help had been expected from Germany, and when news came to MacNeill that this had miscarried, he called off the projected rising. He was not in the full confidence of his lieutenants, who were I.R.B. men, and feeling this, perhaps, he took it on himself to publish a notice in the *Sunday Independent* of April 22nd, cancelling a meeting of Volunteers which had been arranged for Easter Sunday. As the rising was to take place that day, this, to the initiated, meant that it was proclaimed. At ten o'clock on Sunday night, Thomas MacDonagh, Commandant of the Dublin Brigade of the Volunteers, gave an order for mobilization. The Insurrection was going to take place without the Chief-of-Staff.

It was known by the men who made this decision that the German ship carrying 20,000 rifles, together with some machine-guns and ammunition, had been scuttled ; that Stack, the leader in Kerry, had been arrested ; that the plot was known, and that no help could come now from any source. They also knew that the announcement in that day's paper would seriously impair the chances of a successful mobilization, and they knew that the total strength of the organization was 3,000 in Dublin, 18,000 in the country. In the Capital they were also able to count on the Citizen Army numbering 200, and the Hibernian Rifles, numbering less than 50. With this knowledge they were prepared to throw down the gauntlet to the British Empire.

It needs no argument to prove that a victory in arms was never seriously expected. What, then, was the purpose of this apparently senseless rising ? It was the resolution of a very small group of men to lay down their lives in order to sow again the seeds of heroism in a country which had depended too long on the ineffective action of Parliamentary representatives.

The most able, and the man of clearest vision in the group, was James Connolly. He had a very definite aim which was at once national and international. He desired a Republic for Ireland, and a socialist Republic at that. He had no mystical desire to shed his own blood, and he had complained of Pearse's obsession with this theme, but he had come to the conclusion that an armed demonstration was essential to capture the attention of the world, and he was prepared, although a pacifist by inclination, to make that demonstration, if necessary, without the Volunteers, relying on the Citizen Army of 200. Pearse was the titular Commander-in-Chief of the Rebellion, but Connolly was the real director of operations.

The number of men who presented themselves on Easter Monday was 687. The others had acted on MacNeill's order of the previous day. Not many of the young men who reported that morning realized what was on foot, and it must have been a rude shock to unprepared minds to hear that they were ordered to seize the General Post Office and other buildings in the City. From the steps of the Post Office, Pearse read the proclamation of an Irish Republic. In all, not more than 1,200 men took part in the rising on the Irish side, and, with insignificant exceptions, the fighting was confined to Dublin City. The British had 6,000 soldiers in the city within three days when reinforcements were brought in from England. These were attacked as they marched into Dublin, and many were killed on Mount Street Bridge. It is said that the " Tommies " had no clear idea of where they were or what they had come for ; that they were shot down like rabbits, and this was one of the features of the rising which aroused most indignation in the minds of those who were opposed to it. It may well have been that some of the soldiers being Irish (one of the reinforcements to the garrison was a contingent of Dublin Fusiliers), it was regarded as wise policy not to let them know too much. The Curragh Mutiny was a refusal to march against the North. Perhaps, Irish soldiers might have been reluctant to march against Dublin.

In any event, the inevitable occurred, and Pearse surrendered on Saturday, April 29th. Fifteen men were executed for their part in the Rebellion. The executions were long drawn out ; Connolly had to be propped in a chair as he was too severely wounded to stand while the soldiers shot him. The intention of General Maxwell, who was in charge of the British Forces, was, no doubt, to strike the maximum terror into the hearts of the populace. He was not so good a psychologist as his opponents. " The insurrection, though it has failed, will leave a wonderful effect on the country," said Thomas Clarke. " We will die, but it will be a different Ireland after us."

Men like Arthur Griffith, who were bitterly opposed to the rising, now "longed for vengeance," and in a few days the mass of public opinion swung completely over to the "rebels." When General Maxwell wrote to the Bishop of Limerick, asking him to remove from the neighbourhood two priests who had engaged in the Volunteer movement, the Bishop, who was an old man, in his reply to the General, contrasted the fates of the Irish insurgents and the leaders of the Jameson Raid. "Personally," he wrote, "I regard your action with horror, and I believe that it has outraged the conscience of the country."

All the signatories of the Republican proclamation had been shot, and some 1,800 Volunteers and Sinn Feiners were deported to England. This was the second cardinal error. Here, in prison camps, they had excellent opportunities of reorganizing and making plans for the future, or selecting leaders and making friends with their colleagues in England, opportunities which would never have occurred under ordinary circumstances. Internment kept up the revolutionary spirit. Men who before 1916 regarded their membership of the Volunteers as a gesture, were now made aware of reality. They had then been civilians with guns. Now they felt they were soldiers.

It must not be forgotten that the Great War was now raging and at a most critical phase. The disturbance in Ireland was an embarrassment with which the British Government had no time to deal, and the best brains were fully occupied with the task of saving the life of England, let alone her Empire. Nevertheless, after 700 years, the British had clearly not developed the capacity for understanding or ruling the Irish.

For the time being, it seemed that Maxwell's purge had had the effect intended ; there was very little outward manifestation of a change in public feeling. Life, apparently, went on as before, and Kevin O'Higgins, like many other Volunteers, went on with his studies. He was now in Cork, attending law lectures at the University, and he threw himself into the life of the College. Even then the majority of the students' clubs were controlled by committees which showed no sympathy with militant nationalism, but the change that had come over the country soon revealed itself among the students. Politics began to play a dominating part, even in football clubs, and passions were aroused by the efforts of the more advanced party to gain control. There were many angry, noisy meetings. In these, O'Higgins played a prominent part. He championed the extremists, but his manner was noticeably calm, confident and unemotional. He easily gained an ascendancy over louder-voiced and redder-faced companions.

Meanwhile, plans were being made in secret to reorganize the Volunteers. MacNeill's countermanding order had taken some of the glamour from the name of that force, and, in sympathy with the Proclamation of 1916, the title Irish Republican Army, or I.R.A., came into fashion. It was never an official description.

In 1917, Kevin O'Higgins was Captain of the Stradbally Company in the Carlow Brigade, but imposing as this title sounds, it does not denote any active service, for the guerilla warfare had not yet broken out. Doctor Higgins did not approve of the Insurrection although he was a strong Nationalist, but, no doubt, the sons of the family were aware of Kevin's activities. Tom had been an enthusiastic Volunteer from the beginning, and Brian, a younger boy, joined the I.R.A. while still a schoolboy. He had been expelled from Clongowes as a result of an encounter with an old priest who met him sauntering along a garden path after hours. " Where have you been ? " the priest demanded. " At the Curragh Races," was the prompt and unequivocal reply. The reverend father had Brian expelled, not so much for going to the race-meeting as for the brazen way in which he admitted it.

Brian became a very active member of the I.R.A., and spent some time in prison, but Kevin afterwards referred to his own military career as flippantly as he did to his attempt to become a lawyer. He was, nevertheless, one of the active spirits in a somewhat uninspired neighbourhood. There is not a great deal to be said in praise of Queen's County, the land is poor, the country flat ; Huguenots and Quakers settled there, and their descendants still live in the towns, but it has produced few remarkable men.

O'Higgins found it very difficult to instil new political doctrines into bucolic heads until a national issue arose which needed very little exposition to stir the dullest imagination. Early in 1918 it was decided to impose conscription on Ireland. Men were badly needed to reinforce the depleted British Army, and owing to the stoppage of emigration to America, there were, as well as the 60,000 who had gone to France, thousands of young Irishmen who had declined the invitation to volunteer for war service. As we have seen, at the time of the rising, there were not much more than 20,000 Volunteers, and there were four or five times that number of young men in the country at the time. Those who had taken part in the Insurrection were, in Shaw's phrase, fighting with halters round their necks.   They were not cowards. It is not easy to be enthusiastic about the young men who did nothing, even though a keen political sense may well have justified them to themselves.

Many now joined the Volunteers, and Sinn Fein found itself in unison with the Irish Parliamentary Party, which it was destined within a few months to sweep out of existence.   A by-election was due to take place in Offaly, then King's County, and the Irish Party candidate retired in favour of Doctor McCartan, the representative of Sinn Fein. Kevin O'Higgins was a leading spirit in this election, and he spoke at several meetings. When Desmond Fitz Gerald, who had taken part in the rising, came down from headquarters in Dublin, it was arranged that he would speak at a place called Welsh Island, and Kevin O'Higgins was to support him on the platform. Fitz Gerald was treated as an elder states-man, although he was not more than a year or two older than O'Higgins.   Fitz Gerald had to press O'Higgins to speak ; he was extremely diffident, and it was only after a certain amount of encouragement that he could be persuaded to take part in the meeting. When he did so he completely belied the impression of youthful inexperience which he had created by making a mature and brilliant speech, quite out of the common run. It was at this election that he first won a political reputation, but his progress was greatly accelerated by another circumstance.

The critical state of the war may have accounted for the fact that the British Government completely lost its head in Ireland in 1918. People were clapped into jail on the slightest pretext, and a German plot was manufactured as an excuse for arresting all the prominent Sinn Feiners. A single German was discovered on the west coast of Ireland, and this was taken to be evidence of a widespread conspiracy between the Sinn Fein Party and the German Government.

O'Higgins was arrested and charged with the offence that " he did unlawfully assemble and while so assembled did disturb the peace by inciting those present to obstruct the officers of the law." Speaking at Garryhinch cross-roads, he was supposed, among other inflammatory statements, to have declared : " To Hell with England ; to Hell with its rotten Empire," and to have advised the crowd to fight ; if they had no rifles, with a fork, spear, scythe or poker. He was arrested in the yard of the Dublin

Four Courts coming away from a law lecture. After a week in Mountjoy Prison, with one Lynch who was supposed to have offended on the same occasion, he was brought with his companion, both handcuffed, in a heavily-guarded train to Tullamore for trial. He defended himself vigorously,[2] and was unsparing of the two policemen who were State witnesses, inquiring of the sergeant who gave evidence " whether he had ever committed perjury before ? " And when the sergeant admitted that he had not taken down the speech but had made " mental notes," O'Higgins replied : " I suggest that you had a good deal of blank space for that purpose." The constable's account of the speech was remarkably similar to his sergeant's, considering that neither had put down the words until a few hours after the meeting.

" You would have the life of a dog at the barracks if you contradicted Sergeant Molloy in this matter ? " O'Higgins insisted.

" No," replied the policeman before the magistrate intervened to warn him that there was no need to answer the question. " He has answered it," said O'Higgins. The other magistrate then repeated the question, and pointed out that the constable said " No." " He *wouldn't* have a dog's life," O'Higgins explained, and the crowd laughed, and the magistrate wished he had not spoken. The two R.M.'s hoped to get an early train back to Dublin, and O'Higgins, who realized this, was determined to drag on the proceedings until the train had gone. To anyone who had ever heard him speaking, it was obvious that he would never indulge in, what he described as, " a coarse rant." He only defended himself, he explained, to make that clear and not with any hope or wish for clemency. He then made the observation that Sinn Feiners were out simply for the independence of Ireland and not necessarily for the destruction of the British Empire. He was not allowed to continue on these lines, and one of the magistrates observed how wrong it was for young men of education to mislead the people to whom they could give advice and example ; it was particularly unfortunate to think of it on this day when news of an Irish conspiracy with Germany had just been announced in the paper.

O'Higgins remained imperturbable to hear a sentence of three months' imprisonment, to be increased to five if he did not give bail for good behaviour. He served the full sentence. When the news of O'Higgins's arrest came to Tim Healy, he wrote to his brother, Maurice, " Your apprentice was handcuffed before his father and mother to take him to the train, and all Tullamore turned out to see him off, including the priests and Christian Brothers. His mother kissed his handcuffs. The people in the train so put the police out of countenance that they took off the handcuffs until Kingsbridge was reached, when they replaced them to stow him safely in Mountjoy. I think that . . . the police might have spared his parents additional indignities."

O'Higgins never referred to his imprisonment or complained about it. Once in the Dáil he referred to his trial when introducing the Criminal Justice Administration Bill, but he did so good-humouredly. "I remember on one occasion being informed by a policeman that he read from a paper that at a certain cross-roads on a certain date I had said certain things to the great terror and alarm of all His Majesty's loyal subjects. I asked him would he name five or six loyal subjects of His Majesty's within a radius of ten or twelve miles of that particular cross-roads, and he said, ' Begob, you have me there.' "

From Mountjoy, O'Higgins was transferred to Belfast, where there were over 200 Sinn Fein prisoners. They were interned rather than imprisoned, being allowed to live together as though in a camp. O'Higgins was unobtrusive in prison, making one or two friends in preference to joining with a crowd, but he attended Irish lessons given by another prisoner, Ernest Blythe, acted in theatricals, and was a ringleader in water-throwing, which was one of the relaxations of prison life.[3] No one walking down a corridor was safe from the sudden discharge of a bucket from one of the balconies, and it was quite usual, on opening the door of a cell, to upset a bucket which had been placed overhead for the unwary. It was considered in the worst of taste to show any annoyance when the hard edge of a bucket landed on one's skull and the contents drenched one's clothes. It was an excellent training for a politician, and only one prisoner was known to fall beneath the required standards of behaviour. When a bucket landed on his head, he stepped into the adjoining cell and punched the occupant in the face.

Practical joking is not an attractive habit ; it was a weakness of Kevin O'Higgins. Even as a Minister for State, on his way to Geneva, he could not resist taking the laces out of the shoes of a colleague who had fallen asleep in the carriage. He had more subtle forms of humour, and he found an occasion to exercise this when an innocent-looking prisoner asked him for help in pre-

paring a speech which he had been chosen to deliver on the forthcoming release of three of the prisoners. For days he conspired
with O'Higgins, who prepared a most elaborate oration, full of
absurd double meanings. After twelve meetings, the speech was
considered fit for delivery and the novice was profuse in his thanks.
When the night for the celebration arrived, Kevin let some of
the prisoners into the secret, and they were chuckling in anticipation of the absurdities which the gull was about to deliver. The
orator climbed on a barrel to begin. It was noticed that he had
come without a manuscript. He did not require any, for the speech
which he delivered that evening showed all the skill of a practised
demagogue. The joke was turned against O'Higgins.

The prisoners had a manuscript magazine to which he contributed regularly. His light articles were very much appreciated,
but he alternated them with very serious discussion on such matters
as Land Tenure, Democratic Theory, and Law Reforms, which
were not so much to the taste of the readers.

There still exist some verses in manuscript which O'Higgins
wrote ; some may date from prison days. One perhaps may be
given for its subject-matter rather than for any particular merit
in the verses :

> " I made a speech at Garryhinch,
>   I urged the people not to flinch
>   Before the threats of Viscount ' Frinch,'
>   So now I'm here.
>
> The peelers swore I cursed the King,
> (The Tories growled that I should swing),
> The R.M. thought that peace 'twould bring
>   If I were here.
>
> Sez he, ' Five months you'll do in jail,
> We'll strike off two if you give bail.'
> But faith I'll die before I quail,
>   So I'll stay here.
>
> But when my five months' spell is done,
> 'Tis said we're sure to have some fun,
> We'll put the tyrants on the run,
>   And I'll be there."

CHAPTER III

THE MEMBER FOR QUEEN'S COUNTY

WHEN O'Higgins came out of prison it was but a few weeks before the end of the Great War, and when Parliament dissolved, he was invited to go forward as a Sinn Fein [1] candidate for Queen's County in the General Election of 1918. Most of the candidates were in jail at the time, but this did not prevent their nomination being proceeded with. For the first time, women had the vote, but what made the election even more remarkable in Ireland was the declared intention of the Sinn Feiners, if elected, to abstain from attendance at Westminster as a protest against the refusal of the British Government to meet the national desire for independence.

" The two supreme services which Ireland has rendered Britain," according to Winston Churchill, " are her accession to the Allied cause on the outbreak of the Great War, and her withdrawal from the House of Commons at its close." [2] Had the Sinn Feiners come into Parliament, they would in four years have given to the Labour Party an absolute majority, but the Irish were tired from generations of disappointment, and they looked not to Parliament but to the Peace Conference and the new, high-sounding principles of President Wilson.

In his election speeches, O'Higgins made this the issue : Was Ireland's grievance to be a domestic or an international matter ? Nowhere do I find him use the word " Republic," but he insisted on the right of Ireland to independence as a separate nation.

There was now complete hostility between the Parliamentary Party (the Nationalists), led by John Dillon since Redmond's death in 1918, and Sinn Fein. The doyen of the Parliamentarians, Tim Healy, spoke on behalf of the Sinn Feiners. The older party was annihilated at the election, and 73 Sinn Feiners were returned out of a total Irish membership of 105.

At the end of a war which was begun to liberate Belgium from the tyranny of Germany, Ireland had returned to Parliament a majority greater than any party in England had ever enjoyed, the electors having been informed that their members would not sit at Westminster. This resounding victory was won at the end of a campaign during which the majority of the Sinn Fein leaders were in prison and a press censorship was rigorously operated by a hostile Government. To add to these troubles, the Director of Elections was arrested three weeks before polling day.

" So much," wrote Churchill, " was going on all over the world and our own affairs pressed on us so importunately, that the significance of these demonstrations was hardly noticed." In every way the decay of British rule manifested itself ; magistrates sent people to prison for signing their names in Irish in hotel registers, and for displaying green, white and orange flags. The overwhelming victory of Sinn Fein, the end of the war, the approaching appearance of Wilson in Europe, and the Peace Conference, all inspired high hopes that a new day was about to dawn for Ireland. A casual glance at any provincial paper of the period reveals this air of confidence. Now that the British knew beyond doubt what Ireland wanted, it followed that after a short time these wishes would be translated into a reality. Moreover, the gelding of the House of Lords in 1911 guaranteed that the small and influential clique who defeated Gladstone's plans could no longer stand in the way of a serious popular demand.

The Sinn Fein members elected to Westminster now arranged to convoke an Irish Parliament or Dáil, and on the 21st of January, 1919, this met in the Mansion House, at Dublin, and formally declared Ireland to be a Republic, confirming, as it were, the proclamation of 1916. In their solemn enthusiasm this first Dáil passed several ideal and democratic resolutions in the generous spirit that characterizes political bodies who do not exercise the functions of government. When the Dáil met, de Valera was in prison in Lincoln Gaol, and Michael Collins and Harry Boland were in England planning his escape. The man to whom the first Irish shadow-Parliament owed its inspiration was Arthur Griffith.

Poor, unassisted and proud, he had created a political philosophy, and he had hammered out the framework on which a dream could be realized. Pearse and his comrades in 1916 provided by their sacrifice whatever mystical and romantic inspiration was lacking in Griffith's work. Men, although they never realize it, need the stimulus of poetry if they are going to accomplish great enterprises. He had for years advocated the abstention of Irish members from

the House of Commons, and the creation of government departments and institutions in Ireland which would—so far as they
could—operate beside and in defiance of the British Government's
Irish machinery.   Courts were to be held to which people were
to bring their disputes ; rates and taxes were to be collected by the
national authority ; Irish representatives were to be sent abroad.
In furtherance of these plans, the Dáil created a department of
Local Government of which the Minister was W. T. Cosgrave,
a well-known figure in the Dublin Corporation and a participator
in the rising of 1916. The success of this department exceeded all
expectations.   Conducted in back rooms under the pretence of a
private business concern, it contrived to exercise control over
every County Council in Southern Ireland, and every Municipal
Corporation with the exception of Dublin. A fleet of inspectors
toured the country. Sinn Fein rate collectors collected the rates,
and Sinn Fein councils expended them on road repairs, poor law
relief and the like. In vain, inspectors came down from Dublin,
books were not produced, and the banks, which had formerly
acted as treasurers for Council funds, no longer were prepared to
take the risk. The Councils refused to send their minutes to the
Local Government Board in the Custom House, Dublin, and as
a result, the British machinery of local government was brought
to a standstill.

The work was a great deal for Cosgrave to undertake unassisted.
He was in bad health at the time ; moreover he was handicapped
by the fact that his appearance was well known in Dublin, and
the police, once they came to know of his activities, were in a
position to prevent them by shadowing him to his office. No
letters came direct to the new Local Government Department ;
they were received by various agencies, drapers' shops, public
houses, and they were collected by the headquarters staff. Very
few letters, and no minutes, from the County Councils came to
the Custom House, which was the official seat of Local Government, the greater part of the mail directed there was diverted by
friendly postal officials to one of the Sinn Fein clearing houses.

Kevin O'Higgins attended the Dáil and continued his legal
studies, obtaining an LL.B. with first-class honours after six weeks'
preparation for the examination, but events pulled him away
from the law and immersed him in work of a more exciting and
dangerous kind.

An assistant was required by Cosgrave, and O'Higgins was

selected for the task. He became engrossed in the work, and in particular with the reform which this subterranean department was able to effect in the miserable workhouse system which had been imposed on Ireland in 1838. The Sinn Fein ministry, instead of forcing paupers who had small holdings to sell them before they could get aid from the Poor Law authorities (and that only by becoming inmates of the workhouse), began to distribute small sums among the indigent in their homes, an innovation which became, in 1926, the law of the land.

The department consisted of the Minister, the Assistant Minister, a clerk, a typist and an office boy. They flitted from place to place ; Clare Street, Rutland Square and Exchequer Street all housed this department of State. At first, O'Higgins was known as Mr. Casey, but a friend who greeted him by that name in a restaurant was kicked on the shin and warned, in a whisper, that a policeman in plain clothes was at the next table and the name now was Wilson. Casey was dead.

This underground government was sadly in need of funds. De Valera, after his escape from Lincoln, did not delay, but sailed for America to rally support there and to encourage subscriptions to a National Loan which in Ireland was launched by Michael Collins. Each parliamentary representative was put in charge of the collection in his own constituency, and O'Higgins organized the business of the loan in Queen's County. The loan campaign began in August, 1919.

By this time the political temperature had changed very considerably. It was clear that the result of the election had not impressed on the British Government the necessity for any immediate change in their Irish policy. The principle of Partition had been accepted as an essential part of any Home Rule Bill, and Lloyd George announced that as the present condition of Ireland did not allow of any scheme of this nature, the Bill would have to be postponed.[3] Just as with Palestine, the British had embarrassed themselves with conflicting promises, to give Home Rule to Redmond and to keep Ulster out for Carson.

However determined this first Dáil may have been to achieve the independence of its country, it was not in the main composed of violent men, and the pursuit of a bloodless policy was their aim and intention. The spearhead of British government in Ireland was Dublin Castle, and its scouts were the Royal Irish Constabulary, who were stationed throughout the country. A boycotting cam-

paign against the R.I.C. was preached by the Dáil.   Their employment was represented as a degraded one for Irishmen.   It was
hoped by this means to undermine the force, and in fact some
members, more susceptible to national feeling, or apprehensive for
their personal safety, resigned from the police.   In the meanwhile,
Collins had established a spy system of immense effectiveness,
some of the " G " division in Dublin Castle having agreed to give
information to the Sinn Feiners.   So cleverly was this contrived
that when the British evacuated the country in 1922, Sir Arthur
Cope advised Neligan, one of the Castle detectives, to come over
to the British service.   Neligan for three years had been meeting
Collins at regular intervals to acquaint him with all the police
information.   Broy and MacNamara were others in the British
service who conveyed intelligence regularly to Collins.

Sporadic violence took place in various parts of the country.
In Tipperary, Treacy was the first deliberately to shoot policemen, to resist arrest, and later, to ambush a small party of constabulary who were guarding the transport of gelignite at Solo-
headbeg.

At this time, *An tOglach*, the official Volunteer publication,
had declared that a state of war existed ; but there is no doubt
that these acts of violence in Tipperary were spontaneous and
not directed from Dublin.   In the Capital, Collins was organizing
a devoted and ruthless band who, in the summer of 1919, began
the systematic shooting of members of the police intelligence
department, but not, as a rule, without first warning the victims
and giving them a chance to leave the country.

The men of 1916 donned the uniforms of Volunteers and dared
to challenge an Empire in arms.   The leaders were not treated
as prisoners of war but were summarily shot.   The new order of
Irish fighters wore no uniform.   It was objected that they fired
from behind hedges, as though a proper soldier would have taken
up his position in the line of enemy fire and announced his intent
before attempting to shoot.   After the recent world war the various
resistance movements have accustomed people to assassination
and it has not been condemned, but the world, even in 1919, had
not yet graduated in horror and many were unable to reconcile
themselves to the idea of an army which could not be identified,
soldiers who shot, hid their guns, and mixed with the crowd.   It was
not a policy which won the approval of the Church to which nearly
all the Irish fighting men belonged—although the younger priests

were mostly sympathetic—and it was only possible because nationalism had, since the execution of the 1916 leaders, acquired a new significance. The war had intensified nationalism everywhere and the British Empire was not able to keep its subjects immunized from the infection of freedom. There was, throughout the country, a feeling of exaltation, an expectancy of success, such as there had not been since the palmy days of O'Connell, but now there was no longer any faith in constitutional measures. If it was desired to achieve their goal, there was abundant evidence to show the Sinn Feiners that only by stopping at nothing could they hope to succeed.

The provincial press recorded some of O'Higgins's addresses to his constituents during the early summer of 1919. In keeping with Sinn Fein policy, he spoke harshly of the Nationalists, led since Redmond's death by John Dillon, and he described them as "the corrupt and emasculated parliamentary party in Ireland." Of their leader he was unsparing in epithet : "It must be immensely soothing to Mr. Dillon's vanity that his fall synchronized with that of Kings and Emperors and that his Party disappeared amidst the crash of dynasties in many lands."[4] The virtual extinction of the Nationalist Party at the previous election would seem to make this onslaught upon them a task of supererogation, but presumably the Sinn Feiners were afraid of the resurgence of what O'Higgins described as "the poisonous growths of Anglicization that had flourished in the genial atmosphere of 'constitutionalism.'" Regarding the aims of Sinn Fein, he was emphatic rather than specific. "I expect that in the days of slavery there were few so silly as to speak of the 'rights' of the slave. One thing, and one thing only, has Ireland a right to from England and that thing is the recognition of her absolute independence. Ireland is not held, and never has been held, or governed by the consent of her citizens ; she is being held and governed by the Lewis gun."

In order to quash the suggestion that the policy of force was repugnant to them, the Dáil ratified and took responsibility for all the shootings that had taken place ; nevertheless, the direction of these operations was not from the Cabinet.[5] Sinn Fein (the creation of Griffith), the Volunteers, and the reorganized Irish Republican Brotherhood formed an alliance which was something less than a union of souls. The gap was bridged by the personal regard which Griffith conceived for Collins, the supreme organizer of the campaign against the British forces.

O'Higgins came to admire and love Michael Collins, and was for a time a member of the Irish Republican Brotherhood, but, like de Valera, it irked him to take an oath to a secret society in defiance of the ban of the Church, and he resigned from the I.R.B. "Either religion is nothing or it is more than anything" was the phrase he used to a colleague when explaining his action.

When O'Higgins went to Queen's County to organize the loan, he was undertaking a task of considerable magnitude. To get round the country, to carry the money from place to place and eventually smuggle it to Dublin, to avoid arrest in a small county in which he had lived for twenty-seven years, presented innumerable difficulties. His mode of conveyance was a very old bicycle which he christened " Push Omega de Luxe "; his system of propaganda was largely confined to word of mouth, for there was very considerable difficulty in distributing a prospectus. No paper dared to publish a word about the loan, but Dollards, a Dublin firm, undertook to print the bonds and circulars. In each district the local I.R.B. men acted as agents, and visited those whom they thought were likely to give support. Many, no doubt, contributed in dread of what would happen if they refused, but, in fact, no threats were ever used to exact money, nor violence done when help was refused. Meetings were summoned in barns and rooms of friendly shopkeepers, and at those meetings there was usually a " decoy duck " who responded to O'Higgins's appeal by offering £100 to the fund. Such munificence aroused emulation, and the gulls strove to compete in lavishness. In each county there were twenty-five polling areas, and at each of these he had to address meetings.

In each district of his constituency O'Higgins was taken under the protection of the local I.R.A. commandant with whom sometimes he used to stay ; but as a rule there was a window open in the house of a friendly priest, and as he cycled down the dark roads a light ahead promised shelter and comfort. The curate of Timahoe was a devoted friend of O'Higgins, and when the hue and cry grew ominous he stayed in the priest's house, sometimes for weeks at a time. They played billiards, at which O'Higgins was an indifferent performer, but his friend noticed that with all the diffidence of his manner he did not like to be beaten. He also remarked a streak of recklessness which characterized all the O'Higgins family. Passing under the portals of the R.I.C. barracks, they would come in a body to visit Kevin in his hiding place, and it was impossible to keep him cooped up in the house. He carried a revolver, and it would have gone hard with him had he been captured.

He was always able to count on shelter at St. Mary's College, Knockbeg, where he had been at school. The Rector took great risks to help O'Higgins and many others in the movement. One of the teachers, Gearoid O'Sullivan, was a right-hand man of Michael Collins, and when the latter planned the escape of a Volunteer called Fleming from Mountjoy Prison, it was to Knockbeg that he was brought for shelter. Collins himself visited the College occasionally, as did Rory O'Connor and other leaders. When O'Higgins appeared, he was greeted as Mr. Casey, a name suggested by his initials, and he used the school as a place of safekeeping for the loan funds.

The river Barrow runs behind Knockbeg, and the method by which political visitors from Dublin came without attracting undue attention was, after alighting at Mageney, a quiet country station on the Carlow line, to walk down the tow-path between the railway tracks and the river to a certain spot ; then a boat would come over from the College side of the river and bring them across.

One night, when O'Higgins was staying with the priest at Timahoe, he came through the open window somewhat later than usual, and his friend noticed, while they talked, that O'Higgins was twisting in his hand something small and white which looked like a woman's handkerchief. Father Fenelon did not think very much about it for there were many girls in the O'Higgins family ; not for a moment did he think that the former student for the priesthood, now dedicated to a high and dangerous purpose, had either opportunity or inclination for meeting women other than those of his own household. He did not remember that in Knockbeg, as well as friendly priests, there was a lady on the staff, a very pretty teacher of English. It must indeed have been a remarkable school—providing an impressionable pupil with material which Rousseau or Robert Louis Stevenson would alike have envied. Miss Cole, the fair professor, was interested, one evening in December, 1918, by the appearance of a young man with a strong, thoughtful face, a deliberate manner of speech, eyes of disconcerting penetration and hands remarkably white and delicate. He was then on his way to an election meeting. He came back a few times during that campaign, and while the loan collection was in progress he was a regular visitor. Sometimes, when expected, he did not turn up, and his friends sat until late dreading the news of his capture ; but in the early hours of the morning an exhausted and bedraggled figure would ride up the avenue on an old and creaking bicycle with his father's midwifery bag tied with a rope to the carrier.

The object of the organizers of the loan was to give it the dignity of a National Issue, secured by the credit of the Irish Republic, and bearing interest which was to be repaid when the Republic was established. It was not a mere levying of money, although it was hardly an investment which a prudent stockbroker would recommend. The Sinn Fein Government wished to give receipts for money borrowed in order to preserve the legal character of the transaction ; the British Government regarded the possession of a receipt as sufficient evidence upon which to prosecute.

The Sinn Fein Government consisted of a small group of men who met in back rooms and whose Parliamentary attendance depended upon the success with which they had avoided the police. There was, therefore, an air of " let's pretend " about some of their activities : the Minister for External Affairs, for instance, sent representatives abroad whom no Government recognized as such. In the country, raids were made on police barracks which, one by one, were burned or closed down. Parties of constabulary were ambushed, and sometimes British soldiers were attacked in the same manner. As guerilla warfare demands local knowledge and cannot be directed by remote control, it can safely be assumed that the functions of the Irish Minister for Defence were strictly limited by circumstances, and the Minister for Fine Arts was similarly curtailed.

Publicity and propaganda were on a different footing ; on this department fell the essential work of putting the Irish case before the world and answering the attacks which the British Government were making in the Press. The speeches of English ministers were published to the world ; the speeches of Irish ministers were made with someone watching at the door to see if a policeman could have possibly overheard. The difficulties of publishing and distributing a Sinn Fein paper were almost, but not quite, insuperable. Ireland was good copy for a journalist, and it was only by meeting foreign journalists secretly that any propaganda was possible. Desmond Fitz Gerald was in charge of this branch of the Sinn Fein government, and when, inevitably, he was arrested, his place was taken by Erskine Childers, who had come over to Sinn Fein from the Irish Convention, a talking body which had been set up by the British Government in 1917, and met in Trinity College, Dublin, with the object of arriving at a solution to the Irish questions. Many excellent men attended the Convention, but the time and the manner in which it was set up were as appropriate to the case as would be the application of red flannel to a patient in the last stages of galloping consumption.

The Department of Finance, under Collins, was another which had a task as urgent as it was difficult ; but the Minister for Education, in existing circumstances, belonged to the mythical side of the Sinn Fein organization.

Two departments which might equally have been considered illusory became of real importance—the Ministries of Home Affairs and Local Government respectively. Courts were set up by the former which were presided over by Sinn Fein lawyers. The driving of the constabulary from country barracks into the towns left the inhabitants with little order and less law ; it soon dawned upon the unsympathetic property owners, that the presence of a court without a legal jurisdiction, but the judgment of which would in fact be enforced, was something worth trying. When, moreover, it was discovered that the judges in the courts were usually fair-minded and often of high intelligence, the temptation to resort to them was almost irresistible. For a few years, therefore, landlords and others who hated and despised the national movement, as well as the country folk generally, brought their cases to the Sinn Fein courts, and found in these improvised tribunals more sympathy than they were wont to receive from the average Resident Magistrate. In districts where the King's writ limped there was also comfort from the Republican police, who, whenever they were captured removing trespassers or otherwise maintaining the civil law, were, of course, themselves sent to prison. It was a pleasantly Gilbertian situation in an otherwise grim picture.

The Local Government Act of 1898 had been designed to mollify Irish discontents by allowing a more popular representation in the management of civic and rural affairs. It was the first screw that a Chamberlain unwittingly provided for the coffin of the British Empire. Patrician, publican and peasant did not hobnob round the dusty tables of rural councils as the author of this measure hoped. The patrician, in most cases, disappeared from Local Government and availed himself of the provisions of the Land

Act of 1903 to sell his estate to the Land Commission, which had begun the scheme for peasant proprietorship that, had it been introduced in time, would have changed the history of Ireland.

County Councils became popular assemblies which reflected the wishes of the majority far too clearly for the convenience of the British Government. As we have seen, these Councils all went over to Sinn Fein and gave the substance of control to the outlaws, who, in the matters of Education, Fine Arts and Embassies, were pursuing shadows. The realization by the people that there were, in fact, national courts, and that the Sinn Feiners were in fact, controlling Local Government, had a moral effect which was incalculable.

When O'Higgins arrived in Dublin as Assistant Minister for Local Government, Collins made arrangements for his lodging. With characteristic ingenuity, he placed him in a house owned by a Dublin policeman in Synge Street, where he was known as Mr. Casey. Whenever O'Higgins had any difficulty in identifying himself, he had only to ask the police to get in touch with his landlord, who reassured the most suspicious detectives. When O'Higgins, as Minister for Home Affairs in the first government of the Free State, reviewed the police, this man nearly fainted when he recognized his former lodger.

The office of Local Government had many homes—Clare Street, Exchequer Street, Rutland (now Parnell) Square. Always word came in time before a raid and the office was transferred to safety.

In the autumn of 1920, Collins heard from Neligan that Cosgrave was soon to be arrested by the Castle authorities ; he passed the information on, and Cosgrave decided that it was futile in the circumstances to try to carry on the Local Government department. One day when O'Higgins came into the office he found a note directing him to stop the work for the time being. Cosgrave had left Dublin that day. This gave rise to the first clash of policy between O'Higgins and his chief, men diametrically opposed to one another in temperament, intellect and outlook. With the passage of time, O'Higgins came to recognize Cosgrave's rare qualities, and to understand his methods, to which, in the first flush of enthusiasm, his uncompromising nature was unsympathetic. O'Higgins refused to take Cosgrave's advice, and continued to run the department during the absence of the Minister. Writing to his future wife, he refers to his resolution : " I'm going to show that I can steer the ould canoe in a squall, and keep it headin'

right. . . . I'm worrying the opposition—they call me a ' person '
lately. I am hoping to be promoted to an ' individual ' any day
now."

Despite his antipathy to figures, O'Higgins was a first-class
administrator. He was always able to get the best out of those
who worked with him ; his enemies were those who were at the
furthest remove, his friends those with whom he was most closely
associated ; nevertheless, he still retained a style which was not
calculated to endear him to a wide public. On one occasion a
series of official and apparently unnecessary questions came in
which he perused calmly and answered methodically before hand-
ing his replies to his clerk, who noticed that he had written at
the end of a series of comprehensive answers, " Were you instructed
by your Council to propound these queries or is it a piece of
gratuitous insolence on your part ? " He had no illusions about
his reputation, as he disclosed in a letter : " Whenever there's an
abusive letter to be written, Cosgrave says : ' Here, Higgins, you're
a cross-grained divil, you'd better deal with this fellow—and
for God's sake work off some of your spleen on him, instead of
on me.' "

Like most people who have sharp tongues or pens, he did not
realize his power to wound. Once when he was a person of more
consequence in the State, he showed a visitor the draft of a speech
which he had prepared, and asked for a frank comment. The
speech contained many gratuitous personal thrusts which were
quite unnecessary to the argument. When this was pointed out,
O'Higgins put his pen through the offending passages without
demur. He was so intoxicated by phrases that he did not stop to
consider whether it was worth incurring enmity for the sake of a
well-turned sentence. A reproof may be forgiven, but if it has
been accompanied by a sting it cannot be forgotten.

The only weak link in the chain of Local Government was the
Dublin Corporation, which the British held in a grip of gold ;
but pliant officials facilitated raids on their offices to prevent audits
and in other ways helped the Sinn Feiners. The destruction of the
Customs House, which was one of the last acts before the truce
with England, was the final blow to the British administrative
machinery in Ireland.

CHAPTER IV

THE BLACK AND TANS

IN the early days of his courtship, while his fate was still uncertain, O'Higgins called the professor of English at Knockbeg, Défarges, after the lady who knitted under the guillotine while heads were falling.

"Dear Défarges," he wrote in May, 1920, "the country, as I have observed before, is not half settled, but the pace is increasing and prospects are, on the whole, good. Such crude details as human hearts impaled on engines should not blind your little eyes to the beauty of the Resurrection. I expect Lazarus looked in need of a wash and a brush-up when he came staggering towards the light in his grave clothes. The whole history of the world is the triumph of mind over matter. We are backing our Idea against aeroplanes and armoured cars. Have a half-crown on. At least you'll get a good run for your money. Isn't it bad management to run to a second page like this ? But I wanted to tell you that I had a consultation yesterday with another victim of your knitting-needle—to wit Æ. I had never met him before, but I found him extremely easy to get on with and he had some useful ideas in my line. By the way, groping in my pocket I encountered an absurd frivolous piece of millinery not all conducive to brick and mortar reflections . . . I am really getting over-diffuse and forgetting my principles of conserving. Goodbye, may the Lord love you."

Despite the fact that a great many of the Dáil members were wanted by the police, the Dáil itself was not an illegal body, but in September, 1919, the British executive in Ireland issued an order for its suppression as a dangerous association. The entire opposition to British rule had now been driven underground, and this was the state of affairs when Mr. "Casey" arrived in Dublin to lodge with an unsuspecting policeman in 33 Synge Street.

This year of 1920 saw, on the one hand, measures of Local Government reform carried out under the nose of the "official" government ; it saw also the establishment of the Republican courts. These constructive measures were accompanied by such an increase in the tempo of the attack on the R.I.C. that many left its ranks and it was not possible to get more recruits. Sir Henry Wilson and the Army authorities pressed for martial law and "shooting by roster,"[1] but the Coalition Government preferred to leave the task in the hands of the Black and Tans, who were, according to Winston Churchill, "selected from a great press of applicants, on account of their intelligence, their characters and their records in the War." Whatever method was employed in their selection they proved themselves sorry representatives of a civilized State.

The Government, however carefully it may have examined the recruits, did not see fit to take responsibility for their actions. Lloyd George explained to Sir Henry Wilson that it would not be possible to do so until after the American election.[2] At the same time he introduced an Irish Home Rule Bill, which was in Ireland called "The Partition Act." It gave the six counties, which were arbitrarily allotted to Ulster, the power of "opting out" of an Irish parliament and setting up a local one. The Carsonites did not want any form of self-government, but they agreed to work the Act, and, to quote Winston Churchill, "from that moment the position of Ulster became unassailable." Whatever the prospects for this Bill might have been at an earlier date, it now came too late ; Ireland had decided that in the post-war world she could get what she wanted. She could look to the League of Nations, to America, and, for the first time, to an overwhelming vote at home for the extremists (heretofore the constitutional party was always the most popular one). Many acts of great violence, and many which all Irishmen would rather forget, were perpetrated by the Irish in these years, but not anything like the number that usually accompany a revolution. The behaviour of the bewildered British troops in Ireland did not arouse indignation, but the loosing of the Auxiliary Police and the Black and Tans disgusted many who were ordinarily loyal to British Rule in Ireland. The Catholic Hierarchy, who have never countenanced armed violence and who had always been conservative to the point of creating a breach with the more politically intemperate of their flock, condemned the actions of the British Government. Even if one discounts such radical papers as *The Nation*, which were completely sympathetic to the Irish, it is not easy to dismiss the opinion of the cool-minded Asquith, who pointed out, in a letter to *The Times*, that the only logical sequence to the Government's policy was to reconquer Ireland and hold her by force, an action which he declared "will never be sanctioned by the will or the conscience of the British people."

Greatness cannot discard responsibility. Banquo's ghost will invariably turn up to dinner. "If these men ought to be murdered, then the Government ought to murder them," said Sir Henry Wilson to Lloyd George, who danced at this and said, "No government could possibly take the responsibility."[3]

It is foolish to deny that there were atrocities on the Irish side, but England could not hope to keep her prestige when her police first blackened their faces before proceeding to raid the house of the Lord Mayor of Cork, whom they murdered. "We have murder by the throat," said Mr. Lloyd George. He was, in fact, shaking hands with it.

O'Higgins had now changed his name from Casey to Wilson, and moved from Synge Street to Gardiner Street on the north side of Dublin. He was given a new secretary, Rory O'Connor, a young engineer, for whom he had a great admiration, and he wrote in jubilation : "I have had a stroke of luck with regard to business which starts to-morrow, securing Rory as secretary instead of friend Spud. They are to my mind the two extremes. As you can imagine this is a great relief to me ; it will mean less strain and worry when we get going. The old boy has tackled it most serenely—one would imagine he was running these affairs all his life. Glory be, from Spud to the sublime Rory but a step, but what a step ! . . . Wasn't it old Socrates who said that no one knew anything, but that he was a little wiser than the rest of men because he knew that he knew nothing. I think if one took the trouble to analyse that old think of his it's not very clear. But let it pass. A. M. blew in to-day looking for information (wot a hope !) ; he complained that I was beginning to look very serious. I was not in my sweetest mood at the time and I snapped at him 'Why shouldn't I ? What's the ruddy joke ? '—He collapsed quietly and when recovered went out on his toes. . . . Now I wonder am I getting intolerant or autocratic, or bureaucratic, or any other of these kind of mental ailments ; I don't think so ; as a matter of fact the net result of my experience since I am up has been to give me a very comprehensive know-ledge of my limitations. But when a fellow comes in when you're having a crowded hour of anything but glorious life, and starts talking about your face—my face, I mean, he said nothing about yours—why it doesn't seem apt or opportune . . . Pet, love, you see the urgent necessity of coming back soon to old Case ; positively he's getting poetic, morbidly poetic. . . . That mustn't happen, the time suits it not. We must ' be hard, my friends.' Hard and bright and keen as the hob of that place one does not mention to Loreto girls. Hard like Old R. used to be once upon a time, the hardness of Macbeth when he said Mrs. Macbeth should ' have died another time.' Old Carson mobilizing behind the skirts of Britannia to murder non-combatants in the North for propaganda purposes. And the beggar knows that a clear ring for a week would ' stamp his card ' and settle the ' two-nation ' theory for all time. Shop again ! There's a medium between this and the sickness of the duck which we must strive to attain to and maintain. . . . We have all the 31 day month of August before us—in which I have arranged for fine weather. . . . I'll show you how nice Dún Laoghaire looks from the Hill of Howth on a fine day—you haven't seen it since it's had its new name sanctioned by us, looks ever so much better."

Occasionally he reviled himself for having got engaged at such an uncertain and dangerous time, when he " stood committed to the country's cause and doing what I held to be my duty," but he would not lament for long. " I have faith and trust in her and she'll try to have a little in me, and we'll both try to have a great deal in God; Who, after all, can't quite disown responsibility for what has happened." He was extremely solicitous about his fiancée's health. Like many robust countrymen, he had an exaggerated idea of the fragility of town-bred girls, and his letters would suggest that he was engaged to a chronic invalid or the inmate of a sanatorium. As to his own health, he was quite indifferent. Working tremendously hard, under conditions of extraordinary discomfort, he made little of the strain. " Hang it, think of the tremendous reserve supply—untouched as yet—hasn't even been called upon. I could run for years on the energy saved in Knockbeg."[4]

The strain of these years on those concerned in the struggle was greater than they realized at the time, and the strange behaviour of some of the Irish leaders in subsequent years was due to the nervous tax of the years 1919–21. Kevin O'Higgins, apart from the difficulty and risks of his work in Dublin, was anxious for the safety of his family in Stradbally, where his brother, Brian, still of school age, was regarded as a very dangerous character by the authorities. Doctor Higgins agreed with the political views of his wife's family. He was a strong Nationalist and a political follower of Tim Healy. But it was a long step from Tim Healy to the I.R.A., and the Doctor found it compatible with his opinions to retain his place on the bench of magistrates until 1920, when he resigned as a protest against the excesses of the Black and Tans. Kevin read the news in Dublin, and commented : " One mustn't bustle people, just give grace time to work—and it was really the sacerdotes that prevailed upon him to hang on so long. Oh, these sacerdotes ! When will they learn that when a thing is right, man, an animal that walks on his hind-legs and turns his face to the skies, should not be ashamed to stand for it—that it is the people who stand against it that should hang their heads for shame, and the people who, well knowing that it is right, ' pass by on the other side,' like the Levite—the meanest character in the Bible— meaner than Judas, meaner than Pontius Pilate—who, poor man, if he did wash his hands, at least had the courage to speak his mind."

The resignation of the doctor from the bench was followed by a police order forbidding him to use a car for calling on his patients, an obstacle which was overcome with local co-operation, but Woodlands had become a marked spot for military and police. Tom O'Higgins, though the Dispensary doctor in Maryborough, had been turned out of his house, which was commandeered by the police, and he was himself a prisoner at Ballykinlar ; Kevin was wanted by the police, and Brian was most eagerly pursued. In all, eleven raids were made on Woodlands to find him. As a rule, the Auxiliaries came in through a window and surrounded the house, but they never found their prey. On their tenth visit the doctor was feeling rather testy, and when the officer in charge of the raiding party noticed the photograph of a soldier in khaki and asked who it was, Doctor Higgins replied, " My son, Michael, he was killed in the War. He thought he was doing right fighting for small nations." " I am glad," said the officer, meaning, no doubt, that he was pleased to hear of the war service, but the doctor took him to mean that he was glad Michael was dead, and being at all times quick-tempered, he flared up and ordered the officer to get out of the house.

Late that night the soldiers came back ; they could not find Brian, so they took his father instead. Soon afterwards Brian was arrested. The officer in charge of the party who made the arrest said, " Poor Mrs. Higgins, this is the eleventh time," and when a small grandson came out and put his arms round a soldier's neck and said, " Now that you have Uncle Brian, will you let out poor grandad ? ", tears came into the soldier's eyes. He belonged to a Scottish regiment, and, like most soldiers, hated the work he had to do in Ireland.

Father and son were imprisoned at the Curragh, but when Brian very nearly effected an escape, he was moved to Mountjoy Prison. Rory O'Connor was arrested at this time. " The poor old beggar," wrote O'Higgins, " sent his brother a letter of contingent instructions—I take pride and pleasure in the fact that in such a letter he put it on record that I was his very good friend and comrade." O'Connor found himself in prison with Doctor Higgins, who was " keepin' his end up well," having accepted his predicament with philosophical detachment, and interested himself in O'Connor, who had a tubercular cough which Doctor Higgins swore he could cure if O'Connor would come and stay at Stradbally. " Verily strange bed-fellows," he wrote of his father and his friend. " The acquaintance will be good for the old man as Rory is certainly among the best we can show." O'Higgins was very critical of people, and inclined to voice his opinions freely to anyone in whom he trusted, but nowhere in his correspondence is there a word about Rory O'Connor which is not of praise.

Meanwhile the list of horrors mounted. They were not all on one side ; the desperate deeds of the Black and Tans are fully recorded, but there were many horrors on the Irish side. One of the most terrible was the shooting of Alan Bell, a magistrate who had signed an Order for a Commission of Inquiry into the funds in the various Irish banks, with the object of tracing money subscribed to the Dáil loan. Bell was pulled out of a tram and shot on the side of the street. He was an old man, convinced that it was his duty to obey the existing Government. With his training, a refusal to do what he did would have been an act of cowardice. But he had been warned, and, had he carried out his task, the movement for independence would have been crippled, if not brought to an end. No one who knew Collins believed that he ordered these deeds without regret. He was not inhuman, but the Irish had no prisons, and Collins, with his West Cork ruthlessness, was determined to remove any obstacle in the path of freedom. There were other terrible deeds, but the record of the Volunteers had been good in comparison with the indiscriminate shootings, beatings and burnings which became the policy of the Black and Tans.

Then came "Bloody Sunday" (21st November, 1920).   On that morning, fourteen officers were shot, some in the presence of their wives, some in bed beside their wives, others after their wives had been pulled away as they tried to shield them with their bodies.   One must guard against the error of exaggerating the importance of numbers in such a matter. Many people met violent deaths at this time, and it is not less dreadful to kill fourteen men over a period of three months than to shoot them on the same morning. But the effect of mass slaughter on the imagination defies the cool counsel of logic. General Crozier wrote : " Wilson was responsible for the first *sub rosa* murder gang, run by the military early in 1920, which resulted in the murder of Captain A. and others on Bloody Sunday, when Collins put them on the spot in the nick of time in order to forestall a similar action by the British authorities."   And Beaslai, who was in a position to know, has written : " We were satisfied that there was a conspiracy to murder Irish citizens, deliberately carried out by the Intelligence Department of the English forces in Ireland. . . . These intelligence officers lived among the citizens, under disguised names, in civilian clothes, were not only spies, subject to the penalty of spies of war, but had all directly or indirectly been concerned in the murder of Irish citizens."   Seventeen Irishmen had been murdered during the previous month in a manner that suggested an official plan.

If some who were innocent were shot by mistake, the balance was redressed that afternoon when lorries of Black and Tans drove to Croke Park, where a dense crowd was watching a football match, and fired on the crowd, killing fourteen and wounding sixty. A sharp-shooter picked off one of the players with his gun, and when a companion shouted "Fluke," asked him to watch while he aimed at the ball, through which he proceeded to put a bullet at a distance of perhaps a hundred yards.[5]

" There are times," wrote O'Higgins to his fiancée on the following day, " when I am glad my little Bird is out of the hurly-burly and in comparatively peaceful surroundings, for I fear these times will have more than a passing effect on those who are in close touch with the crude horrors that occur from time to time."

The police were in a state of nervous tension at this time, and O'Higgins had two escapes ; he was held up on " Bloody Sunday," but the police let him pass ; on the Thursday following, a Black and Tan thrust his head into the office where O'Higgins and his staff were working and ordered them downstairs. Some time before this, the police had discovered the former whereabouts of the office, and O'Higgins and his staff had only escaped with their papers two hours before the office was raided. After a few days they set up their department in a large room at the top of the Dublin County Council offices in Parnell Square. This was the very first day in the new office, and it now seemed more than likely to be the last. Downstairs the County Council staff were lined up against the wall, and when O'Higgins and his assistants joined them, they moved away so as not to be confused with a group of people whom it might be dangerous to know. The Council staff did not know who their neighbours were, but Dubliners have a shrewd instinct for other people's business, and, no doubt, many made inspired guesses.

While some of the raiding party rushed upstairs, others took the names of the occupiers of the building. If they thought a face unsympathetic they gave it a crack under the jaw with the butt of their guns. " What is your name ? " an officer asked O'Higgins. " Wilson," he replied, giving his home address, where he was known as a law student. " How would you like the con- tents of this, Wilson ? " the officer inquired, digging his revolver into O'Higgins's ribs to illustrate the question. " Well, I'd hardly feel the last half-dozen of them," was the reply. It did not please the questioner.

" None of your bloody impudence," he cried, striking O'Higgins on the face, " or you will get them."

Meanwhile from upstairs came the sounds of desks being smashed, cupboards and doors ripped open. As the incriminating papers of the Sinn Fein Local Government Department lay open on the tables in their rooms, it seemed inevitable that in a few minutes the Auxiliaries would return with their capture. That would mean the summary departure of the departmental staff in a lorry and the end of the political activities of Kevin O'Higgins. After some time the raiders came rushing down the stairs, ran out to their lorries and the whole party drove away. They had come in search of account books which the County Council had refused to present for audit, and had confined their search to the floor which con-

tained the Council offices, the contents of which lay in a mass
of broken furniture and scattered papers. [6]

It required considerable faith to maintain belief in the eventual
success of the Sinn Fein campaign. Funds were limited and difficult
to conceal or employ. Britain had control of the sea and the ports.
President Wilson was showing no inclination to break a lance
for the cause of Ireland. De Valera had, in one sense, an amazing
success in America. He was fêted by the huge Irish-American
population, who refused to call him by any less title than President
of the Irish Republic. He was, of course, Prime Minister of the
Dáil, but, the constitutional position being still somewhat chimerical,
the larger title was more effective for the purposes of propaganda.
The American political parties were on the eve of a general election,
and the Irish-American vote was a factor which neither could
overlook. De Valera has been blamed for not securing from one
or other of the political parties a pledge to support the Irish case
at Versailles, but the fact is that both were using him for their own
purposes, and were not concerned with Sinn Fein save in so far
as it affected domestic issues.

Even though de Valera's American adventure did not prove
him a Talleyrand, it would have taxed the resources of the wily
Bishop himself to have emerged with profit from America
immediately after the 1914-18 War.

Despite the gradual disillusionment about America, and the
increasing pressure of the Black and Tan regime, O'Higgins
remained sanguine. "Things will come all right," he wrote ;
" are in fact coming right at the moment. They say we have our
heads in the clouds—perhaps, but our feet are on the ground and
we're feelin' it at every step, can they say as much ? When we
gain the goal, the price will seem ludicrously small. The individuals
have their moments of loneliness and blankness—'tis human—
but the mass will stick—and win—because we don't all get the
hump at the same time and hump passes " ; and in another mood
he wrote : " I think we are living five years in one these times,
tant mieux, ' the sooner it's over, the sooner to sleep.' I wonder
is the national character (is there such a thing ?) changing much
as a result of it all ? And, if so, for better or worse ? Mineself
thinks that fundamentally it must be for better. I think that anything that makes the individual think less of and for himself and
more of and for the community in which he is a unit is good. At
the worst we are raising standards ; at a guess one would say that

it will be a long time before counterfeit coin will pass freely again in this green land."

His own career as a lawyer was faced with an insuperable difficulty ; if he presented himself for the Solicitors' Final Examination, he was certain of arrest. Nevertheless, he had not abandoned the idea of a legal career, and in October, 1920, he talked of borrowing notes (" quis currit legat ") from Cussen, who was then the leading grinder for law examinations. At the same time he was carrying on the Local Government office ; as he put it, " doing his damnedest and finds that by taking his work very seriously, perhaps even a little savagely, he is able to carry on." The weekends were mostly spent with his future wife's family in Dundrum where sometimes he had to lie low, for the coming and going of a young man to a house, composed entirely of women, had begun to attract attention. On one occasion the local priest sent him a message not to venture to Mass, and for some weeks at Christmas, following " Bloody Sunday," he never left the house. Some of his own relations lived in Donnybrook, and that was the only other house he went to, although he was a regular attendant at the Abbey Theatre on Saturday afternoons. At Maynooth he had won the prize for elocution, and in prison, theatricals had been one of his principal occupations. There was some risk in going to a small theatre, but he rarely missed a new play. The distance between Carlow and Dublin, and the difficulties of transport, made his meetings with his fiancée few and precious. He wrote regularly, and his letters, though seldom about himself, are revealing. They display, in their numerous appraising references to his family, that strong clan spirit which he inherited from his mother's people, the Sullivans. He never praised himself except in terms of his family. For instance, at the thought of life without his hoped-for wife, he writes : " I don't think I'm soft, none of us are ; I believe I could stick any physical calamity with a degree of decorum and fortitude—but this thing is different." He had no belief in those who wanted to stop the dreadful routine of assassination and reprisal. A rumour of a proposed " Truce of God " met his immediate scorn. " The Scripture warns us against the kind of fool that cries 'Peace ! Peace !' when there is no peace— there be many whereabouts as old Caspar remarked of the skulls."

Sir Henry Wilson's Diary describes his anger with the Cabinet, which refused, even after " Bloody Sunday," to impose martial law on Ireland. Lloyd George, on the contrary, began to search for ways of peace. It is the sad truth of Ireland's relations with England that she always did best when she was most violent. The ruthlessness of Collins achieved more than the chivalry of all the Irish leaders who endeavoured to treat England as an honourable friend.

O'Higgins, like all Sinn Feiners of his generation, had nothing but contempt for Redmond, whose worst fault was that he believed it possible to succeed in politics and treat his opponents as gentlemen. His judgment was at fault, but his young critics failed to give him the credit that was his due. For better or worse they had committed themselves to a more dangerous course. It was but natural that they should minimise the efforts of unsuccessful constitutionalists.

" Child," he wrote to his fiancée, " you ask me if I can understand the point of view of the Jacques—the man on the hedge. I think I can just glimpse it, but I haven't much sympathy with it. There ought not to be any man on the hedge at present, and if there were none, the load wouldn't be cutting the breasts of those who are pulling it."

One great and generous gesture by England at any time would have worked a miraculous change in the relations between the countries. In 1920, according to Miss Macardle, 203 unarmed people, including six women and twelve children, were shot by Crown forces, and thirty-six prisoners killed in custody ; while 184 of the British forces and sixty-five unarmed civilians, believed to be their secret agents, were killed.[7] The late Desmond Fitz Gerald, who was in charge of Sinn Fein propaganda, admitted that there was a good deal of exaggeration in the complaints he used to receive, just as the books written by Sinn Fein supporters give an exaggerated picture of the amount of spontaneity in the national effort and the numbers engaged in it.

Except for the work in his own department, O'Higgins was not much in the councils of the army leaders of Sinn Fein. Collins, whom he revered, he met but rarely, and the military men had no connection with the work which he was doing. His admiration for Rory O'Connor has been made evident. Of Arthur Griffith he wrote : " He is a good sort and has more strength than people give him credit for. Sometimes I think of his words ' We will win through to our goal. Before that goal is attained, many will have fallen and all will have suffered. But—we will win through to our goal.' "

O'Higgins thought that Griffith was a bad judge of men. He had the same opinion of Cathal Brugha, the Minister for Defence. Whenever an applicant for a post presented a testimonial signed by Cathal Brugha, O'Higgins used to say, " Now if only that had been signed by Arthur Griffith as well, we could be certain it was safe to refuse the application."

The stress of the times, and the strain of his work, did not interfere with O'Higgins's wooing, even though it had to be mostly by letter. In holiday time the young lovers used sometimes to get a few days together. One of their favourite haunts was the Hill of Howth, and while they sat there, looking across the bay, Kevin would produce a copy of Pearse, or Mitchel, or some other patriot, and read aloud in his firm, clear voice, while the white sails of yachts, coming out from the harbour at Dun Laoghaire, drifted across the water like small ducks in procession, and the sun glinted and danced on the hazy silver of the sea. All around were other young couples, no happier, if more traditionally employed. From the Kish lightship a warning gun would boom and die upon the air, increasing the sense of warm and lazy peacefulness, a stone dropped into a pool of silence.

In his letters, O'Higgins sometimes, in reply to a question, to resolve a doubt, or excuse some previous shortcoming, wrote about himself. Love develops introspection : lovers become interesting to themselves. " Kevin never let himself be known by anyone, I believe, and he suffered greatly for this great reserve," wrote a friend of his to the biographer, but in his courtship he occasionally pulled aside the curtains on his mind. And asking himself the question that everyone who has known love must at some time have asked themselves, " Why should this person care for me ? " he expatiated on himself : " There is no hard side to my character . . . she knew that she could ask me things and tell me things that she could tell no other man and very few women. . . . It seems such a strange inexplicable thing to me that my girl should care for me even a wee bit that sometimes I wonder is she seeing aright—or is anything due to the setting and circumstances in which she came to know me first. I have thrashed it out with myself . . . her little heart is soft and the sight of you blowing in out of the night on your old Push-Omega and blowing out again after a few days' rest may have made an appeal out of all proportion to what the facts warranted. . . . Supposing she had met you . . . pre-1916 for instance ? You weren't a very admirable, not always even a very respectable, citizen in those days, O'Higg—slacked your work, well pleased not to get stuck in exams, drank—like old Joe Addison—not because you liked it but because it set your foolish tongue free and you thought it was a fine thing to spin out words to the admiration of your friends. No—you have no pre-'16 record— the little good that's in you dates from that." He denies that he is a superman, a mover of mountains, and "he is not nearly as good as he would wish to be; if he is not innately vicious, it is due to the fact of a saint-mother and decent home influences."

Love, like drink, has an influence that borders on the maudlin, but most of his letters were on a lighter note. "Darling—A wet Sunday! Why the devil doesn't someone come driving along in his coffin—just to cheer us up a bit? And there's a man next door singing (?) 'She is far from the land'; having listened attentively for a few moments, I am strongly of opinion that— for the moment at any rate—*she* is more fortunate than I am." He had been to the theatre and met "a superfluity of friends of me salad days knocking about, some of them (tell it not in Loreto Hall, whisper it not in the National Library), while not theologically drunk, inclined to be over-effusive in their offers of liquid hospitality."

If this seems incongruous, in the dark setting of those days, to a reader who did not know them, it will not surprise anyone familiar with the times. For they were very incongruous times; people continued to live normal, even cheerful, lives in Dublin, while lorries, fenced with wire, in which hostages sat, surrounded by their captors in black berets with rifles cocked, dashed through the streets. Very few people were taking part in the struggle which was being carried on in their midst. Races, dances, theatres flourished, but violence was intermittent, sporadic, like death which occurs every day everywhere, but of which we are hardly conscious until it turns its eye on someone near us.

While outrages were mounting in number and horror, and Wilson and the Army clamoured for martial law, Lloyd George was busy negotiating with Collins and Griffith through the good offices of Archbishop Clune from Australia, and while he was declaring at the Guildhall that "we have murder by the throat," he was hoping for a compromise. Certain individuals in Ireland began, without consulting the Dáil, to send out olive branches and this was interpreted by Lloyd George as an indication of a crack in the rebel structure. One of these was Father O'Flanagan, a very prominent Sinn Feiner, who sent a telegram to Lloyd George. At the same time, six members of the Galway County Council, in the name of that body, called upon Dáil Eireann to negotiate a truce. "The West," O'Higgins wrote, "as you may have noticed, is awake—woke somewhere ahead of the rest of us and consulting its watch decided it was time to rat— . . . 'tis eminently a time for a cool head and warm feet—unfortunately, there be many suffering from the reverse. Altogether . . . the situation is grave but not serious."

At this time it seemed obvious that the prospects of carrying on the Department of Local Government were hopeless. It must have been a period of great strain for O'Higgins. Fortunately, Rory O'Connor had come back to ease what would have otherwise been an impossible situation. Lloyd George suddenly announced a new policy of martial law for parts of Munster. This was a compromise between the advice of the army chiefs, of whom Wilson, for one, was perpetually advocating a full military policy for Ireland, of Liberals, who were inclined to examine the Irish demands, and of legalists, who were ashamed of the Black and Tans, but were emphatic that the *status quo* should be maintained in Ireland. Wilson's Diaries contain innumerable contemptuous references to the "frocks," as he called the politicians, who were allowing the situation to deteriorate. Lloyd George admitted that he could not allow the Cabinet to take responsibility for atrocities until the American elections were over. In pursuance of this policy, Sir Hamar Greenwood, a Canadian, the Chief Secretary for Ireland, announced in the House of Commons that he had no knowledge as to who were responsible for burning Cork, while General Macready, who was in command of the forces, has admitted in his *Memoirs* that the burning was done by the Auxiliaries.

A combination of events must have determined Lloyd George's change of policy—the unauthorised Irish peace feelers, the conclusion of the American election, with the defeat of Wilson, the passing into law of the Government of Ireland Act, which ensured "the security of Ulster," and growing indignation among the British people at the reign of terror in Ireland by the Auxiliaries and the Black and Tans. By the end of 1920, they had become completely out of hand, and it was clear that demoralization had set in.

Winston Churchill appears to have preferred the rough justice of the Auxiliary Police to the policy of authorized reprisals which came into force in 1921. Certainly the burning of creameries, which was a popular form of reprisal, punished a class who were by no means concerned in the fighting, and the burning of country mansions, as an answer, was the only result of the new method. Moreover, the activities of the Black and Tans increased in fury, and one night the Lord Mayor of Limerick, his predecessor, and another leading citizen were murdered in their homes by men in disguise. " The armed agents of the Crown violate every law in aimless and vindictive and insolent savagery," wrote General Gough.[8]

But the pressure on the weaker combatant was beginning to tell ; supplies of ammunition were running out, and the Executive was driven underground more and more. The Dáil Courts had practically ceased to function, and the position had deteriorated in all respects save one—world opinion was definitely shocked by the British methods.

The negotiations before Christmas had been with Collins on the Irish side ; in the Spring there were fresh indications of a will to peace. De Valera was now in charge. He had returned from America on Christmas Eve. O'Higgins regarded de Valera in the light of a deity. But he had been an absent deity : to the young men of the movement, Collins had become the bulwark against the Black and Tans, and the chief hope of victory. Collins was a loyal comrade, and if inclined to be impatient with inefficiency, he never spared himself when another was in trouble. His charm and superabundant vitality have often been recorded, but, having gone to London at fifteen to make a living with others of his class, it was not unnatural that he should have had a rough, hard-swearing way when he was crossed. His abruptness was not resented by subordinates, but some of his colleagues found it no salve to their rising jealousy of his reputation. Chief of these was Cathal Brugha (Charles Burgess), the son of a Yorkshireman who had settled in Dublin. O'Higgins was fond of pointing out how half-Irish patriots were more intransigent than those of the whole blood. At the time of the Civil War they went on the side of the Irregulars. Brugha had been riddled with bullets during the Easter Week Rebellion, and was a man of epic courage. He was of rigid mind, narrow and determined. As Minister for Defence, it riled him to see Collins made so much of by the Press. Brugha's most original contribution to the war effort was the suggestion that machine-guns should be smuggled into the House of Commons and turned on to the Ministerial benches. When this was voted impracticable, he suggested, as an alternative, shooting into London cinemas. This plan was not adopted either.

Soon after de Valera's return, Brugha made persistent inquiries about funds which Collins had handled, and de Valera ordered an inquiry. This galled Collins very much. He was also amazed when de Valera, on his return to Ireland, ordered him to go to America to continue the work there. It would be easy to explain this on the ground that de Valera was unconsciously jealous of Collins, as O'Higgins believed. But it was also in keeping with his expressed policy of easing off the campaign of violence that de Valera should decide to send the mainspring of that campaign out of the country. It is quite understandable, after the way in which he had been fêted in America, and hailed as President of the Irish Republic there, that de Valera should have wished to be associated with a more orthodox kind of warfare than that which was being waged by Collins's gunmen and the flying columns of Volunteers. Realists, however, had a firm grip on the grim situation : the notion of field fighting was not given a hearing. And Collins refused to go to America.

In all this, de Valera was probably encouraged by Brugha who, as Minister for Defence, was Collins's nominal superior and also by Austin Stack, Minister for Home Affairs, who had conceived a dislike for Collins. Both of these men had practical limitations and they got on Collins's nerves. "Your department is only a b——joke, Austin," he said to Stack. The remark was not forgiven, nor had he taken the pains to disguise his opinion of Brugha as an administrator. So much has been written of the debonair side of Collins's character that the domineering and aggressive element in his nature, which was very strong, has been overlooked. It made him enemies.

When de Valera came back from America he was prone to regale his companions with accounts of his experiences. These had been pleasanter than theirs and the repetition of the topic irritated Collins. "Oh, I have it off by heart," he interrupted on one occasion.[9] A paragraph in one of Collins's letters to de Valera in America is a revelation—of the recipient particularly—"For God's sake ' Dev ' don't start an argument about its being from the prospectus only, etc. Don't, please. It's quite all right."[10] It is not difficult to believe that de Valera listened to Brugha and Stack. He was strictly impartial. But Collins felt that, in the circumstances, to be judicial was to be unfair. He had carried the whole load; the magnanimity should have been theirs, and de Valera should have had the generosity to tell them so. O'Higgins was very depressed to see how de Valera, whom he still revered, kept silent when Collins was attacked in the Cabinet.

De Valera's first suggestions to the Cabinet were to "ease off." He criticized the tactics of the army in so far as their methods were provoking reprisals on the civilian population and he expressed disapproval of the lengths to which the Department of Local Government and Home Affairs had gone. They should, he thought, "make the burden on the people as light as they could."[11] Afterwards de Valera publicly defended the policy of ambushes on the grounds that the Irish had no armoured cars or tanks and stone walls were their only protection, as surprise was their only hope, in battle.

O'Higgins was desperately disappointed by de Valera's criticism of his department's activities. "I will never put myself in the ridiculous position," de Valera said, "of an engine running away without its train."[12] But despite any conflict about departmental policy de Valera soon formed a high opinion of O'Higgins. Turning to him one day in the Dáil, he invited his attendance at a Cabinet meeting where he could take every part in the business of the Executive except voting. It was a signal act of recognition. "Things are looking up all round," he wrote to his fiancée in the spring. "I take pride in the fact that I sensed the psychological moment early in March and duly informed my much better and wiser half. At the same time . . . our friends may decide on another bout of the rough and tumble business; failing that, they may well be relied on to try every trick in their dirty bag to stampede a not very wise or highly-educated people."

And a few weeks later he was jubilant. "Things be movin' rapidly and magnificently in real sober earnest now. . . . You know I don't lose my head and talk wild as a rule. . . . Even if events don't move quite so well or so rapidly you can take it that there has been an advance which puts the issue absolutely beyond a shadow of doubt. . . . You and I are good stickers, little one—if this thing goes wrong—as, of course, it may—why we have a bit left still, but the child may hope and MUST pray that this bud will flourish and bloom and will require no more of 'war's red rain' to bring it to fruition and maturity."

CHAPTER V

THE TREATY

IN August the Dáil met and there was a renewal of the air of hopeful confidence which had permeated the first Dáil of 1919. There was also a great display of mutual regard : it is both comic and sad to see how soon uncritical admiration gave way to the bitterest personalities. This Dáil had been elected in May under the Government of Ireland Act, 1920. The Act prescribed an election for the parliaments of Northern and Southern Ireland : the Sinn Feiners, while refusing to recognise the Act, used the occasion to elect a new Dáil. The Irish Party did not contest any seats and in every constituency in Southern Ireland a Sinn Feiner was returned unopposed except in Trinity College which returned four Unionists without a contest. In the North twelve Sinn Feiners and Nationalists were returned and forty Unionists. In Tyrone and Fermanagh the unionist candidates were beaten by 7,831 votes.

De Valera was now called An t-Uachtarain (President) instead of Priomh-Aireach (Prime Minister)—an amendment of his own suggestion which had some significance, because in the Treaty debate de Valera claimed that he was President of the Republic. This and other technicalities were important because the efforts to pursue a legalistic attitude towards them and to preserve the sacred character with which they were endowed were to some extent responsible for the Civil War.

It was one of the characteristics of Kevin O'Higgins, for which he was most hated in later years, that he never lost an opportunity to tell the truth about the façade which he and his former colleagues had maintained. Once the moral necessity for it ceased, it became mere humbug and as such O'Higgins treated it without ceremony. Speaking in March, 1922, at a public meeting in Dublin he said : "During the past two years the 'existing republic' had existed very much in a couple of backrooms in Dublin."

When, therefore, the new Dáil met in August, 1921, de Valera was again in fact Prime Minister of the underground government, his title, however, was changed to that which is the Irish version of President in the present constitution.

In his speech at the opening of the Dáil, de Valera gave his view of the republican issue, an explicit analysis which made it clear that de Valera was no fanatic but a practical statesman ; but parts of this speech reveal that incapacity for producing his thoughts in words which has made it difficult at times to follow the workings of his mind or to understand what precisely he means.

On the following day de Valera made a longer speech on the same subject and again one is faced, perusing it, with an almost impossible task if one seeks to find a coherent statement. It is not a speech but a man thinking aloud and not thinking consecutively or clearly. Anyone listening at the time, visualizing a moment of crisis, would find it difficult to predict what de Valera would do in that crisis. In his heart was a sincere and obvious devotion to the ideal of Irish freedom, but if he were to trust to his intellect to put him on the path leading to that ideal, no one could predict where he would eventually find himself. In matters of judgment a man must use his mind and abide by its decisions : a heart in a statesman is to be desired, but it is to be feared, if in an emergency, it is the organ by which he resolves what to do.

De Valera's method of argument was to state two premises and then, without drawing any conclusion, to start talking about something which the minor premise suggested to his mind.

He argued in the course of this remarkable speech that Ireland could not be offered Dominion Status because Ireland was cut in two. Then he stated that it was not in the nature of things that Ireland could be offered Dominion Home Rule " because that status depends upon the fact that Australia and Canada and South Africa and the rest are not neighbours of Britain."[1] From that point he argued at great length to arrive eventually at the conclusion that Ireland and England are neighbours by nature and should, therefore, be neighbourly. The problem had to be settled—" the fundamental problem " as he described it. But the only solution he could offer was that it should be settled " simply on the basis of that which everyone knows to be right and good." The last word gave birth to a new thought and the speaker's mind hurried off to peep into the cradle.

The word " fundamental " appeared with the frequency of a

preposition but, alas, its persistence seemed only part of a scheme to delay the discussion of fundamentals. Again and again it seemed that de Valera must take the plunge and arrive at a conclusion, again and again expectation was heightened by bounces on the logical springboard : the dive was anxiously awaited, but there was no sound of the splash.

The only tangible suggestion in this long speech was a hint that " an association consistent with our right to see that we were the judges of what were our own interests, and that we were not compelled to leave the judgment of what were our interests or not to others " would commend itself to the majority of his colleagues. The British description of the Commonwealth fitted in with such a notion, but the Dominions were free to secede if they wanted to ; " We are told that we must stay in whether we like it or not."

At this point one feels that in the obvious sequence of ideas de Valera would conclude by saying, in effect : " The English don't really intend to allow us to be a Dominion and the world can judge the sincerity of their so-called offer of Dominion Status." But this speech was not on the conventional pattern. " We are not claiming any right to secede," he continued. " There can never be in the case of Ireland a question of secession because there has never been a union. They talk as if there was a union. I say that, even if there was, that union was severed here on the 21st January, 1919." A remark which brings to mind the reply a foreigner received when he asked an Irish lady politician to explain the high rate of lunacy in Ireland. " That is a lie," she replied, " propagated by the English. And even if it is true, they are responsible for it."

This speech of de Valera's was not lightly thrown off. At its commencement he remarked that he spoke in English because what he had to say " will be heard by the whole world " and he also made it clear at the beginning that his purpose was to let it be known that the terms then offered by Britain would not be accepted. It is unlikely that he spoke vaguely of set purpose. Vagueness of that kind is usually expressed in well-ordered sentences in which each word bears the stamp of careful selection. De Valera's torrential repetitiveness does not give this impression. In truth, perhaps, he was groping for a formula which would preserve the national self-respect and yet satisfy England and Ulster. Into an Irish Republic he must have known that the

North would not come. Some of the speech suggests that he may have been, in part at least, endeavouring to interpret another man's ideas. It was, for instance, a theory of Childers that Ireland could never have the same status as Canada in fact, because England would interfere with Ireland which was near her, while Canada, out of reach, would be left alone.

The responsibility was tremendous and the dangers very great. An exchange of letters began between Lloyd George and de Valera in which the latter always insisted that he could only negotiate as the leader of an independent sovereign state. At the same time he was aware that a compromise was essential. Joseph McGrath and Harry Boland were sent with one of these letters to see Lloyd George at Gairloch in Scotland and McGrath, afterwards in the Dáil, said that Boland confided in him that he was to be sent to America by de Valera to prepare Irish-American opinion for something less than a Republic. Griffith, in a burst of anger, some months after the Treaty, said that before he went to London de Valera had said : " Get me out of this strait-jacket of the Republic."[2] De Valera publicly denied the statement but it did not, after all, mean so much. There was the fact of Ulster, the fact of the inequality in strength between the two negotiators and the military aspect of the situation. In the light of these an uncomplicated form of separation for a United Ireland was impossible of achievement. How much was it necessary to give away ?

The attitude of the British was made clear ; they did not regard de Valera as an impossibilist or a dangerous man. Seán Mac Eoin, a gallant and redoubtable fighter, was only released from prison when Collins refused to have anything to do with negotiations to which his release was not a preliminary, but some weeks before negotiations began de Valera was arrested and promptly set free. Kevin O'Higgins, for one on the Irish side, regarded Collins as the die-hard, de Valera as a constitutionalist and a moderating influence. " Patience, wisdom, tolerance, a great compassion for the multitude, struck me as distinguishing marks of Mr. de Valera when the responsibility of national leadership was his," wrote O'Higgins afterwards. When, therefore, in London on his honeymoon he heard that there was a sharp division of opinion between the Irish plenipotentiaries, he never doubted but that Collins was making difficulties and that de Valera and Griffith would come to terms.

Collins invited O'Higgins to come as secretary to the delegation, then about to set out for London. He asked to be excused on account of his marriage so long delayed and now arranged. This refusal is surprising in view of the Cato-like qualities which O'Higgins was later to exhibit; but there was no conscious neglect of duty in his attitude; he was diffident about his own abilities and did not consider that he would be an exceptional acquisition to the team.

His marriage to Miss Cole took place in the last week of October, 1921, a time of extreme political tension. Among the guests was de Valera and the best man was Rory O'Connor. A photograph at the wedding shows the three men together. In the light of after events it has a tragic significance—a symbol of the poisonous effect that politics can have on human relations.

O'Higgins gave Collins all the credit for the fact that an Irish delegation was now sitting in conference with the leaders of the English Cabinet. The Irish party consisted of Griffith, Collins, Edmund Duggan, Robert Barton and George Gavan Duffy who had for some years practised as a solicitor in London. Fitz Gerald was press representative. The secretaries were : John Chartres, who lived in London ; Diarmuid O'Hegarty, who was afterwards to become the Grey Eminence of the Free State Government, and Erskine Childers. The English team was led by the Prime Minister, Lloyd George, and with him were Lord Birkenhead, Winston Churchill, Austen Chamberlain, Sir Hamar Greenwood, Sir Gordon Hewart, Sir L. Worthington Evans, and other Ministers took part in the discussions.

After wearisome parley the Irish delegation returned on the 3rd December to Dublin with a draft which did not win the approval of de Valera or two of his Ministers, Brugha and Stack. Griffith agreed not to sign it. The document was modified and then, under pressure, the extent of which has been variously described, articles of agreement were signed on 6th December, 1921. De Valera, Brugha and Stack repudiated them, although a majority in the Cabinet agreed to accept. The events that followed led to Civil War.

In London Griffith and Collins were alone able to impress ; their colleagues were quite overshadowed. Two camps began to form, Childers, Barton and Gavan Duffy forming an opposition which was purist in principle but not effective in practice. Personalities played a great part. Griffith abominated Childers.

He would break off conversation when Childers entered the room and only resume it when he left. In Ireland Stack disliked, and Brugha hated, Collins who, in time, became more and more in harmony with Griffith. De Valera was aware of Brugha's jealousy of Collins. Nevertheless Collins expected that de Valera would overrule Brugha and Stack. From them he expected opposition to any compromise he made.

*   *   *

O'Higgins and his wife were in London on their honeymoon while the Irish delegation stayed at Hans Place and Cadogan Gardens. Busy as he was at conferences and shadowed by press-men, Collins never forgot other people. Presents arrived for the bride; there was a box at the theatre. One night a dinner was given to O'Higgins and his bride by the delegation. It became painfully obvious that the gaiety was forced and a basic gloom found its way through the outward appearance of a party spirit.

O'Higgins remained in London for three weeks. He became increasingly depressed by the deterioration in the relations between the delegates. He thought from the first that it was a great mistake to send Childers, with his breeding and record, to London. Griffith did not want him and he irritated Griffith exceedingly, which was not a good beginning. His presence might well have been resented by the British. At night Childers sat up writing long memoranda which he posted home, and an uncomfortable feeling that these were critical took possession of some of the delegates. Childers was frail and coughed continually. O'Higgins, a doctor's son, suspected ill-health and he mistrusted the judgment of sick men.

The dislike for Childers was not confined to Griffith : his precise manner and air of aloofness gave an impression of conscious superiority which was probably misleading. Griffith had refused his offer to come into Irish politics, and had advised him to stay in England ; when he ignored this suggestion, and became known to de Valera, Griffith, who had a hatred of English people in Ireland, was very much annoyed. He regarded Childers as an English Radical politician, who, seeing no political future for himself in England, and having taken up Ireland as a specialist's subject, decided to make a career in the Sinn Fein movement.

Childers's mother was Irish, and much of his childhood had been spent in Ireland. His political interest had gradually developed, for he wrote a long book on Home Rule in 1912—which treated Irish secession as out of the question. In 1914 he owned and navigated the yacht which brought to Howth arms for the Irish Volunteers, and when he returned from war service in the Air Force Intelligence Section, he was appointed Secretary to the Convention which Lloyd George set up to study the Irish problem, and which met in Trinity College. Thence he progressed to Sinn Fein, meeting Desmond Fitz Gerald, who introduced him to Griffith.

"When I came home from the United States, Deputy Childers was introduced to me by the Minister for Finance," said de Valera once in the Dáil. "God forgive me," ejaculated Collins.[3]

A rational basis for criticism of Childers was the fact that in his adoption of Ireland's cause there was an element of adventure —a romantic enthusiasm such as that which sent Byron to Greece and La Fayette to America. Neither of these men was ever accorded anything but honour for their disinterested chivalry, why the feud with Childers? Firstly, because neither Byron nor La Fayette took sides against the country of their birth, and then there was the difficulty of Childers's idiosyncrasies—a red-tapish observance of the orthodoxies of diplomatic routine and mannerisms, which gave rise to a disproportionate antipathy. He had been chosen by de Valera. The popularity of the President misled a great many people into believing that he had a particular affection for plain people and a corresponding antipathy to the grand manner. In fact, de Valera has never shown a distaste for the political companionship of the polite. During this period it was some of the adherents of Collins who displayed at times an unreasonable disinclination to trust political support from people who had been educated in "Ascendancy" circles.

Admiration for the sane, manly and devoted qualities of Arthur Griffith need not blind one to his defects. He could be sour. He did as much as anyone to arouse the bitter anti-English feeling which is only now beginning to die. He frankly suspected Childers's credentials. He thought he might be an English secret service man, acting as a spy and *agent provocateur*. He said so. No one believes this now ; it was an illusion of Griffith, but he sowed the seeds of distrust and anger which made the death of Childers certain when he was captured in the Civil War. The practical element in Collins revolted against Childers when, in a discussion

with Admiral Beatty on coastal defence problems, Childers said :
" Supposing Ireland were not there," and Beatty replied : " But
it is there."[4]

The final crisis in the Irish Cabinet was over the question of an
oath of allegiance. De Valera had dictated a form of oath which
he was prepared to recommend, and the English draft contained
an oath in a more imperial form. De Valera's apologists declare
that his version was dictated without the elaborate care which he
usually gave to any expression in words, and misinterpreted.
Some years later, O'Higgins described the circumstances : " We
sat there and waited while de Valera chewed his pencil. Two
of the plenipotentiaries took out their notebooks ready to take
down what the great man would say. . . . After five or seven
minutes of silence the form of words was dictated. Barton then
read it out."[5] De Valera also agreed to vote an annual contribution
to the King's revenue.

The Treaty provided that the Irish Free State was a Dominion
with the same status as Canada ; that six Northern counties had
the power to secede ; that certain defence facilities were accorded
to England ; that Ireland should bear such a share of the British
national debt as should be decided, if necessary, by arbitration.

During the week-end visit of the delegation to Dublin, after
the British had presented their final draft, Brugha, with unamiable
vigilance, inquired why Griffith and Collins had formed the habit
of meeting British representatives without the other Irish delegates.
When Griffith replied that the arrangement was approved by
his colleagues, Brugha remarked : " Yes, the British Government
selected their men." This observation so incensed Collins and
Griffith that they refused, on their return to London, to accompany
their colleagues when they went with a new proposal to the British
Government, embodying the idea of an externally-associated
Republic. The document contained de Valera's dictated oath
and an offer to give a contribution to the King's revenue.

Griffith, Collins and Duggan refused to bring the completed
draft to the British. It was, in their opinion, the end of negotiations
if they did so. At length, when Barton and Gavan Duffy rose to go
alone, Griffith agreed to accompany them. He fought his hardest
to gain acceptance of these proposals, for which he had no responsibility. (Griffith was prepared to accept a very slight improvement
on the original English offer.) Lloyd George regarded the Irish
proposal as a return to the original position, and the break came

when Gavan Duffy said : "Our difficulty is coming into the Empire."[6]

Lloyd George then saw Collins privately and managed to convince him that if a Treaty was signed, and Ulster refused to remain in the Free State, the Boundary Commission would award so small an area to the North that it would be forced by economic necessity to forgo the luxury of a separate government. Other sops were held out by Lloyd George, and by the end of the interview he had succeeded in making a deep impression. An appointment was arranged. One further meeting with the British ended with Griffith promising to sign. On the way back to Hans Place, Collins announced his intention of doing likewise. Duggan then agreed. Barton took a long time before he could be convinced. He and Childers were confidants as well as cousins, and before he gave his decisions he saw Childers alone. He then agreed to sign if he could at the same time say he was doing it under duress. This was not agreed to. The result of a break meant—or so the delegates were convinced—a resumption of war on a more terrible scale with the advantage all on England's side. This factor decided Barton ; and Duffy, not long afterwards, agreed also to sign.

Of the five who signed the Treaty, Griffith was best satisfied with it ; Collins, who knew the military position and who had been sent to England against his will, came to the conclusion that he made the best bargain in the circumstances, and, being essentially practical, decided that certain peace was preferable to certain war. Having signed it, he was too much of a man to apologize for his signature.

In view of the fact that de Valera insisted that he believed no treaty could be signed which had not been first referred back to him, it is interesting that neither Childers, Barton nor Duffy thought of this. Griffith has been accused of breaking his word to the Cabinet in this matter, but the fact is that the final British Treaty proposals had been fully discussed by the Irish Cabinet and turned down ; the delegation had succeeded in obtaining substantial modifications in the original proposals, and, realizing that the issue was " sign or break," thought their responsibility to Dublin at an end. They were plenipotentiaries by de Valera's express wish. Moreover, it was clear that the Irish solution would not be accepted by the English, although Griffith, against his wishes, had done all he could to make it succeed.

After the delegation had returned to London on the 3rd

December, rumours of a break were widespread, and in Ireland there was talk of a renewal of war. On the night of the 6th December, while the Treaty was being signed, de Valera was in Limerick, where he had been reviewing Volunteers. When he heard the news of the Treaty he was on his way back to Dublin to preside, in his capacity as Chancellor of the National University, over a Dante Commemoration Meeting in the Mansion House. Brugha and Stack were waiting to tell him that the news was " Bad," and when Duggan arrived with a copy of the document, he brushed it aside, and, according to Beaslai, " turned round to discuss whether he would wear his Chancellor's robes or not, muttering some remark about ' Soon being back to teaching.' " A rough outline of the agreement had appeared in the evening paper, and this was the only information which de Valera had received before he sat in dignified rage at the lecture in honour of the Italian poet.[7]

Outside, crowds cheered the prospect of peace.

CHAPTER VI

DEBATE ON THE TREATY

KEVIN O'HIGGINS, when he heard of a settlement, wrote a triumphant letter home to tell the news, but when the terms of the Treaty were disclosed, he expressed disappointment. This was the feeling of all Separatists. It must not be thought that there was a party who liked the terms in the ranks of the Republicans. There was not. But there was a sharp division as to the advisability of accepting or rejecting them. De Valera summoned a Cabinet meeting which Kevin O'Higgins attended; a vote was taken and the Treaty agreed to by a majority, de Valera, Stack and Brugha dissenting.

On the way home from England, Collins and other members of the party had tried to forecast the reactions of the Dáil members to the proposals. No one thought de Valera would reject them. Childers had a long discussion with one of the law advisers as to the method by which the constitution could be brought into being. He did not like the idea of having it conferred by an Act of the British Parliament. He gave no hint that he thought the Treaty might be—or that he wished it to be—cast aside, but seemed to accept it as an accomplished fact.

To O'Higgins, the essential matter was unity; if the Cabinet could work together, the best could be got out of the Treaty. To him, as to Collins, the great thing was that now the British forces would evacuate the country and Dublin Castle would be handed over to an Irish Government. O'Higgins was one of the many who begged de Valera not to have a split. He reminded him of the Parnell split and the ruin it brought to the Irish cause. "It will," said O'Higgins, "be like releasing the west wind." "Aye," cried de Valera, striking his chest, "the west wind." [1] On the 8th of December, following the vote at the Cabinet meeting, de Valera sent a letter to the papers announcing that he, Brugha and Stack "cannot recommend the acceptance of this Treaty," and ending with a paragraph which made a lasting impression on the memory of O'Higgins: "The great test of our people has come; let us face it worthily without bitterness and, above all, without recriminations. There is a definite constitutional way of resolving our political differences—let us not depart from it, and let the conduct of the Cabinet in this matter be an example to the whole nation."

While Collins's biographer has written of this letter: "It is hard to speak with patience of the man who, entrusted with the leadership of the Irish people in a great moment of crisis in their history, could fling such a torch in the powder magazine," Lord Pakenham, ten years later, considered that: "Holding the principles he did, de Valera had no course but to write a letter of this kind." [2]

No one, it can be said, showed such bitterness in the discussions that followed as Brugha; nor can it be said that any of the three dissidents showed a tender regard for constitutional ways of resolving difficulties as they multiplied reasons for delaying an election while the country was rushing to a state of seething disorder and indiscipline.

The Dáil then met in private session, and here de Valera produced his plan, which was to be offered as a substitute for the Treaty to the British. This, as *Document No. 2*, became the King Charles's head of Irish politics. It was voted upon by the assembly and rejected, whereat de Valera sent round to collect the distributed copies, but one member kept his and took it away. In this Document the word Republic is not mentioned; but there is no Oath, no Governor-General, and it provides that " for purposes of common concern Ireland shall be associated with the States of the British Commonwealth." Moreover, " His Britannic Majesty " was to be recognized as " head of the Association."

In no other practical aspect did the Document differ from the Treaty. The provision for port and defence facilities to England and for the Northern right to self-determination remained.

In most respects it is the status which the Twenty-six Counties now enjoy and that, de Valera has more than once declared, is, according to accepted definitions, the status of a Republic. De Valera's proposals were in most particulars the scheme of external association which, for the last time, the delegates had tried to get the English to agree to on the day before the Treaty was signed.

The chief criticism of de Valera's behaviour is that he did not go on the delegation. He forced Collins to go against his will, and entrusted the leadership of the delegation to Griffith whom he knew to have moderate views. When the delegation returned to Dublin on 3rd December for the last meeting, they carried the final British offer. It was not unlikely that Lloyd George would refuse to allow further delay while the plenipotentiaries went back for instructions. Lloyd George was leading the British delegation, his counterpart should have led the Irish party. And it was de Valera who was warmest in his insistence that no restrictions whatever be put upon the delegation. "Remember," he said, "what you are asking them to do. You are asking them to secure by negotiations what we are totally unable to secure by force of arms."[3] Is it possible that de Valera wanted the negotiations to break down so that he could at the last moment come to terms himself? Griffith in the Dáil gave an account of a conversation with de Valera when the delegates were being chosen in the course of which de Valera said: "There may have to be scapegoats."[4] Collins did his best not to go to London. With a price on his head, he thought it better to preserve his legend than to come out into the open. The legend might be needed again. Once gone it was gone forever. Moreover, he was an oath-bound member of the Irish Republican Brotherhood which put him in the position that if he, the architect of the counter-terror, signed any Treaty the extremists would regard him as a traitor, while, if he failed to get a settlement, the country would hold him responsible for the resumption of war. De Valera and Griffith were the obvious negotiators. Neither of them had said or done anything which made it inconsistent for them to compromise. If Collins endorsed the terms that were acceptable to them, who in the country would have had the authority to challenge the settlement? It did not appear thus to de Valera; and Collins went with a heavy heart to London convinced that he went to his ruin. "I am signing my death warrant," he said to Birkenhead as he put his name to the Treaty.

The document which de Valera produced as his alternative to the Treaty differed from it in such a minor degree that it is hard to believe de Valera was prepared to risk Civil War for the difference. The fact that a Treaty was signed seemed to annoy him more than the contents of the Treaty itself. If he felt disappointed with the work of the delegation when he had his own way in composing that delegation, was it not his duty to find

" a constitutional way " out of the situation instead of advertising so precipitously a division among the leaders of the people ? A Cabinet should act as a Cabinet. A minister can always resign. It would have been better for de Valera to have done this if he considered his honour was at stake. But, looking at these events a quarter of a century after they took place, and with the cool judgment with which one reviews conduct in a crisis which has been resolved, if the negotiators had definite instructions not to sign anything before the Cabinet knew what they were signing, it would seem as though Lloyd George had stampeded the jaded Irishmen. Sir Henry Wilson may have looked forward to a full scale military campaign in Ireland, but was his the sort of mentality that foresees the impartial judgment of history ? Or did that military mind reflect the general mood of a war-weary world ? Would the English people have tolerated it ? Possibly not. But if there was a break in the negotiations world sympathy would not have gone out to Ireland. Charity begins at home and thins rapidly as it travels : we are always impatient with others if they refuse to settle questions on account of points of detail. What is a principle to them is obstinacy to us.

Acute sensitivity on the moral dignity of his country was one of the outstanding features of O'Higgins's character. In this crisis he had only one impulse—to put aside any feeling of disappointment, to keep a united front, and to embark on a policy of construction in the country.

He had no doubts whatever as to whether it was better to implement this Treaty, make a constitution for the country, take over immediate control of its government and resources, or to embark on a further period of guerilla war, impending bankruptcy and general demoralization. Against a policy which was endorsed by Griffith and Collins, he was not prepared to jib. He respected one, he hero-worshipped the other.

The Dáil met in public session in University College in Earlsfort Terrace on the 14th December, 1921. The room was crowded and stuffy. It was remarked by journalists that only two of the assembled deputies kept on their overcoats—de Valera and J. J. Walsh. De Valera looked deadly pale, thin and ill. Prayers were said by the Reverend Doctor Browne and then de Valera opened the proceedings in a few sentences of Irish which have been translated :—" My Irish is not as good as I should like it to be. I am better able to express my thoughts in English and so I think I had better speak wholly in English,"[5] and then he proceeded to say :—" Some of the members do not know Irish, I think, and consequently what I shall say will be in English." His object was to make clear the instructions which were given to the delegates and he expressed his willingness to discuss the matter in private. Collins pointed out that the articles of agreement were not a treaty, the Dáil had to ratify them and the signatories need only recommend the document for acceptance. In the same manner the British Parliament had to pass legislation to ratify the agreement. Both had power to reject what their representatives had signed.

This fact should be kept in mind. Those who, like de Valera, did not approve, had only to win a majority in the Dáil to repudiate the Treaty. If the Dáil decided otherwise, then the democratic principle asserted itself, and the minority would have to give way. And this Dáil was composed of members picked on a very selective basis, not as representatives of public opinion, but purely on a basis of acknowledged extremism. " Time and again," wrote O'Higgins, " in Dáil Eireann private session he (de Valera) assured the assembled Teachtai that he never made the mistake of regarding them as representatives of the nation in any real sense ; his view being that they were but a selection from the left wing of the nation."[6]

After the discussions of the first day the Dáil had a private session during which de Valera expounded the policy of Document No. 2 which Cathal Brugha described as " a supreme effort by the Captain of the ship to pull it off the rocks on which it had been driven by the incompetent amateurs who had seized the helm."

Writing to his brother, Maurice, on the 15th December, Tim Healy said : " Your apprentice Kevin made the best speech to-day in the Dáil and although hitherto friendly with de Valera, he laid into him brilliantly and told him his hasty action was the cause of the trouble and that he had been appealed to again and again not to send out his condemnation, especially as, until the previous week, he had been in full accord with the delegates."[7]

In any event neither Griffith nor Collins showed a disposition to go back on the document they had signed, and a majority in the Dáil decided not to accept de Valera's proposals on the unlikely possibility that, having been in substance offered and rejected, they would now be acceptable to the British Government.

When the Dáil reassembled in public, the Speaker announced that de Valera had withdrawn his proposals and they "must be regarded as confidential" until he brought them forward formally.

Griffith and Collins both protested against this tying of their hands. If the Dáil were to discuss the Treaty and decide whether or not to accept it, why should the public be deprived of the essential information what the alternative was ? De Valera explained that his suggestions were only put in "to elicit views. I am ready to put my proposition in its proper place before this assembly and before the Irish nation."[8]

The Treaty debates make strange reading. There is much latent hysteria which would have provided Dostoievsky with material. There is the calm and courteous—and as the future disclosed— entirely incorrect reasoning of Childers ; the restless, sometimes effeminate emotionalism of de Valera ; the moderation of Collins ; the firm manliness of Griffith ; the withering blight of Mary MacSwiney ; the naïvety of the other women ; the weakness and candour of Barton ; the sterile bitterness of Brugha ; the incorrigible idealism of Mellowes ; the cynicism of Walsh ; the intelligence of two young men, O'Higgins and Patrick Hogan, destined to become to one another as David and Jonathan. It is, perhaps, significant that Miss MacSwiney, in the course of an oration that lasted for more than two hours, referred to each of them as having spoken "in a slightly superior voice."

Coming away from the meeting, O'Higgins asked Patrick McCartan what he thought of his speech. McCartan replied : "Very clever but very bitter." O'Higgins was genuinely surprised. "Bitter," he said, "I was not bitter." Reading that speech now one finds no trace of bitterness. It is very direct and forthright if, in places, ironical. No doubt what influenced McCartan was, what Miss MacSwiney described as, " a slightly superior voice."

O'Higgins had a magisterial manner. Addressing an audience, he spoke, as it were, from a height. This had a different effect on different people : to some it conveyed compelling moral purpose ; to others imperiousness. It was not a manner which tempered the point of witticisms ; the man seemed too solemn to joke for pleasure ; he had nothing of the gamin about him, nothing of that exquisiteness which gives a safe conduct to the wisecrack. Two great Irishmen, Wilde and Shaw, have taken liberties with their tongues and made no enemies, because they always appeared to be on the best of terms with the world, even when they were saying the rudest things about it. O'Higgins in public, so far from seeming to be on good terms with the world, appeared rather to be preoccupied with the amount of original sin he found in it, and his parliamentary style sometimes suggested the pulpit during Lent. It has been said of Shaw that he has no enemies but his friends don't like him. The contrary was true of O'Higgins. He had good friends and he made many enemies ; but then, Shaw has never held any political office and O'Higgins, to quote Garvin, "crushed anarchy in Ireland under an armed heel so that it has never lifted its head again. To do this he had to crush some of the dearest impulses of his own heart, and to sacrifice within himself, in the flower of his age, every possibility of extended life."[9]

Everything about O'Higgins suggested a completely integrated personality. The first impression he gave was, indeed, of a man "cast in bronze." That impression remained and people having formed it were unprepared for any bending, any lightness of touch.

We do not associate such a character with the lighter side of mind ; yet after his death, *The Times* referred to "his sparing whimsical speech." This side of him was only disclosed, as a rule, in conversation. He was a man whom one would believe to mean always what he said ; such men require a subtle and sophisticated audience for their lighter moments. The members of the Dáil were O'Higgins's audience. They did not, as a whole, answer to that description.

We are not here concerned with the arguments used by the various speakers in the weary, word-spattered days of idealism, realism and flatulence, when the Dáil debated the Anglo-Irish Treaty, except in so far as they concern the subject of this biography.

O'Higgins[10] began by alluding to the keenness with which he felt the separation between himself and those with whom he was at variance and "the great-hearted man who leads them." "It has been the purest pleasure of my life to work with them." In view of all the terrible words and deeds that were to follow, it is well to realize that these were sincerely the feelings of the speaker, just as Griffith was sincere when he said of de Valera : "There is scarcely a man I have ever met in my life that I have more love and respect for." O'Higgins was never effusive. He was never one of that too common and so tiresome species— the gushing Irishman. When, therefore, he spoke well of anyone, he meant what he said. It is worth remembering that he could say in December, 1921 : "I pay willing tribute to the sincerity and to the lofty idealism of those who hold different views from ours on this issue." In his exposition of his reasons for supporting the London delegation, there is no hint of fog, no rhetoric and no rambling. He knit the issue at once, endeavouring to keep the discussion "on lines that are severely relevant." The question to be decided was whether the Dáil should accept the Treaty— not whether the delegation ought to have signed the agreement— "They are within their rights in signing ; no one, I think, questions that. We could have given terms of reference to the pleni- potentiaries ; we gave none." He threw a new light on the much discussed point as to whether Lloyd George exacted the signatures under a threat of "immediate and terrible war." It is a well-worn device in bargaining to offer some advance on previous terms at the price of immediate acceptance. The adversary has to assess the relative strength of the parties and decide whether he can do better by waiting. This, in O'Higgins's opinion, was what Lloyd George had done. "At the last moment there were terms put up, not for bargain, but as the price of the signatures. There were big improvements on the *final* document—improvements affect- ing Trade, Defence and North East Ulster—and they were not put up to be brought back for consideration." O'Higgins made it abundantly clear that the assembly had full powers in law and honour to reject the proposals. He spoke without heat, but he made fun of Erskine Childers, "who took a lot of unnecessary time and trouble in explaining how much nicer it would be to get better terms than these. He did not tell us, as an authority on military and naval matters, how we are going to break the British Army and Navy and get these better terms." But O'Higgins, if advocating the acceptance of the Treaty, was not overestimating its value. "A sovereign and independent Republic was our claim and our fighting ground." The fact that negotiations were begun, and delegates selected, showed that there was something to be given away. "We would do well to scrutinize carefully the document they have produced, not so much in relation to the inscription on our battle standards, but rather in relation to our prospects of achieving more."

He spoke without interruption until he began to review the terms presented by the British and with which the Irish had returned on the Saturday before the signing of the Treaty, terms which quashed the " external association " idea—Ireland outside the Empire and attached not inside and absorbed—and brought Ireland definitely within the British Empire, pledging the members of her Parliament. At this stage, de Valera broke in. These were Cabinet matters not to be discussed. O'Higgins thought the " Irish people are entitled to hear the genesis of the present situation," a remark which won applause from some, but de Valera was adamant. A general discussion then began, O'Higgins contending that it was not fair that the public should be left under the impression that the alternative to the Treaty was the full Irish claim for a Republic. They should know the narrow margin between the Treaty men and the Anti-Treaty Party. This brought up the question of Document No. 2. It had been discussed in secret session for three days. " Are the Irish people," Griffith intervened, " not to be allowed to see that Document ? " De Valera protested. His proposals were put forward " to remedy what I considered a serious mistake for the nation." They were now withdrawn ; in due course, he would put forward his own proposition.

O'Higgins expressed his dissatisfaction at not being able to discuss the relative merits of the Treaty and the proposals which the Cabinet could have agreed on. " I do not," he urged, " wish to be forced into a stronger advocacy of the Treaty than I feel. . . . I do say it represents such a broad measure of liberty for the Irish people and acknowledges such a large proportion of its rights, you are not entitled to reject it without being able to show that you have a reasonable prospect of achieving more." " The man who is against peace," said the English Premier, in presenting his ultimatum, " must bear now and for ever the responsibility for terrible and immediate war." And then O'Higgins made the point upon which he based a great deal of his future antagonism to those who created the circumstances which led to the Civil War : " The men there knew our resources and the resources of the enemy, and they held in their own hearts and consciences that we were not entitled to plunge the plain people of Ireland into a terrible and immediate war *for the difference between the terms of this Treaty and what they knew a united Cabinet would recommend to the Dáil.*"

He went on to summarize the advantages of the Treaty—
fiscal freedom and control of internal affairs. " When England
is at war, Ireland need not send one man or contribute one penny.
I wish to emphasize that. This morning the President said the
Army of the Irish Free State would be the Army of His Majesty.
Can His Majesty send one battalion or company of the Army of
the Irish Free State from Cork into the adjoining county ? If he
acts in Ireland, he acts on the advice of his Irish Ministers." And
then he used the phrase which, more than any other, crystallized
the difference in method between himself and de Valera : " Yes,
if we go into the Empire, we go in, not sliding in, attempting to
throw dust in our people's eyes, but we go in with our heads up."

Far from feeling defeated, O'Higgins was anticipating with
intense excitement the task of nation-building that lay ahead.
Already he had given thought to the peculiar, undefined relations
between the different members of the Commonwealth of Nations,
and was speculating on the possibility of moulding that system
into something nearer to the heart's desire. " I believe the evolution
of this group must be towards a condition, not merely of individual
freedom, but also of equality of status. I quite admit, in the case
of Ireland, the tie is not voluntary, and, in the case of Ireland,
the status is not equal." He could not take the responsibility of
voting for war in preference. " To ratify this Treaty, it has been
said, would constitute an abandonment of principles, . . . would
be a betrayal to those who died for Irish independence in the past.
. . . Now, principle is immortal. If the principle of Ireland's
nationhood could be vitally affected by the action of a representative body of Irishmen at any time, it has died many deaths." The
Irish chieftains had sworn allegiance to Henry VIII ; Grattan's
Parliament pledged allegiance to George III. Irish members at
Westminster had pledged like allegiance for 118 years. Never
was it suggested that the men who went out fighting for a Republic
were bound, or behaved, dishonourably, because of the allegiance
sworn by their ancestors. " There has been too much talk of what
the dead men would do."

Quite apart from the ingenuity which his speech revealed, there
was everywhere apparent a sophisticated, mature and statesman-
like approach to the subject. Here was no hot-headed fanatic, no
careerist using patriotic cant to forward his own interests, and
yet there was no tincture of materialism which, in a revolutionary
epoch, when men are taking desperate risks, has about it something

particularly uninspiring. He dwelt upon the significance of the clause in the Treaty which guaranteed to Ireland the practice and constitutional usage of Canada. This had been brushed aside by Childers, who seemed to believe that England would never allow Ireland to enjoy a tittle of the freedom which remoteness insured to Canada. It is interesting to note how completely and hopelessly Childers, a British soldier and civil servant, educated in England, with a life-study of constitutional law, misjudged the situation, and how near the truth the inexperienced O'Higgins was proved to be by the course of events. Indeed, some of Childers's remarks give the impression that he was unaware of the existing position. " Are we," he had inquired, " by our own act to abandon our independence ? " (As though Ireland, instead of being a country securely, if uncomfortably, in the grip of what was then, perhaps, the greatest power in the world, was an independent nation which for no reason at all was walking into bondage.) The Treaty, according to Childers, " places Ireland definitely and irrevocably under British authority and under the British Crown." Where, then, was Ireland in the year 1921 ? Where had she been for 750 years ? Passionately, Childers, the son of an English father, a former servant of the Crown, pleaded with the assembly not to believe that England would be as good as her word, while Collins, who had treated England frankly as an enemy, admitted that the Treaty " gives us more recognition on the part of Great Britain and the associated States than we have got from any other nation. . . . America did not recognize the Irish Republic."

With a barren legalism, Childers argued " whether this assembly shall, or ever can, surrender its own independence and declare itself subject to the British Crown and Parliament." O'Higgins, more hopefully, more helpfully, stated his view of the English attitude : " I think it unwise and unstatesmanlike that England's representatives have thought fit to insist under threat of war on certain clauses of that Treaty. I do the English people the justice of believing that they would gladly have endorsed a more generous measure. I hardly hope that within the terms of this Treaty there lies the fulfilment of Ireland's destiny, but I do hope and believe that with the disappearance of old passions and distrusts, fostered by centuries of persecution and desperate resistance, what remains may be won by agreement and by peaceful political evolution." And apart from this quiet optimism, which events have proved to be well-founded, his speech abounded with phrases which showed that he did not think only in terms of "the left wing of the Irish people." "We have responsibilities to all the nation and not merely to a particular political party within the nation," he said, and, in the same spirit : "The welfare and happiness of the men and women and the little children of this nation must, after all, take precedence of political creeds and theories."

When O'Higgins was speaking, the debate was only on its second day, and the tone of the proceedings was still at its meridian, but as day followed day, and each side busily calculated its chances, there was a rapid deterioration. In the middle of the debate, de Valera suddenly proposed his own resignation, a political expedient against which Griffith protested with such strength that the proposal was not proceeded with. Trying as the days of debate must have been for de Valera, he had not once been subjected to personal abuse or treated with anything but deference and respect. Griffith, who sat patiently and silently while his own honour was attacked, expostulated : "Why we should be stopped in the middle of this discussion, and a vote taken on the personality of President de Valera, I don't understand ; and I don't think my countrymen will understand it." Here, de Valera revealed a somewhat effeminate tendency which Griffith alone had the knack of provoking.

"I am sick and tired of politics," he cried, "so sick that no matter what happened I would go back to private life. . . . Only I see mean things. . . . It is because I am straight that I meet crookedness with straight-dealing always. . . . I detest trickery. . . . Insinuations about me have hurt me. . . . I know what others didn't know : where the verge of the precipice was, and nothing would have pulled me beyond it—not even Lloyd George and all his Empire could have brought me over it. Therefore, I am straight with everybody and I am not a person for political trickery . . ." [12]

It was rather naïve, as his proposal was obviously a strategic move to postpone a vote on the Treaty.

It must be said that from this debate only a few emerge with credit. Collins had grand passages, but he was diffuse. Mary MacSwiney and Cathal Brugha revealed what angel voices de Valera was hearing in private council. Brugha's speech degenerated into an attack on Collins. "I think it is of great importance that an authoritative statement be made (a) defining the real position Mr. Michael Collins held in the Army ; (b) telling what

fights he has taken an active part in. . . . He is merely a subordinate in the Department of Defence. . . . He was made a
romantic figure, a mystical character such as this person certainly
is not. . . . In charity to Mr. Collins, I will not repeat here what
a participant in one ambush said about Mr. Collins." [13] Griffith,
he did not spare. " The chairman of the delegation thinks the war
is won, so far as he could win it, for England " ; nor did O'Higgins
escape castigation.

Brugha's political doctrine was radically different from
O'Higgins's. He, like Childers, regarded Ireland as in a strong,
England in a weak position, not that the relative strength of the
combatants mattered to him : " Why, if instead of being so strong,
our last cartridge had been fired, our last shilling had been spent,
and our last man were lying on the ground and his enemies howling
round him and their bayonets raised, ready to plunge them into
his body, that man should say—true to the traditions handed down
—if they said to him : ' Now, will you come into our Empire ? '
—he should say, and he would say : ' No, I will not.' " Brugha
ended his remarkable speech by reminding Griffith that when he
stood down in favour of de Valera in 1917, " men have respect
for Arthur Griffith second only to Eamon de Valera," and he
suggested that the members of the delegation should refrain from
voting for the Treaty. " If Arthur Griffith will fall in with this
suggestion now . . . I tell him if he does this, his name will live
for ever in Ireland." [14]

Griffith refused the invitation to dishonour his signature and
become immortalized in Irish history, and adhered to the more
orthodox opinion that " the man or nation that dishonours its
signature is dishonoured for ever." Ironically, he accepted the
suggestion that he was unknown in public life before 1916, and
owed such fame as he had since attained to Cathal Brugha. And
then he spoke of Michael Collins : " He was the man whose
matchless energy, whose indomitable will carried Ireland through
the terrible crisis, and though I have not now, and never had, an
ambition about either political affairs or history, if my name is
to go down in history, I want it associated with the name of Michael
Collins."

The final speech of Griffith is by far the most effective, reasonable
and persuasive in the whole debate. He had heard himself taunted
with the charge of treachery and he had never stirred or replied
in personalities. One of his remarks showed a keen appreciation

of the spirit that was stirring abroad. "Ah! democracy is, to some minds, very good in theory when democracy fits in with their own ideas ; but when democracy bends the reins contrary to their own ideas, they get back into a caustic vein." His speech may not have turned any votes. Speeches rarely do. It certainly lost none, and the Treaty was passed by 64 votes to 57.

The articles provided that a Provisional Government was to be set up to take over the administrative machinery from the outgoing British. The opposition in the Dáil had no intention of allowing matters to proceed on such easy lines, and their next step was to propose de Valera for re-election as President. He had broken down after the result of the voting was declared, and it was obvious that he would not, and could not, in view of his attitude, put into force the provisions of the Treaty. Another difficulty arose from the fact that it was known by this time that the Army was split in its allegiance. Mellowes and Stack had, at an early stage, visited every corps and sown the seeds of dissension. In order to keep the Army together as much as possible it was thought necessary by the Treatyites to pretend that Ireland was still a Republic. When, therefore, de Valera was defeated in the vote of President, and Griffith elected, a series of questions were fired at Griffith as to how he could reconcile his position with his policy. As President of the Republic, how could he plot its destruction ? It was mere casuistry, and Griffith must have been sorely tempted to blow through it, but the desire to propitiate the Army predominated, and he bore patiently with Mary MacSwiney and de Valera "putting pharisaical questions." It was only when Childers added his weight that Griffith's patience broke down. "I will not reply to any damned Englishman in this assembly," he cried after striking the table with his fist. He had on the previous day selected his Ministry, with O'Higgins as Minister for Economic Affairs.

In order to get over the constitutional difficulties, it was decided to maintain the Dáil with Griffith as President, and call the Southern Parliament under the 1920 Act—the same people plus the four Trinity representatives—and from that form the Provisional Government to take over the machinery of government from the British. In deference to extreme sentiments, Collins was to be Chairman of the Provisional Government, and Griffith played no part in it.

Brugha had been succeeded by Mulcahy as Minister for Defence, and the last words spoken at this ill-omened session of the Dáil were his : "If any assurance is required—the Army will remain the Army of the Irish Republic."

No one knew better the condition of the Army, and it must have seemed to him also that this announcement was necessary for discipline and morale. But the fact was that the Dáil had voted for the status offered by the Treaty, which was represented by the title, "The Irish Free State," and the Republic, which had never been a reality, was now a very dim possibility. The most likely alternative to the Free State was the return of the British Government and more fighting, for Great Britain of 1922 had an attitude to her Imperial dowry very different from that which prevails in these days of waiver and easy settlement.

Mulcahy's own speech had been restrained and sensible. He disliked the Treaty, but had heard of no alternative. Unlike Brugha, who spoke as though the ambushes by flying columns had driven the English into the sea, Mulcahy told the sober truth when he said : "We have not been able to drive the enemy from anything but from a fairly good-sized police barracks."

Nevertheless, cold logic was not enough and there was another difficulty : as well as the purists who wanted nothing if they could not get the "whole thing," the Army had been swollen by new recruits who had taken no part in the earlier fighting and joined when hostilities ceased. These "Trucileers" were, many of them, young loafers who dreaded a return to normal conditions. They liked to swagger round looking like gunmen, inspiring awe in miserable, and apprehension in responsible, minds. A shrewd judge of his countrymen, who had played a leading part in the revolutionary movement, remarked after a short holiday in his native place that there were many young men in the country who were determined never to do an honest day's work again.

The fighting with the English had been done by a few thousand men ; there were now nearly 100,000 in the I.R.A. and the pulse of this armed force was under constant and anxious pressure by those who were bidding for its support. It is a pity, if it were necessary, and fatal, if it were not, that the policy of make-believe had to be kept up for the benefit of the Army. No one wished it to be said of him that he disparaged the Republic, yet all like Mulcahy, who voted for the Treaty, knew that a Republic in fact was not to be the form of government in Ireland. Those who opposed the Treaty knew that their policy meant certain chaos and, at best, a return to the pre-Truce horrors. The ordinary men and women knew only that there was now peace and hope for the future.

On 14th January, 1922, those members of the Dáil who had voted for the Treaty and the four members for Trinity College met in the Mansion House and elected the Provisional Government —Collins as Chairman, Cosgrave, Duggan, O'Higgins, Hogan, McGrath, Finian Lynch and Eoin MacNeill. The ministry of the Dáil under Griffith as President was Collins, Gavan Duffy, Duggan, Cosgrave, O'Higgins and Mulcahy. It may well be asked how such a duplicate arrangement could function. The retention of the Dáil Ministry was a gesture. It signified that the country did not recognize the Southern Parliament which elected the Provisional Government and it was an earnest that the machinery of the Republic was being preserved intact if the people voted against the Treaty at the general election. In practice it was fatal to the maintenance of order.

" The country," said O'Higgins on the 18th of March, " is drifting into anarchy now owing to the concurring lack of jurisdiction of Dáil Eireann, the British Government and the Provisional Government. Those who shirked asking the country for a straight vote are responsible."

It was one of the great triumphs of de Valera that he had always continued to keep the peace between the fighting men and the constitutionalists, such as Griffith. Now some of the principal men of action—Collins, Mulcahy, MacEoin and McGrath— had gone over to Griffith ; others, such as Brugha and Mellowes, refused to hear counsels of moderation : by going with them de Valera was in fact giving up leadership : with the extremists, he followed and did not lead. Collins had personal supporters all centred in Dublin. Mulcahy and MacEoin had also the support of many Volunteers, but in the Army itself were many who took no part in politics, who, during the fighting, did very much what they pleased in their own areas and who now saw themselves about to become subordinate to a government which had, in their view, lowered the Flag.

It was never certain that the Dáil would approve the Treaty, but it was clear that there was a definite desire for peace in the country and the Dáil was more than likely to reflect the popular opinion. Without waiting for the result individual Volunteers began to secede and many of the headquarters staff spoke of the Dáil as a body to which they no longer owed allegiance. They called for a Volunteer Convention and the requisition was signed by Rory O'Connor, who was not in the Dáil, and other officers, including Liam Mellowes, who was a deputy. This demand was served on Mulcahy on the 11th January, 1922, a few days after the passing of the Treaty and his appointment as Minister for Defence. The purpose of this convention was to establish the Volunteers once again as a self-sufficient body free from parliamentary or ministerial control. Mulcahy was hard pressed to postpone such a step and, at the same time, endeavour to conciliate the mutineers. No one knew what was going to happen. The police were the British police and were being disbanded. The Army was a few bands of guerillas who had never obeyed the government of a sovereign state. The only method by which it was found possible to avert this Army crisis was by impressing on O'Connor that a split in the I.R.A. would hold up the evacuation of the British troops which was then proceeding. He and his friends were now openly hostile to the Dáil. Ernie O'Malley repudiated any duty to the Minister for Defence or the Chief-of-Staff. O'Connor said of de Valera : " It doesn't matter to me what he said. Some of us are no more prepared to stand for de Valera than for the Treaty." And on another occasion when it was put to him that the majority of the people might want the Treaty and if they were to be refused the right to take it, the alternative was a dictatorship, O'Connor replied : " You may take it that way, if you like."[15]

The Army Convention, meanwhile, was postponed for two months while in civil affairs the Gilbertian system of two governments continued its uneasy way.

When the Dáil rose after the Treaty debate it was not to meet for a month. The holiday was spent by O'Higgins in the herculean task of taking over the finances of the British administration. He had no time for lobbying in that month of ceaseless political activity. An Ard Fheis, or meeting, of the Sinn Fein organization assembled on the 21st February to consider the situation before the Dáil sat again. It was from this body that the candidates for the Dáil had been most carefully selected and there is no doubt that the majority of those present on the 21st February were opposed to the Treaty. Collins and de Valera conferred and it was agreed not to vote on that issue, which was an advantage for Collins, and to postpone a general election for three months, which suited de Valera. Nearly half a year would elapse after the Treaty was signed before the Irish people were to be given an opportunity to declare their will.

When the Dáil met, de Valera and his followers asked questions of the Ministers in their official capacities, refusing to recognize the existence of the Provisional Government and pretending that in fact the Dáil commanded the resources of the country. The pretence also involved the fiction that, prior to the Treaty, the Government of Ireland had been carried out by the Dáil. De Valera pressed the Minister for Education for an answer as to whether he held a mere nominal office or was responsible for the education of the country. In fact the system of national education was under the control of the Intermediate Education Board which was handed over by the British to the Provisional Government who provided the funds for running it. The Dáil had no funds. Similarly solemn questions about Land Purchase were addressed to Patrick Hogan, Minister for Lands, and he was reprimanded for answering a constituent from the offices of the Provisional Government where he was also Minister for Lands. The Ministers did their best to keep up appearances in this play-acting which was being conducted to soothe the susceptibilities of extremists. It was O'Higgins who was the first to revolt against the inquisition. "In my capacity as a member of the Provisional Government," he said in answer to one of de Valera's questions, " I am engaged in taking over certain departments of the British Government—the Ministry of Transport, Mercantile Marine, Department of the Board of Trade, and so on. When I am doing these things certain people—a minority in this House—say I am a national apostate. Now, in my capacity as national apostate, I will not answer questions to the minority of this House."[16] He had seen a request from the Lord Mayor of Cork which was addressed to the Minister for Finance in the Dáil for 2,000,000 pounds for the rebuilding of that city. " Mr. Collins, Minister for Finance, Dáil Eireann," said O'Higgins, " is not in a position —and the Lord Mayor of Cork knew it—to put up 2,000,000 pounds for the rebuilding of Cork but Mr. Collins, Chairman of the Provisional Government, is in a position to secure from the British Government payment in advance which will be settled by an inter-governmental commission. And the Provisional Government is responsible to the body that appointed it. It was not this body that appointed the Provisional Government and, as one member of the Provisional Government, I will not answer questions here regarding actions I take as member of the Provisional Government."[17]

Apart from the unwearying efforts of de Valera's supporters to embarrass them in the Dáil, those Ministers who had also to work in the Provisional Government were subject to an endless campaign of rowdyism and abuse whenever they appeared in public. The leaders of the heckling campaign were women. Hysteria was in the air. They might have uttered the words of Macbeth's redoubtable wife :

> " Come you spirits
> That tend on mortal thoughts ! Unsex me here . . ."

or, as O'Higgins put it, in the cold sobriety of prose :[18] " To form a just appreciation of developments in Ireland in 1922, it is necessary to remember that the country had come through a revolution and to remember what a weird composite of idealism, neurosis, megalomania and criminality is apt to be thrown to the surface in even the best-regulated revolution. It was a situation precipitated by men who had not cleared the blood from their eyes, and reinforced by all the waywardness of a people with whom, by dint of historical circumstances, a negative attitude had tended to become traditional. With many it was the reaction from a great fear. With others it was fanaticism pure and simple. With others still it was something that was neither pure nor simple, an ebullition of the savage, primitive passion to wreck and loot and level when an opportunity seemed to offer to do so with impunity. Instincts of that kind are not an Irish monopoly. They are universal to human nature, but in the conditions which exist in modern civilized states they are, for the most part, successfully held in check, manifesting themselves only in occasional isolated outrages of a revolting character or in sporadic local outbreaks, easily countered by the organized forces of the State. But in Ireland in 1922 there was no State and no organized forces. The Provisional Government was simply eight young men in the City Hall standing amidst the ruins of one administration, with the foundations of another not yet laid, and with wild men screaming through the keyhole. No police force was functioning through the country, no system of justice was operating, the wheels of administration hung idle

battered out of recognition by the clash of rival jurisdictions."
While in the Dáil, impotent Ministers longed to fly from their
tormentors to the places where they could do some constructive
work, a state of anarchy was coming to life behind the smoke-
screen of talk which de Valera's supporters were putting up in
the Dáil.

In different parts of the country cadres of Volunteers, who
refused obedience to the Government, were taking over barracks
from the retiring British. In March there was very nearly open
warfare in Limerick. The Brigade Commandant in that area had
repudiated the authority of General Headquarters, and when the
British were prepared to hand over the barracks in the city to the
Irish Army, the Commanding Officer of another division was
ordered to take them under his control. At this the soldiers of
the local company seized hotels and buildings in the town and
only by prolonged and difficult negotiations, in which civilians
took part, was peace preserved.

The Government decided to act and the proposed convention
of the Volunteers, which had been postponed, was now cancelled.
The consequence of this was an open act of mutiny. The anti-
Treaty officers held a convention on their own on 18th March
in the Dublin Mansion House and elected an executive.

This body which was attended by Cathal Brugha now decided
to reimpose the "Belfast Boycott" and to extend it to the Six
County area. Trains were derailed and their contents seized as
a result of this policy and, worst of all, the Orange pogrom began
again, more violently than ever before.

There was by no means a clear-cut division in the Army.
Desperate efforts were being made by the more responsible leaders
on both sides to effect a compromise. Joint action against the
North was one recipe for reconciliation and Joseph McGrath
and Seán MacEoin both called for Volunteers for such an enterprise. The Provisional Government as such would have nothing
to do with an illegal enterprise but the I.R.B. continued to
exercise its secret influence and there were many on the side of
the Treaty simply from personal loyalty to Collins.

Trains going to pro-Treaty election meetings were derailed.
The platform on which Collins was to speak in Killarney was
burnt down. In Cork shots were fired at a meeting which he was
addressing. Collins, unarmed, captured a man who was trying
to shoot him. It was not a premeditated effort at assassination ;

the man was unaware of the identity of his target and had only the intention of stealing his motor-car. In April fighting took place in Kilkenny and elsewhere.

The Irregulars captured with astounding ease a British naval tug at Cobh in Co. Cork and seized the plentiful store of arms and ammunition she had aboard. It seems, and Collins suspected, that there were people in England who wanted to encourage the Civil War which now seemed certain. The fiction has been propagated that there would have been no Civil War if the British Government had not ordered the Provisional Government to bombard the Four Courts in June. So early as April Liam Mellowes in the Dáil was saying: " There would be no question of Civil War here now were it not for the undermining of the Republic. . . . The sphere of the Army is to maintain and uphold the Republic". Miss MacSwiney on the same occasion was even more explicit. " The responsibility for every act of trouble in this country, for all the disunion, all the killing, and all the wounding that may take place, rests entirely on the heads of those who have tried to subvert the Republic."

The acts of the " Irregulars," as it became the fashion to call the seceding Volunteers, included the smashing up of printing presses, the raiding of shops and post offices and on 1st May about £275,000 was taken from branches of the Bank of Ireland. They justified these acts by saying that the Army of the Republic was not having its debts paid and there was an outcry by some of de Valera's followers in the Dáil when these practices were described as illegal. On the 14th April the Irregulars seized, without opposition, the Four Courts, the Fowler Hall, the Kildare Street Club and the Masonic Hall in Dublin. The Four Courts became their headquarters and from there they delivered their ukases.

O'Higgins was impatient that some steps should be taken to bring this condition of affairs to an end. Collins, beset with difficulties, negotiating with Churchill on the one hand and Craig on the other, made desperate efforts to reach a compromise. It is said that he weakened but it is not well-founded. Once the Civil War began he was determined to see it through. He wished to avert it as long as possible. He always cherished a hope that he could come to terms with de Valera. " If only I could see ' the Long Fellow ' alone, I could settle this thing," he would sigh, " but he is always surrounded by people."

In the Dáil an objection was raised to the state of the election

register, and the enfranchisement of women was proposed as a
necessary preliminary to an election.   It was objected that this
would further postpone the election and Griffith was adamant
in refusing to agree.   He did not believe in the sincerity of the
proposal which was advocated by some who had actively opposed
votes for women when the question was debated on its own
merits.

All this time election meetings were taking place in the various
towns in Ireland.   In March de Valera made a tour of the south
and uttered the words over which there has been so much
controversy—" They would have to wade through Irish blood "
—He repeated this phrase more than once.   Torn from its context
it reads more violently than in its place.   He had himself denied
that he intended an exhortation to violence.   His meaning was
clear enough.   If the Treaty was passed and if a government
was set up under it and *" if our Volunteers continue, and I hope
they will continue until the goal is reached,"* then of necessity they,
" in order to achieve freedom, will have, I said yesterday, to
march over the dead bodies of their own brothers.   They will
have to wade through Irish blood."

It is true that de Valera was only foretelling what he believed
would happen if the Treaty were to be accepted by the people.
But even if he can be acquitted of the charge that he directly
encouraged the violence which was then breaking out everywhere and which was soon to reduce the country to chaos, he
cannot be said to have paid tribute to the democratic ideal.
Why, if the Irish people wanted the Treaty, were they not to
have it ?   Because, said de Valera, " there are rights which a
minority may justly uphold, even by arms against a majority "
and " the people have never a right to do wrong."[19]

Why, if the people elected to have this Treaty, did de Valera
express the hope that the Volunteers would wade through their
blood, if necessary, to get them something better ?   The truth
may be that de Valera, disappointed and suddenly taken down
from his eminence, gave way to the less noble side of a complex
nature.   It must also be remembered that his sensational welcome
in America and the unreal atmosphere in which he lived there
—as though he were a visiting monarch—must have made a
remarkable impression on a man who, reared in a country cottage,
had been used to the life of a school teacher until he was thirty-
five.   At first there had been nothing but failure and disappointment

over a scholarship in Trinity, a professorship at Cork : then the tragedy of 1916. But after Easter Week, in which he showed courage and resource, luck changed. His American citizenship probably saved him from the fate of the other leaders : the only Commandant to survive, he became " the hero and darling of the Rising."[20] In Lewes Jail he was elected Commandant by the prisoners who were detained there in 1917, later he was transferred to Lincoln Prison from which he escaped : then came his return to Dublin and his election as President of the first Dáil : then America and a sudden and unexpected world of roses. It is significant that Miss Macardle, the literary apologist for the anti-Treatyites, makes no reference, in her very full account of these times, to the words spoken by the former President. Instead, she writes of the way in which " the authority of Dáil Eireann was being rapidly undermined in favour of the Provisional Government," and expresses surprise that Griffith had only pro-Treaty men in his Cabinet, who " treated the vote in the Dáil as giving them licence to carry out the British Government's programme."

The Treaty provided that a Provisional Government should take over from Britain. On the strength of this, British troops were now evacuating the country, and the police forces were being disbanded, while all the resources of the Government of Ireland were being transferred from British hands. Griffith and Collins would gladly have held an election on the Treaty issue in February, and agreed to hold a plebiscite for all adults, but this was refused as a " stone age " proposal ; and it was de Valera who had the election date postponed, and wished it to be longer postponed. The Republicans continued to talk as though the Dáil was being deprived of an omnipotence which it never possessed, and, while complaining that the powers of this body were being filched from it, stumped the country, urging the people to vote in a manner which was certain to reduce an impoverished country to bankruptcy, restore a period of guerilla warfare and terrorism, and throw away the first substantial measure of self-government enjoyed by Ireland for over seven hundred years. When asked what his alternative policy was, de Valera said : " When a man's house was burning, the only policy was to put out the fire," and he advised the Irish people " to go for another round in the race and who knows whether the other fellow would be able to finish." [21]

Opening a paper for one day (3rd March), we find three examples of how the young and brave were putting out the fire. Max Green, a son-in-law of John Redmond, was shot dead when he attempted to stop an armed robber who ran into his arms in St. Stephen's Green. On the same day, police vacating a barracks in Tipperary were held up by armed men. One was shot dead and two wounded, one so seriously that he died within a few days. A band of 200 men stopped a police escort of lorries and stole property valued at £12,000. On the feast of St. Patrick, armed youths entered the ward of a hospital in Galway and shot dead three patients there, two of whom were policemen suffering, one from nephritis, the other congestion of the lungs.

Speaking in Cork, Collins described de Valera's words, in the circumstances of the time, as "the language of madness," and spoke severely of the behaviour of Brugha who had encouraged the Army split, and Stack, who had obstructed the creation of a police force : " Such tactics were those of a discredited and defeated faction."

On the Northern boundary, the troops of both Free State and Republic made forays into the Six Counties. At Belleek, British troops were called up to drive them out. These affairs, combined with the resurrection and intensification of the " Belfast Boycott," were followed by dreadful disorder in the North, of which the worst incident was the murder of the MacMahon family in Belfast. Collins reached an agreement with Craig in an effort to bring about peace, but both parties were handicapped by the behaviour of their more disorderly followers. The British Government stood or fell by the success of the Treaty, and, for this reason, sought to modify criticism of happenings in the South. Churchill referred in disparaging terms to greater chaos in the North when (*Irish Times*, 29th March) Sir Henry Wilson wrote an open letter to Sir James Craig about " the dangerous conditions which obtain in the Twenty-Six Counties," which, he prophesied, would increase and spread unless " Great Britain established law and order in Ireland "—a remark which shows that reoccupation by British troops was not a remote possibility—or " a man in those counties rises who can crush out murder and anarchy and re-establish law and order."

In Kevin O'Higgins, the South was to see that man, but his time was not yet. His impatience at the delay, while the country was rushing to ruin, broke out occasionally. He urged Collins to grasp the nettle and bring his collected forces to grips with the Irregulars. " By God, we will," cried Collins, thumping the table ; but always he postponed the bloody issue and tried to compromise. " If we don't take action," said Griffith, " we will be considered the greatest poltroons in history." [22]

It is alleged that the Provisional Government attacked the Four Courts only at the behest of the British Government. Whatever prompted the action—Churchill did send a telegram—it was one which was inevitable in the circumstances. Before the event O'Higgins presented a memorandum to his colleagues which is of interest as evidence of his attitude.

" The condition of things in Ireland which faces the Government is unquestionably very grave. To my mind, the Election results count for very little in the way of alleviating that condition. Our problem was not at any time parliamentary, not a matter of counting heads either inside or outside the ' Sovereign Assembly.' It consisted, and still consists, in the fact that a section of reckless desperate men, prompted by a variety of motives, ranging from the highest to the lowest, are prepared to resist the writ of an administration set up in conformity with the Anglo-Irish Treaty.

The internal morale of the country, and its prestige abroad, are at very low ebb indeed, despite the fact that after a struggle, gallantly maintained for five years, we have won a very considerable victory against enormous odds. Economically, the country is heading straight for ruin ; there is no enterprise because of no security ; no credit because the writ of no Court is effective ; unemployment is increasing daily, and ominous processions of workless men are becoming a familiar feature.

In the North the position seems to be drifting from bad to worse, murders and burning follow each other with dreary monotony, and refugees of one colour or the other are either fleeing the country or pouring across the ' border ' into counties already menaced by famine. The shooting of Sir Henry Wilson is simply another barrel of oil on the flames. Assassination is a game that two can play, and men may be lost to Ireland of greater potentialities and more constructive ability than Sir H. Wilson.

What lies ahead ? Civil War ? A social revolution ? Reoccupied by the British, with the goodwill of the world, and a ' moral mandate ' such as they never had before with regard to Ireland ? These possibilities, none of which are attractive, are not mutually exclusive. With regard to the first, it is unnecessary to point out that even a highly-disciplined veteran army might break under the strain of a Civil War waged against men who had been their comrades in trying times. Could our forces, composed mostly of raw lads, the great majority having no experience of fighting, be expected to wage an effective fight against men who claim to be ' the custodians of the Separatist ideal ' ?

Moreover, in our struggle with the British we developed a type of war by which a comparatively small number of men can harass and hamper a government and finally reduce it to impotence and futility. While that process would be at work, the second possibility mentioned above would certainly be looming nearer with the increased stagnation and consequent unemployment, and when that stage would be reached, the situation would be ripe for British intervention and the world's applause. The position is so grave that there is at least this advantage—nothing we may do, no desperate bid we may make, is likely to make it worse. I, therefore, put forward for your consideration the following suggestions :—

Sir James Craig, Lord Londonderry, and other North-East leaders, must be gravely concerned by the prospect that is opening up both in the Six and in the Twenty-six Counties. For even supposing all was well in their bailiwick—and all is far from well—a paradise divided only by an imaginary line from hell is unthinkable. Therefore, these men's minds should be receptive to any suggestions, even remotely calculated to alleviate conditions in their area and in ours.

On the other hand, I cannot believe that Messrs. de Valera, Brugha, Boland, O'Kelly, etc., can view the situation that is developing with equanimity. While they need never be expected to admit as much explicitly or implicitly, they must be conscious of grave personal responsibility for the evils that threaten the country, and might be expected to handle rather carefully any development in the general situation which would provide even the smallest opportunity for face-saving and escaping from the position in which their public utterances have placed them. It is clear that they hoped for such an opportunity in the Constitution, but British suspicion was roused to such a pitch by the ' Pact ' that every unpleasant form was insisted on, and even Mr. de Valera could find no loophole through which to slip away from his ' rock.'

I dismiss the idea of a British [compromise ?] on either the

Treaty or the Constitution as a political impossibility for the British signatories. The die-hard forces were never stronger. Where, then, is there even a remote possibility in the North-East when the frenzy that may be expected to follow the ' taking off ' of Sir Henry Wilson dies down and has its reaction ? The question arises, what could be put up to Sir James Craig and his colleagues ?

I wonder if anyone here, or in England, or in North-East Ulster believes very strongly in the Boundary Commission as a piece of constructive statesmanship ? I don't. The proposition I would like to see put up to Sir J. Craig would be as follows : On condition of an immediate cessation of hostile activity against his Parliament, and a general acquiescence in its jurisdiction by Nationalists resident in his area, met on his side by ameliorative measures to be defined later (disbandment of Specials, release of prisoners, etc.), he would undertake within six months of the confirmation of our Constitution by the British Parliament to take and abide by a plebiscite of the *Province* of Ulster on the question of whether the Six Counties should or should not come within the Free State, such plebiscites to be taken at intervals of, say, a year until unity is reached. In consideration of this, the Boundary Commission proposal to be waived.

In 1911, the Province of Ulster contained roughly 900,000 Protestants to 700,000 Catholics. On a plebiscite, the 700,000 Catholics would vote against 700,000 of the others, leaving 200,000 people scattered over nine counties, all Protestants, all Ulsterites, and most of them ' Unionists ' (in the old sense), as a *board of compulsory arbitration between the North-East Corner and the rest of Ireland.*

I may be asked, in the unlikely event of the Northern Government looking kindly on this proposal, where does any lever or bargaining power come in for the ' upholders of the Separatist tradition ' ? Not very definitely, I admit, but de Valera has frequently said : ' I would make great sacrifices for the unity of Ireland.' They have all stressed partition in their anti-Treaty propaganda, and we would have the powerful cry against them, if they continued their antics, that they were imperilling the unity of Ireland and lessening the chances of a favourable result in the plebiscite.

Is it too much to expect that under this pressure they would subside into constitutional agitation ? Examining their activities in recent months, one finds that it is chiefly with regard to the North-East frontier and in the matter of the Belfast boycott that they come up against the Provisional Government. If we could rob them of these two sources of trouble and objectives for their activity, they would have nothing left except to attack their own, which, to do them justice, they seem to have little stomach for.

I put forward these suggestions rather in the hope of stimulating thought on this subject than in the belief that they embody any final scheme which could be adopted or acted upon as it stands."

The preceding months had been busy ones for O'Higgins, and his relative silence in the Dáil and at public meetings was rather the measure of his activity than the reverse.

With Collins, he went to England in January to make arrangements for the transfer of government and to discuss questions, of which the most pressing was who was to pay for the enormous damage to property done during the previous years. Later, with Griffith, he strove to get agreement on a Constitution which would soothe the injured pride of those who felt that the Treaty contained too large a sacrifice of national aims.

He was extremely effective in negotiation. His method was to allow his adversary his say, listening attentively and displaying no feeling or impatience. When everything had been said on the other side, he then had his say, and insisted that his opponent gave him the same hearing. It may have been that membership of a large and opinionated family made this a habit. A young Higgins had to wait his turn to speak at table, and having secured it, was determined to make the most of it. At one of the early conferences Sir John Anderson, for the British, explained that his Government would only pay compensation for what was commandeered by their armed forces and not for what was confiscated. That would be an Irish liability. Sir John spoke with the technical exactness and detailed grasp of his subject which characterized him. When he had finished, O'Higgins began to laugh quietly. Sir John Anderson is not a man who provokes humour, as a rule, and he looked with some irritation at the Irish representatives, while his colleagues were obviously surprised that so factual a statement should be treated as a joke. O'Higgins begged their pardon. " I was thinking," he said, " of old Pat Murphy who has been riding on his bicycle from Maryborough to Dunamase. He gets tired and sits by the side of the road while he rests himself and takes a few pulls at his pipe. While he is sitting there some Black and Tans, who are driving past, stop the lorry, put his bicycle on it and go away. I can see poor Pat Murphy puzzling out for himself : ' Now was that bicycle confiscated or was it commandeered ? ' "

There were, after all, certain difficulties which Sir John's ordered exposition had not made allowances for.

Writing from London to his wife, O'Higgins, for the first time in contact with the English political leaders, gave his early impressions : " We were at it all day yesterday from 11 a.m. to 6.30 p.m. with a luncheon interval. We had lunch at the house of a brother of Churchill's (a major)—Winston was there and X. who just used his toothpick and tried to look wise while Michael (Collins) and Winston talked frantically."

During the Treaty negotiations, Sir John Lavery and his attractive American wife made open house for the Irish representatives. A rule they adopted, not to accept English hospitality before the conclusion of peace, handicapped them, as it meant there were no opportunities of unofficial intercourse with their opponents. The Laverys played a very important rôle by providing a meeting ground for both sides. Lady Lavery's attractions had made her a figure in the most interesting, if not the most exclusive, sections of London Society. Politicians and artists flocked to her house, and if Debrett was not so well represented, no one was the duller for that. Lady Lavery developed a romantic attachment to Michael Collins which was notorious. Rumour gave colour and exaggeration—and Lady Lavery, it must be confessed, gave rumour wings—to what was, after all, a fancy on her part. Collins was unaware of the rôle which he played in the lively imagination of his hostess. He was engaged to be married, as he stated in public on one curious occasion in the Treaty debate, when Countess Marckievicz announced the prospect of his marriage to Princess Mary. Lady Lavery persisted in the belief that Collins was unattached, and when he died, put on widow's weeds which only the firm tact of a friend prevented her from wearing at his funeral. Letters from Collins were shown to Lord Birkenhead by Lady Lavery, and he noticed that the occasional romantic passages were interpolated in a woman's handwriting valiantly, if unsuccessfully, disguised. It was all very odd, very unreal but not unpleasant, when one became accustomed to it and accepted the romantic convention. O'Higgins was destined to take the place of Collins in Lady Lavery's romantic imagination.

When he arrived in London he was immediately invited to the Lavery's entertainments. He described his first visit : " The Lavery evening passed pleasantly enough—the two Churchills and their wives and some other lady whose name I missed and

the Lavery pair—who are awfully fine folk—but I want to go
hoam. Hump again. I only straighten up when Dublin Castle
—represented by Hamar (Greenwood) and Sir John Anderson—
is facing us across the green table—Hamar crossing his hands over
his stomach and turning his eyes to Heaven at any suggestion
that he has any motive other than effervescing affection and good
will towards ourselves personally and the new order generally.
The other fellow is a more dangerous type—the well-trained Civil
Service . . . plausible, vigilant . . ."

Winston Churchill is not generally considered a good friend
to Ireland. At times he has spoken of the Southern part with
asperity, but the Irish delegates found him helpful and easy to
work with, and for him O'Higgins developed a warm admiration
which grew in time to something stronger than mere regard.
At first meeting he appeared as "not a bad fellow, emotional and
enthusiastic—he's like a child with a new toy about this New
Departure, and would be utterly inconsolable if there was any
hitch or calamity." It is perhaps natural that the approach on
both sides at this stage was careful and suspicious. Men do not
fall in love at first sight with their enemies, and the fact that
O'Higgins was determined to make a success of the Treaty did not
mean that he felt grateful to those who were responsible for its
defects. O'Higgins, for all his imperturbability of manner, was at
heart a young countryman, who did not feel happy in "this
atmosphere of wooden men and painted women." He describes
"a beastly fog" with the minute particularity of one who had
never encountered the "pea-soup variety" before. Collins was
on his way over, and until (he writes) "a particular document
on which we are working is completed," he cannot get home.
"Pinin' he is and very cross—but workin' it off on Hamar."

Collins arrived on a Saturday afternoon, and on the following
day O'Higgins accompanied him to meet Lloyd George. "We
met the P.M. on Sunday afternoon, we were about an hour with
him—he's certainly a remarkable devil—he flirted with his eye-
glass and faced us, now with the beaming ingenuous face of a
boy and now like a very, very old fox."

Of the British representatives, O'Higgins was most attracted
by E. S. Montagu, the Secretary of State for India, who "never
raises a point against us. Whenever there is a hitch or deadlock
he comes lumbering in, puts *our* proposition into a different form
of words and stands foursquare for its acceptance. He always

introduces his remarks by emphasizing how little he knows about our affairs but it seems to me he knows more than most of them."

It was interesting to see Michael Collins at grips with these men, the experienced leaders of the Empire. O'Higgins felt that he " stands the test very well with any of them and certainly does not suffer by comparison—you will say that not unnaturally I am a partisan, but I am telling you what I see reflected in their own behaviour while they are dealing with him. In ability I would put Montagu on line with him—but Montagu is a big slouching devil with a lurking smile for everything and he has never played for the crowd as earnestly or as skilfully as his better known colleagues."

CHAPTER VII

THE SPLIT

"LOOKING back over the controversy we have had in Ireland since December last," said O'Higgins in the Dáil, "it seems to me that the wisest words that were spoken in the course of that controversy were spoken by the Deputy for East Clare : 'There is a constitutional way of settling these differences of ours ; in God's name, let us not depart from them.' Those were the wisest words that were spoken in this six months' controversy. Would that the speaker had adhered to them." When O'Higgins went on to quote the reference to "wading through Irish blood," de Valera hotly denied the expression. "It is an absolute misrepresentation." Continuing his speech, O'Higgins mentioned that the question had been asked : "Is this Treaty of yours worth civil war ?" To that he answered : "Perhaps it is," and then he voiced his democratic faith, which he had long reflected over, and which became the corner-stone of all his political actions. To him the democratic idea was in conformity with the Law of God, and all the actions of a statesman had to be referred back to the idea and were valid only if they accorded with it. "The Treaty," he said, "in my opinion, confers very great benefits, very great advantages and very great opportunities on the Irish people and I would not declare off-hand that it is not worth civil war. But if civil war occurs in Ireland it will not be for the Treaty. It will not be for a Free State versus anything else. It will be for a vital, fundamental, democratic principle—for the right of the people of Ireland to decide any issue, great or small, that arises in the politics of this country. Never before in Ireland by Irishmen has that right been challenged. That right is sacred. That right, in my opinion, is worth defending by those who have a mandate to defend it. We have a representative character here. From that comes our authority ; from that comes any power we have ; from that comes any moral strength in our position or in the things we do. In so far as we carry out the will of the Irish people, we have authority ; if we flout that will, we have none."[1]

The election was to be held on the 16th of June. Unfortunately, the firing of platforms, wrecking of trains, shootings and threatenings which enlivened the campaign did not augur well for the unintimidated exercise of the franchise. In fact, unless some compromise was reached, there was going to be a travesty of a General Election. With this in mind, Collins made a last effort to come to terms, and, as a result, concluded with de Valera an arrangement by which each side was only to put forward candidates in proportion to their numerical strength in the outgoing Dáil. The object of the device was to secure a new assembly from which a coalition cabinet could be drawn. Collins insisted that independent candidates should be allowed to stand, and the result of this was that so many of these were returned, in addition to the supporters of Griffith, that the Republicans lost the benefit of the pact. The British Government was furious at what they regarded as a betrayal by Collins ; and Griffith, who was not consulted, was also annoyed. His temper had gradually worn thin, partly from strain and justifiable irritation ; also, it appeared, from a decline in health of which his colleagues, and perhaps himself, were unaware.

He became very bitter in the Dáil, and resumed his attack on Childers with greater vehemence than before. He certainly conveyed the impression that he suspected Childers of being a member of the British Secret Service, and, it must be owned, went beyond the limits of fairness in his attack. Childers had been in the Intelligence Section of the R.F.C. during the European War. It was not just to confuse that with the Secret Service. Admirers of Griffith must regret that in the heat and strain of these times he allowed prejudice to warp his sense of justice.

It had been agreed that the Constitution of the Irish Free State was to be published before the election. A committee had been appointed to draft this document, and it was one of O'Higgins's tasks to obtain agreement on it with the British Government. When the time came to introduce this Constitution to the Dáil, O'Higgins recalled that " every time we crossed to England to negotiate points consequential on the Treaty, things happened here that were meant to be mines under our feet," and he described how " with President Griffith I met representatives of the British Government. I had intimate personal knowledge of the situation that had to be faced and of the very considerable difficulties and embarrassments that arose by reason of the situation existing here."

The upholders of the Treaty were at a serious disadvantage
with their Republican opponents in Ireland, who had no official
duties and could give all their time to propaganda. The absence
of Ministers in London was another difficulty : " I do not think
we will be here a second longer than is absolutely necessary,"
wrote O'Higgins, " as it is a bad business to have so many of us
away at the moment. . . . There is much hump again and I
want to go *hoam*—it's not so bad spittin' at the beggars across
the table but once we knock off it's a dismal business—very unlike
my last visit."

Three drafts of the Constitution were prepared, and an unsuccessful effort was made to obtain British agreement to a form which
did not entail the taking of an oath of allegiance by members
of the Dáil. Collins had been advised by Hugh Kennedy, afterwards Attorney-General and later Chief Justice, that an oath was
not mandatory in the Treaty. " As little of that as possible," said
Griffith to the Constitution committee, putting aside a volume
which contained the Constitution of Canada. The Irish delegates
realized that an oath would keep men out on the hills who, in a
constitutional assembly, might in time turn their minds to
constructive purposes.

In an address to a society at Oxford, in later years, O'Higgins
disclosed a full appreciation of this mentality in Ireland, where
" a people emerging from a period of revolution were thrown
upon their own resources, unaided by any fabric of administration,
for the maintenance of order and the decencies of life. Who will
say with any confidence that a similar situation in France, in Italy,
in America, even in England, with its long tradition of sober
responsible citizenship, would not produce substantially similar
results ?

" Add to the picture which I have outlined the fact that the
guerilla territorial force, which had been the Irish Volunteers,
was divided on the issue of the Treaty and that throughout the
country, supplementing the frenzied eloquence of Mr. de Valera,
the fair were inciting the brave to sanguinary wadings in defence
of what was called ' the existing Republic ' and the problem which
confronted the Provisional Government emerges in somewhat
definite shape. On that problem there could be but one decision.
This new tyranny had to be met and smashed. The right of the
people to found a State on the basis of the Treaty which had been
signed by their plenipotentiaries and endorsed by their Parliament

had to be vindicated beyond question. Weak and reeling from their conflict with British administration, the people of Ireland had to defend from internal enemies their hard-won right to be the masters in their own land."

O'Higgins's address to the electors of Leix and Offaly was temperate in its tone. He made one point which the Dáil might well have considered before it embarked on its depressing debate on the Treaty—rejection by the Dáil would have been a final step ; acceptance had to be followed by an appeal to the people. He believed that the people, as a whole, preferred the Treaty to its alternative : " War, on a different scale, and in different circumstances, from those which marked the conflict up to this point ; on a different scale, because it was to be expected that Britain, having called a formal truce and held formal negotiations, would, if these negotiations proved fruitless, proceed to make what had not yet been made—formal war." And this war would have been waged against a people that had lost its solidarity, because there would be many who would say that the Dáil had no right to reject the Treaty without reference to the people. He saw no prospects of better terms resulting from such a war, and he ended his short address with words which well express the attitude of the men who honestly accepted the position created by the Treaty : " I stand now for getting the best out of the Treaty, for making the fullest use of the power and opportunity it gives us to develop to the utmost the moral and material resources of the nation. I have not abandoned any political aspirations to which I have given expression in the past, but, in the existing circumstances, I advise the people to trust to evolution rather than revolution for their attainment."

The signing of the electoral pact between Collins and de Valera had the effect of making an election possible. It had other consequences. The number of candidates returned who were independent of the two major groups upset de Valera's plans and the British were now adamant that the new Irish Constitution should contain an oath of allegiance to the Crown. Collins was not happy about the compromise with de Valera, into which circumstances had forced him, and he cannot be said to have adhered conscientiously to the agreement. When speaking in Cork, he urged the electorate to vote for the candidate they thought best. The Republicans received a little more than a quarter of the poll. Of the 128 members elected, fifty-eight were on the pro-Treaty panel, thirty-five anti-Treaty (one member was on both), and there were thirty-five members representing other interests. These, in fact, all accepted the Treaty. Miss Macardle describes the result as a victory for the coalition only and sympathizes with the simple-minded Republicans who had voted for their opponents and now saw the mandate for a coalition government interpreted as a mandate for the Treaty.[3] The vote could more truly be described as an expression of irritation with the pact and the politicians who produced it. Never has the Labour Party returned such numbers to the Dáil, never have there been so many Independent members. The Irish may not be politically wise, but they were not so foolish, even in 1922, to forget what was at stake when they voted on that occasion. Speaking in the Dáil on the 17th May, Gavan Duffy emphasized the real issue in the election : "There are differences between us that are serious enough but that cannot be one of them. If you have an election now, it must be on the Treaty whether you say so or not." On the day previous to the election, the Constitution was published, and it appeared in the morning papers on the day of the election. There can be little doubt that its proposers did not want to give their opponents an opportunity to make it an issue. At the same time, it is difficult to believe that Miss Macardle's picture of tens of thousands of credulous Republicans tramping to the polls, before reading their morning paper, in the honest belief that it would be a Republican Constitution, is a faithful description of the event. The judgment of Republicans may have been unsound, but they were not necessarily the least intelligent section of the population. A year later, there was another General Election. By this time the people had had ample opportunity of studying the Constitution, but they refrained from electing a Republican majority.

It had been an article of the Collins–de Valera pact that the Executive should be formed out of their respective members in the proportion of five to four. The result of the election was announced on the 24th of June, and the new Parliament was to meet on the 1st of July. While the election was proceeding, the Irregulars in the Four Courts were planning to give the English seventy-two hours' notice to evacuate the country. Two days after the election, a party, under the leadership of Henderson, "Director of the Belfast Boycott," raided a garage in Dublin and seized motor-cars to the value of £9,000. He was arrested and sent to Mountjoy. That evening his colleagues, as a retaliation, seized J. J. O'Connell, Commander-in-Chief of the Government troops, and held him in the Four Courts as a hostage.

The pact had angered the British Government, who began to suspect the sincerity of Collins. The failure of the Provisional Government to check the raids on the Border, and, finally, the murder in broad daylight in London of Sir Henry Wilson, brought their impatience to near cracking point. Churchill, for one, had staked his immediate political career on the Irish experiment; were the Provisional Government going to let it fail through their supineness?

The election had given the Government what, up to then, they lacked—a mandate from their own people. They sent for the Army chiefs to inquire what would be the reaction of the troops if they were asked to bombard the Four Courts? On such a delicate balance turned the destiny of the country. Had the Army refused to move, the Treaty position was lost and the return of the British a strong possibility. But the Army did not refuse. An ultimatum was presented to the Four Courts garrison and rejected. At 4 a.m. on Wednesday, the 28th of June, the ultimatum expired. "As you have probably heard by this time, we moved against the Four Courts last night," wrote O'Higgins to his wife. "This action—inevitable in any case—was precipitated by the arrest by the Irregulars of 'Ginger' O'Connell as a set-off against the arrest of a man who was in charge of a gang stealing £10,000 worth of motor-cars in the name of the 'Belfast Boycott'—which, as you know, has been extended of late to cover all the sins on the calendar. The action is proceeding according to plan—our forces are using three eighteen pounders and it is expected that what is left of the Four Courts will be evacuated before night. . . . I think it possible that a situation may develop in which the movements of Ministers will be somewhat restricted—I think we may have to sleep here (Government Buildings)—or together somewhere—under guard. I outlined these possibilities to Molly and she is quite sensible about it. You must be equally so. There is absolutely no reason for anxiety as far as my welfare is concerned and while the situation is sad enough the action we have taken was absolutely necessary. In a few days the position will be clearer." He was too sanguine. The men in the Four Courts stood up to the bombardment at close range for two days. They suffered casualties but no loss of life. Before surrendering, they laid booby traps and mines which destroyed the Record Office, adding further proof that the history of Irish culture owes little to her patriots. But this was not the end ; the fighting in Dublin lasted for eight days, and the sorry affair was redeemed by one event only—the bravery of Cathal Brugha, who, by the manner of his death, assured himself of a place in Valhalla.

Disorder spread like a rash over a sick country. Civil government became impossible. O'Higgins, to whom the building of the State had become the first object of his life, saw with bitter impatience the general surrender to the genius of destruction.

The Army of the Provisional Government was so badly equipped and trained that the guns which fired on the Four Courts had to be borrowed from the British, and as only one knew how to fire them, gunners had to be borrowed for the purpose.

Collins, O'Higgins, and other members of the Government, joined the Army, Collins becoming Commander-in-Chief ; O'Higgins, Assistant to the Adjutant-General in Portobello Barracks. The troops at the disposal of the Government were estimated by Beaslai in his *Life* of Collins, at 4,000. The possession of artillery turned the scale in Dublin, but it was by no means certain that the fighting in the country would end so quickly, or for certain in favour of the Provisional Government. In the event, the troops of the Provisional Government marched from success to success. The Irregulars were not able to live on the country as the Volunteers had done, and with approaching defeat, their methods and morale alike deteriorated. " The best and bravest of our nation," de Valera described the Irregular forces. Idealism, chivalry and courage were plentiful among the leaders, but many were killed or captured in the early fighting, and those who remained were not able to control the undisciplined, untrained youths who adhered to them. But it is difficult to endorse de Valera's opinion that the Irregulars " would most loyally have obeyed the will of the Irish people freely expressed." Their spokesman, Rory O'Connor, even before the election, had denied the right of the people to disagree with his views, and de Valera himself expressed grave qualifications of the principle of majority rule.

To O'Higgins, the issue was very simple. Was there to be an Irish State ? Was democracy to be possible in Ireland ? For him, those considerations were paramount, and he never forgave the crime of causing Irishmen to fight for their realization over the dead bodies and burning homes of fellow-countrymen.

Arthur Griffith died suddenly on the 12th of August, 1922, leaving behind him an unmatched record of selfless devotion to his country. His qualities were not of the kind that excite the imagination; he made no appeal to the passions: he was not less great for that. O'Higgins felt an intense humiliation at the way in which the unostentatious life-work of this patriot had been rewarded. Men who were unfit to hold his coat had called him traitor to his face. His patience—especially when, as it afterwards appeared, he laboured with declining health—was remarkable: a few outbursts and his roughness with Childers being his only lapses from a rugged stoicism. The bombardment of the Four Courts, he regarded as a step that had been forced upon him, and it is ridiculous to suggest, as pretended apologists have done, that he died full of remorse for his agreement with the British. " He died of a broken heart," said O'Higgins when he heard the news. But worse was in store. Within ten days of the death of Griffith, Collins, while making a tour of inspection, was shot through the head in an ambush not far from his birthplace. The news of this was telephoned to Dublin, and O'Higgins picked up the telephone in Portobello Barracks to learn that his hero was dead.

To him fell the task of telling his comrades, and with them he marched down to the quays to wait in silence for the gunboat which was bringing the body back for burial. It was a moonless night. After many hours of waiting, a white ship was seen gleaming in the dark, drifting in on the tide. The engines were off. Two lights hung on the bridge, and the ship seemed to be deserted; as it came alongside, a man was seen standing alone, motionless on the bridge, a soldier's cap in his hand. It was Emmet Dalton, who had been with Collins when he died. When he came down to meet the group of men waiting on the pier, they noticed that the cap he held was soaked with blood. A procession was formed behind the coffin, which was carried through Dublin to St. Vincent's Hospital. It was now almost dawn, but O'Higgins, unable to face his loneliness, drove down to Greystones where his wife was staying. He came into her room, and, unable to speak, cried with the painful, terrible intensity of a man unaccustomed to the refuge of tears. When he had regained control of his emotions, he vowed, so long as he lived, to carry on the work for which Collins had given his life.

To O'Higgins, Collins symbolized the whole national movement. "The shining lamp of the Gael," he called him. As Danton had "summed up France" of the Revolution, so, for him, Michael Collins summed up Ireland. A new intensity settled on O'Higgins from that evening. It can be seen in a photograph that was taken when he was one of the pall-bearers at the funeral. It appears in an article of commemoration which he afterwards wrote. "But now I have looked upon the calm face of my friend and chief, have touched his pale hands, have borne his coffin on my shoulders, and in common with his countrymen I face the fact that Michael Collins, the greatest man that ever served this Nation's cause, lies cold in death—slain by a fellow-countryman in his native county."

By the time that Collins died, the result of the Civil War was beyond question, but the rescuing of the country from anarchy was going to be a longer and more difficult task. There was an immediate danger that a wild desire for revenge might undermine discipline but there was no outbreak, and a great deal of the credit for this must go to General Mulcahy, who took over command and issued a message to the Army, calling on the men to "let no cruel act of reprisal blemish your bright honour."

If the Army, as a whole, responded to this appeal, there is no doubt that there was a deterioration in morale after Collins died. Individual soldiers who knew him became savage, and such acts as the shooting of three Republicans out of hand at the Red Cow Inn at Clondalkin, did a great deal to discredit the Government's effort to restore order.

The death of Collins was one of the turning-points in O'Higgins's life. Now that both the leaders of the new Free State were dead, it must have seemed to the Republicans that their prospects had enormously improved. There were only three political personalities who could be said to have had a wide following ; now, within ten days, two were gone. De Valera had no rival as a personality. In the months of crisis that had passed, O'Higgins had ample opportunity to take the measure of his colleagues. He was modest about his own abilities, but he was clear-sighted and without illusions. He knew that the burden would fall on him now, and he was prepared for it. His was one of those natures which take fire in a crisis ; he lived most fully when he lived dangerously, and he had no desire for luxury, safety, comfort or any of those stars which light the bourgeois way. Superficially, he was a very typical Irishman of his class, but, in essentials, he had qualities which made him quite alien. His intellect was subtle, but his nature was direct and his thought clear. He disciplined a mind naturally quick, waiting sometimes painfully long for exactly the right word when he was speaking ; and his thought matured before he spoke.

Of all his colleagues, he was most drawn to Patrick Hogan, a young solicitor and farmer from Loughrea in Galway. Hogan was quick and brilliant, unsurpassed as a popular speaker. No matter how unpropitious the subject, how hostile his audience, after a few moments, Hogan attracted a hearing. He shared many of O'Higgins's tastes and sympathies. Very well read and a student of French, he had a detestation of any form of pretence or humbug. His mind was Gallic and cynical, but his manner was so racy and robust, his humour so irrepressible, that he never failed to arouse enthusiasm. In intelligence, the men were well matched ; in moral force, O'Higgins was supreme. With his other colleagues, with the exception of Desmond Fitz Gerald, O'Higgins was not on intimate terms. But only with Cosgrave were his relations in any sense uneasy. When it came to the choice of a successor to the premiership, O'Higgins favoured Mulcahy, but there was so general an agreement that Cosgrave should be appointed, that he withdrew his opposition. For many years, Cosgrave had taken part in the politics of the Dublin Corporation ; this gave him a knowledge of procedure which most of his colleagues did not enjoy. A man of doubtful courage would not have been acceptable at such a time, and, in this respect, Cosgrave had proved himself by taking part in the Rebellion of 1916, after which he was condemned to death, the sentence being later commuted to imprisonment. He was older than his colleagues by some ten years, and a more suitable choice than a military man for a democratic parliament.

When the Dáil once more assembled on 9th September, Mulcahy proposed Cosgrave as President of the Dáil. The other Ministers were : Desmond Fitz Gerald (External Affairs) ; Ernest Blythe (Local Government) ; Patrick Hogan (Agriculture) ; Joseph McGrath (Labour) ; Eoin MacNeill (Education) ; Richard Mulcahy (Defence) ; J. J. Walsh was Postmaster-General ; E. J. Duggan and Finian Lynch, Ministers without portfolios. Kevin O'Higgins was Minister for Home Affairs and Vice-President of the Executive Council. He was now thirty years of age.

The members of the Government who had joined the Army, returned to civil life when Collins died; it was no longer possible for them to live with safety in their homes, and, with their wives, they took up residence in the Government Buildings. This was no mere policy of caution. O'Higgins told Churchill how, when he went on the roof at night to get air and lit a match, a sniper's bullet shot the cigarette out of his hands. On their return from the honeymoon, Kevin O'Higgins and his bride had set up house in Terenure in the Dublin suburbs, which he called Dunamase after the rock-fort near his boyhood home. It proved to be no fortress, and when rumours of an attack on it reached the Government, Mrs. O'Higgins had to leave at a moment's notice and take refuge with a neighbour. Shots were fired into the house, and, on the following morning, it was closed up and the young wife moved into the safety of Government Buildings.

Living under these conditions, the Ministers set about their task, the enacting of the new Constitution. This task accomplished, the Parliament's life as a constituent assembly would be over. The date agreed upon with the British was the 6th of December, 1922. Arthur Griffith had been over in London with O'Higgins when the negotiations in connection with the draft had been going on. Now O'Higgins was alone, and to him fell the duty of putting the Constitution through all its stages in the Dáil.

Under great difficulties, the work of construction had been resumed. Eagerly he pressed forward to see it accomplished, as though he sensed that he had only five years to live, and there was a great deal to be done.

*   *   *

There was, indeed, a great deal to be done. It has not been given to many to create a new State. It is a task that would seem formidable to the most experienced politician even in propitious times. States, as a rule, have grown gradually; they have not been built up from the foundations. The makers of the Irish Free State had not only the usual difficulties, such as those which the Americans encountered after their War of Independence; they had not only to begin after bloodshed and destruction, but they had to start their work with bullets flying round their heads, with saboteurs roaming the country, burning houses, robbing banks, blowing up bridges, living by the gun. They had to start without police and with a dual judicial system, one of which was anti-national by tradition, the other makeshift by force of circumstances. Moreover, they had to create an Army Police which, like the Civil Service, would be independent of politics and faithful to any government in power.

All these matters would have required the co-operation and support of the citizens, and particularly of the politicians. In the conditions that obtained, it required great faith and great courage to undertake the task. With their lives in daily peril, the Provisional Government undertook that task, and, whatever criticism may legitimately be urged against their methods, whatever their shortcomings, individually or as a team, there is something lacking in a nation which has given so little recognition to the men who, in the circumstances, created the machinery with which the State has travelled ever since. They would have been more than human, these men, if they did not feel bitterness towards those who, however well-intentioned, made the bomb and the petrol can their only contribution to the problem of nation-building.

The reassembly of Parliament, even though the Ministers were living in Government Buildings, was a triumph and a portent. The opening ceremony was interrupted by Laurence Ginnell, a veteran Nationalist, who demanded whether this was the Dáil, and, if so, whether members from the Six Counties could sit in it. He was at length ejected from the building, and if this distressed Republican opinion, it was hard to expect, after what had passed, that the country could afford another session of metaphysics in Parliament while the storm blew outside. There was a job to be done, and a limited time in which to accomplish it. Gavan Duffy emerged as the champion of procedure early in the session when he inquired whether there would be the old duality ; that is to say, a Dáil Government and a Provisional Government. Cosgrave answered that both Governments were now assimilated.

O'Higgins, from the beginning of the session, became the chief spokesman of the Government. When a Labour Deputy asked questions about the attack on the Four Courts and the subsequent acts of the Government, it was O'Higgins who answered him, and his uncompromising manner, his fearless defence of any steps taken by the Government, made him appear to the Republicans and to the world at large, as the strong man of the Government and the originator of its policy.

" I want to get rid of humbug and get down to realities." That was the text of O'Higgins's first speech in the new Dáil ; that was the basis of his political philosophy. It is not, perhaps, the most inspiring policy, but there are times when it is the only policy for an honest man. " The principal reality with which this Parliament is faced," he continued, " is the object for which it came into being—the establishment of the State with a Constitution in accordance with the Treaty signed in London on the 6th December last," and later in his speech he echoed a thought that must have predominated in the public mind : " I submit that the thing that matters most to the Parliament is whether this Parliament is to be a mere talking shop or whether what it says holds in this country. You cannot build if foundations are challenged ; the issue must be decided one way or the other, and the chief business of this Parliament is to decide it, . . . one does not usually build in the path of a forest fire."[4]

There is no doubt that in the rapid recruitment which the emergency made inevitable, undesirable characters found their way into the Army. The *Morning Post* correspondent described the Government troops as the Bogsturm and the Lootwehr. The C.I.D. or " Oriel House men," as they were called, although highly effective, were very far from gentle in their methods. Accommodation was unavailable for the batches of prisoners which the Government was taking, and, generally speaking, conditions for the Republicans were very uncomfortable.

O'Higgins refused to adopt a sentimental attitude towards them, and he read out a letter which one of the prisoners sent from prison :—

> " Monday night, Galway Gaol, No. 4 Cell,
> 7th year of the Republic.
>
> " Dear Billy,
> " All that I am thinking of is where to get guns when we get out, because I want to talk to some Bank Managers and a few railway clerks."[5]

This severely practical approach to the political controversy was, O'Higgins thought, more common than the idealists allowed, and he pointed out that no one who was prepared to give a satisfactory undertaking would be detained in prison. The gentleman who wrote from his cell had completed such a form and denied any connection with the Irregulars. If this letter had not been intercepted, he would have been automatically released from prison.

The man was a type, and in his letter, said O'Higgins, was "embodied the disintegration that is at present proceeding apace in this country—the moral disintegration." If the Parliament did not do its duty, "this will not be the Irish Nation for it will go down in chaos, in anarchy and in futility." These words, spoken with the emphasis and gravity which had become habitual, made a deep effect. The earnestness of manner was heightened and emphasized by the great brow of the speaker, the pallor of the face and the air of repressed passion suggested by the trembling arm and the long forefinger of the protruding right hand. He revealed that the attack on the Four Courts was made in anticipation of "conditions that would have brought back the British power—horse, foot, artillery and Navy—in hostile relations to this country." He appealed to the Labour Party, which was the chief opposition, for "a measure of strong support to establish the sovereignty of the people's will."

As well as the Civil War, and the great unemployment in the country, occasioned partly by existing unrest and also by the general slump with which the world was faced in 1922 after the post-war boom, there was a phase of labour unrest which had extended to the Civil Service. The Post Office workers were on strike. O'Higgins defended the right of the Government to deny this privilege to Civil Servants, in which he found himself in conflict with the Labour Party.[6] Had O'Higgins listened to the argument which their speakers advanced that a State servant should be in exactly the same position as a person in private employment, he would, as he said, have done a criminal thing. "Here, at the very birth and infancy of this State, I would have set a precedent which, enlarged and acted upon later on, would lead to the destruction of the State."

The Constitution was introduced to the Dáil by the President on 18th September. The Treaty was put in a schedule to the Bill, and it was provided that any provision of this Constitution which was repugnant to the Treaty would be void and inoperative. The Constitution was, broadly speaking, separated into three sections : firstly, those articles upon which the British had insisted ; secondly, the provisions for the representation and protection of Southern Unionists ; thirdly, articles of a general nature which were not matters of agreement with anyone, and which could be discussed on their merits and altered if Parliament so desired. Having explained the general nature of the Bill, Cosgrave left to O'Higgins the responsibility of guiding its passage. He described the Constitution as "a strict but fair interpretation of the Treaty,"[7] and if it was not as broad a document as some had hoped for, the fault, to some extent, lay with those who had embarrassed the negotiations with the British by shooting at the departing soldiers while the Irish representatives were trying to obtain better terms. Then he embarked on one of those candid commentaries on the national character which became habitual with him and won him many enemies among those who disliked to hear the truth. His remarks were not meant to be provocative ; he believed : "There are occasions in the lives of individuals and in the lives of nations when it takes more courage, and courage of a higher order, to face facts than to face machine-guns." He hoped that the effect of having a written Constitution of their own would help the people to realize that they were, in fact, the authority. "Back through the ages we have had a traditional outlook on law and government which no reasonable man expects to change in five or seven or even ten years." This attitude of protest, negation, sometimes of sheer wantonness and waywardness and destructiveness—"very evident at the moment"—had been to a large extent, the attitude of the Irish people. It was a fact that the first four Irish Governments would have to bear in mind "while keeping a firm, cool grip on the land."

There arose in Ireland two different causes of complaint against the Government, both voiced by people of the same way of thinking. On the one hand, it was maintained that the Irish Volunteers had driven the English out of the country, which was a matter for glory, and, on the other hand, it was asserted that the British had by duress imposed a Treaty upon Ireland. Recommending the Constitution, O'Higgins made the position painfully clear : "We did not drive the British out of the country ; we were not able, and there was no great prospect that we ever would be able. Many would have liked to do with the British what we read that Brian Boru did with the Danes, not far from here. But we did not do it ; we were not able to do it. If we had been able to do it, the things that are in the Treaty and that are in the Constitution, that many here find irksome, would not be there. And we felt that only by doing that could 100 per cent. of our war programme be attained. And so we took less than 100 per cent. of our war programme, and we abandoned something of those inscriptions which were written on our battle standards, and we abandoned them for the sake of the Irish Nation, the living Irish Nation, and the Irish Nation of the future. No man abandoned them lightly and no man abandoned them without pain." He would go through the Constitution clause by clause, although upon some of them " the Government stands or falls. If the Government falls, we will give every support to our successors in any effort they may make to attain better."[8]

This was a manner of speaking which had not become hackneyed in public affairs. There was an absence of heroics, a lucidity of thought and phrase, a completely adult approach to the conduct of affairs. Speaking of de Valera when supporting his election as President of an earlier Dáil, General Mulcahy described him as " a boy among boys." The description did not fit O'Higgins, but the times had changed ; the spirit of big adventure had gone for ever. It was clear, that when he spoke, the intellect and will controlled the other faculties. His manner of speaking was the antithesis of de Valera's : logic took the place of vagueness. There was no rambling, the mind led the tongue on a tight leash which allowed no impulsive dartings down blind alleys, no rushing round in circles, but a straight progression to a clearly-defined objective.

To follow the progress of the Irish Constitution through the Dáil would tax the patience of the reader beyond endurance. The document itself has been superseded by another, and is therefore of interest only to constitutional historians. It must, however, be considered in a very general way if one is to understand the attitude which O'Higgins and his Party were taking at the time. Those clauses upon which the Government insisted were concerned with the relations of the Irish Free State to the Commonwealth and the Crown. The new State was described as enjoying the same relation with the Crown as that which existed in " law and practice and constitutional usage " between the Crown and Canada, and as being co-equal member of the British Commonwealth of Nations. " There is no constitutional hybrid between a Republic and a Monarchy," O'Higgins declared. " Mr. de Valera had thought he had begotten one, but nobody loved it and he abandoned it himself."[9] On this occasion, O'Higgins had not the gift of prophecy, for de Valera has, in fact, evolved a State which he describes as a Republic associated with the British Commonwealth, using the Crown for certain purposes so long as it suits the Republic's convenience.

It can be said that O'Higgins, had he lived, and had he the power to do so, would not have accepted that position ; at the same time, it must be admitted that he would not have believed it possible that such a position could arrive. It arose in this manner. The oath of allegiance to the King was said to be the rock upon which the Sinn Fein Party split. Gavan Duffy, one of the signatories of the Treaty, expressed the belief that the Constitution need not have contained any such oath. Now, O'Higgins never encouraged that hope. "You will find," he insisted, "reflected in the Constitution the weaknesses and the imperfections which are inherent in the Treaty." A Constitution in which "the King was relegated to the outer darkness," as Gavan Duffy put it, would have been Republican. And O'Higgins was emphatic that "this Constitution is not a Republican Constitution ; perhaps, I would not be wrong in saying that it is as little a Republican Constitution as a British Constitution. It contains the trappings, the insignia, the fictions and the symbols of monarchical institutions, but the real power is in the hands of the people. Anyone who has studied the grim constitutional struggle between the British Parliament and the British Crown knows well the net result of that struggle, knows that the Parliament won, and that the Parliament wisely or unwisely saved the face of the Monarch, while depriving him of any real power. England has been called a Republic with a Monarchy. The position to-day in England is that the humblest member in Westminster wields a more real power and more authority than the British King, and that the King has become a useful fiction, an imposing symbol, but that His Majesty is the majesty of the people." [10] Here, no doubt, O'Higgins over-simplified the position. The influence of the English king must depend to a large extent on the personality of each holder of the office. High place of its nature confers influence, because men do not walk about with the Bill of Rights in their pockets, and the humblest Member of Parliament will only have more real power than a monarch when men are immune from vanity, incapable of flattery, unimpressed by tradition, regardless of personal distinction, and when the nature of women has undergone a corresponding change. O'Higgins desired to stress the fact that in the Irish Constitution the King, by his representative, could only act on the advice of the Executive Council, who were responsible to Parliament, and through Parliament, to the people.

Without straining that point, we can pass to the real crux— the Oath. "There are likely," observed O'Higgins, "to be many words said about this oath before we are through with this business and it is just as well to have the advantage of saying the first word." He proceeded to explain in some detail that the form was less full-blooded than that administered in Canada, Australia or the Union of South Africa. From that he proceeded to attack the attitude, for which Gavan Duffy was sponsor, that the Treaty provided what the form of oath was to be, but omitted to add that an oath was obligatory. This, O'Higgins described as the " whiskey and soda argument . . . because the Treaty only says ' the oath to be taken by members of the Parliament of the Free State shall be so and so,' that is only the same as saying that the whiskey to be taken by members of a certain club shall be John Jameson's ' Three Star ' . . . just in the same way where it was not prescribed or intended by the Treaty, that all members of the Parliament should take this oath, but it was meant if they particularly wanted, and if they insisted on taking an oath, then this would be the oath they would take. I would like that some Deputy other than myself would take the task of arguing that particular point across the table with British Ministers." [11]

It was not to O'Higgins's mind " a serious argument ; it shows a finicky, irresponsible outlook, which should be no part of those responsible for the government of this country to cater for." O'Higgins had no doubt, and urged that " the reverse is not arguable," that the oath in the Treaty was intended to be taken by Members of Parliament before taking their seats.

On account of this oath, the Civil War was fought, and when the Republicans laid down their arms, it was on account of this oath that they refused to enter the Dáil. On the 23rd June, 1927, de Valera led his followers into the Parliament building, but refused to sign the declaration when it was put before him. An Act was passed, as a result of the murder of O'Higgins, which made it compulsory for a parliamentary candidate to agree to take the oath before he could stand for election. De Valera did what his most recent biographer described as " one of the bravest things he has ever done," and once more entered the precincts of the Dáil, but on this occasion, putting the testament to one side, wrote his name under the oath. It was better than the undesirable alternative—withdrawing from politics.[12] In due course, de Valera obtained a parliamentary majority, abolished the oath, and when King Edward VIII abdicated, seized the opportunity to pass an Act of Parliament which prescribed the functions for which the services of the Monarch are retained. He is not mentioned in the present Constitution.

To have foreseen all this, O'Higgins would have first had to foresee that he had only five years to live.

These, then, were the points upon which the Government were not prepared to accept amendments, because it "might react disastrously upon the fortunes of the country." If these clauses went, the Government went with them. Having presented this part of the Constitution in general terms at the second reading of the Bill, O'Higgins turned to the clauses upon which the Government were likewise prepared to treat any disagreement as a vote of no confidence. These were the articles expressive of the agreement reached by the Ministry with representatives of the Southern Unionists. This was the class which not many years before had been commiserated with by the *Pall Mall Gazette*, for, that paper alleged, Irish Home Rule would be followed by their massacre.

In the Civil War, many of them did suffer, and their homes had been burnt during the Black and Tan regime as a reprisal for the burnings of cottages and shops by the British forces. If innocent people suffered because their sympathies were assumed to lie with the Black and Tans, it is equally true that innocent people of the poorer class lost their homes because they were assumed to sympathize with the Volunteers. Rough justice is only satisfactory to those who administer it. There is no doubt whatever that Eamon de Valera, Arthur Griffith and Michael Collins were all prepared to go a long way to win the support of the Unionists for a new Irish regime. Unfortunately, the habit of arson had become fixed, so that the more high-spirited Republicans were not prepared to overcome it as soon as the British forces left the country. It could now be indulged in more freely and at less personal risk. In common, therefore, with the participants, the adherents of the old regime suffered grievously in the Civil War, in which they took no active part. O'Higgins, by insisting on the incorporation of Griffith's concessions to the Unionists in the text of the Constitution, showed that the new Government was anxious to break down the barrier which had formerly separated the Unionists from the Nationalists in the life of their common country. As the question of minorities has played a vital part in modern European history, lies at the root of the Indian problems, and obstructs the unification of Ireland at present, it may be worth while to pause and examine the position of Irish Unionists in 1922.

By the expression "Southern Unionist" is usually meant members of the old Protestant Ascendancy. In fact, many Catholics had Unionist politics, many Unionists had no property or ascendancy, but such people were not representative, and were not so vulnerable as the rich Protestant landlord or merchant. As a rule, Protestants identified themselves with British interests, although they had supplied Ireland with all her earlier eminent national leaders and rebels, excepting only O'Connell. The Protestant Ascendancy did ensure that privilege was reserved for a tiny fraction of the population, and it was likely that a national government, elected on a broad franchise, would imperil or remove these privileges. But a statesman, wishing to do what was best for Ireland, was bound to admit that there was in this class, at that time, however acquired or preserved, a disproportionate share of culture, enterprise and professional skill. Such a statesman would wish to preserve this source of real wealth for the nation. Such a statesman was Griffith, Collins and O'Higgins, and such, too, was de Valera, but his later affiliations drove him for a time in this, as in other respects, to the left of his own convictions. Before the Treaty was signed, Griffith, with de Valera's consent, had given the assurance to Lord Midleton, Mr. Andrew Jameson and the Provost of Trinity College that in an independent Ireland they would be represented, and their interests safeguarded by a Second Chamber in the Legislature. Griffith was attacked by Countess Marckievicz—one of the few representatives of that class in national politics—for trucking with the Unionists, but he was not perturbed. "I met them," he said, "because they are my countrymen . . . and as far as I am concerned they will have fair play." [13]

Now, in this Constitution which O'Higgins was expounding to the Dáil was enshrined the fulfilment of Griffith's promises. As a matter of good faith the Government stood firm in these proposals. Representatives of that small section of Irish womanhood, who formed a Greek chorus in the Irish tragedy, were particularly demonstrative while O'Higgins was speaking. One by one they were removed from the Visitors' Gallery, from where their feelings had excited them to join noisily in the debate. The fears of the Unionists, O'Higgins thought, "may be unfounded. We here may think that there is very little substance in them,

but of the reality of those fears there can be no doubt. . . . I
think it was true statesmanship that dictated to the late President
the making of very considerable concessions along that line. . . .
We now know no political party. We have taken quite definitely
a step forward in our evolution towards completion of nationhood. These people are part and parcel of the nation, and we,
being the majority and strength of the country . . . it comes
well from us to make a generous adjustment to show that these
people were regarded, not as alien enemies, not as planters, but
that we regard them as part and parcel of this Nation, and that
we wish them to take their share of its responsibilities." [14]

Later, in his reply to the debate, he took up the cudgels on their
behalf with more vigour. "Try to remember," he urged, "that
British soldiers and British ex-policemen who were covered by
the terms of the Amnesty that had been issued were being shot
almost daily, almost as a matter of routine. Try to remember
that certain people differing from the majority in religion, and
perhaps also, and I am not sure of that, even in political outlook,
were driven from their homes and from their positions in greater
numbers than I was aware of until quite recently." He would
not admit that the violence in Belfast offered a pretext for retaliation
"in the territory over which we have theoretical jurisdiction." [15]

The privilege of representation in the Senate could have been
a merely theoretical one for there were few of the class whom
it was intended to benefit who would have been elected on a
popular franchise. To make this concession a reality the power
to nominate one-half of the original Senators was given to the
President on the understanding that it would be exercised in favour
of people who would not otherwise be elected. "It is better,"
O'Higgins concluded, "to err on the side of an over-generous
advance than on the side of what would appear to be a rebuff
or a slight to people who will gradually come around to what
is the general view of the Nation."

In its workings O'Higgins was often impatient with the Senate.
While he was always a good listener and very ready to accept
suggestions, he had an almost overbearing eagerness to see his
ideas translated into action. Having seen the light himself, as it
were, he felt that after sufficient explanation every man of goodwill would see it too ; if they did not, they were wilfully blind.
Sometimes the Senate did not see the light. O'Higgins, although
he made a strong appeal to the Unionists—who, as men of

property, rather liked a martinet for discipline and order—was himself too convinced a democrat to approve of the principle that an unrepresentative Senate could block a decision which was considered of urgent importance by the popular branch of the Legislature. He had, in consequence, many stormy passages in the Upper House. But at the breakfast table on the day he died, he said that he hoped the State would institute some equivalent to the Order of Merit which could be awarded to those who, like Senators Samuel Brown, K.C., and Andrew Jameson, gave to the Nation valuable and unostentatious service which by its nature would never otherwise receive the recognition it deserved.

Of the other proposals for the Constitution one only need occupy us here. An attempt was made to break through the narrowness of party government by allowing eight members of the Cabinet or Executive Council, which was to consist of not more than twelve members, to be chosen from outside the Dáil. The idea allowed the best men irrespective of Party to be made heads of departments and would allow them to retain office even after the Government had been defeated. Like so many political inventions, this one did not work in practice and was afterwards abandoned.

When O'Higgins had completed his task, a barrage of criticism against the Constitution was levelled, principally by Gavan Duffy and Johnson, the leader of the Labour Party. In his reply, O'Higgins took no pains to conceal his opinion of their objections. "We find at the end of all the ridiculous mush a certain amount of vague generalities, a certain amount of poetry, a certain amount of emphasis on the desire which many here share for better things if such were obtainable, but very little practical useful criticism of the Constitution."[16]

Johnson had suggested that there was no necessity to have a Constitution and Gavan Duffy recommended that the matter be shelved until after the next Imperial Conference. "There is," O'Higgins complained, "to be no finality. We are to wait for some far-off Imperial Conference which, he made me remember, was mentioned in a resolution of 1917—and after that the millennium. . . . He warns us not to mould in cast iron our country's rights. . . . Apparently he doubts the capacity of this country to develop beyond the full stop of any written document. I have no such doubts."[17] He wanted above all to get the matter settled, to stop talking and to go ahead " with the main business of the Irish Parliament—reconstruction and the dealing with the social and economic problems of the country." "This Constitution," he declared in the Dáil at the end of the debates upon it, "should be prized by the people. It was won in toil, in danger and in stress. It was negotiated on the cliff's edge, and it gives to Ireland the care of her own household. . . . The greatest man that ever served the cause of an oppressed nation achieved this thing and having achieved it gave, as the last final proof of his conviction of its worth, his gallant life."[18]

CHAPTER VIII

THE IRON HAND

A S a candle burns most brightly when it is about to burn out, so the Civil War became more violent as it spluttered to a close. O'Higgins grew more impatient every day and could not understand why the Army could not round up the Irregulars. The country was reaping some of the harvest which it had sown ; not long before assassination had been adopted as a legitimate weapon to use against the British, and a form of warfare in which combatants wore civilian clothes was a particularly difficult one for an army to deal with. An apparently innocent-looking pedestrian could hurl a bomb at a passing motor car and disappear into the crowd with very little fear of capture. Moreover, a form of ambush had grown to be common in which parties of Free State soldiers were fired upon and when they were about to respond the attackers would surrender. By this means a toll of opponents could be taken with an absolute minimum of casualties. On occasions the dicipline of the Army did not stand these tests and from time to time they shot prisoners out of hand.

Angry as O'Higgins was at the Republican excesses, he felt deeply mortified at any lapse by the Government troops. He had no patience with tact when it took the form of winking at illegalities. He preferred a crisis to a crime and was at his best in a crisis. He despised all policies which could not bear upon them the full light of day. Bitterly opposed to the policy of leaving preventative measures to the initiative of the soldiers, he pressed for more control of the Army by the Cabinet. General Mulcahy, the Commander-in-Chief of the Army, was Minister for Defence in the Government. A Volunteer from the beginning, a member of the Irish Republican Brotherhood and Collins's successor, he believed that he understood the mentality of the men in a way that O'Higgins—who described his Army career as " very short though very brilliant "—could not.

Temperamentally, Cosgrave and O'Higgins were antipathetic ; now a cleavage began to appear between O'Higgins and Mulcahy. It was part of Cosgrave's task to keep these two mutually uncongenial people from splitting the Executive Council asunder. As well as this growing sore in the Cabinet, the temper of debate in the Dáil sharpened very considerably as O'Higgins became increasingly impatient of the Opposition, in particular Gavan Duffy. It began with the discussion on the part that the King was to play in the Constitution. To O'Higgins, it seemed unreasonable that a member of the delegation who had signed the Treaty should maintain that, in the matter of the Constitution, the Irish team could refuse to pay any attention to the demands of the British Government. " It is," he complained, " a very safe position for one who feels he has a comfortable minority to take up, and a very safe position for one who is not primarily responsible to the country for what may befall." " Every member," he held, " should cast his vote on every subject as if it were going to be a tie in the Dáil and as if his vote should mean the difference one way or the other."

O'Higgins was an intense believer in democracy, and it was not a happy time for a democrat. On the one hand, there was a body of men in arms who defied the enactments of what the majority of the people had willed ; on the other, there was the difficulty of suppressing these people by normal methods. Were the Irregulars entitled to kill, rob and burn at will, and, in capture, claim that they were prisoners of war ? If not, what was their crime ? By whom was it to be tried ? A juryman required to be a hero, and heroes do not grow at random on a sheriff's panel. Was the country to die of exhaustion ? Were the majority to be denied the fulfilment of their will ? It would be pharisaical to pretend that a majority of the Irish people wanted, in any real sense, an agreement with England in the terms of the Treaty, to which many were indifferent and some hostile, but the great majority wanted peace, and a surrender to the Irregulars meant a return to the position before the Treaty. " It is better to make certain peace with us on the chance of a recurrence of war with England than to fight us and accept the bad bargain you have made." That, in essence, was the Republican suggestion. To yield to it meant to surrender on the very fundamentals of democratic government. But, behind the scenes, efforts were made to see a way out. General Mulcahy, to the intense indignation of some of his colleagues when it was afterwards disclosed, met de Valera. The Cabinet had agreed not to hold private parleys with individual Irregulars. There is no doubt that when General Mulcahy was approached by an ecclesiastical intermediary, he accepted the invitation with the best motives, but it was a blow to the principle of collective responsibility in the Cabinet, and it increased the antagonism of O'Higgins. At this meeting, Mulcahy urged de Valera to exert his influence to stop the war. " There are men of faith," said de Valera, " and men of reason. Now, I am a man of reason, but when a man of faith like Rory O'Connor says he will carry on, I am only a humble soldier behind him." That ended the interview.[1]

Organized fighting had for the most part broken down by September, but the resistance continued. It was not possible to organize civil government, and an unarmed police force was a mere touch of comic opera in such conditions. Courts could not function, and grazing rights were acquired by automatics instead of auctions. Discipline in the Army, which in some districts, notably Kerry, was weak, threatened to become difficult to maintain everywhere. In these circumstances, the Government proposed to give to the Army full power to hold military courts to deal with defined offences, which included any action against the National Forces, as well as arson, possession of firearms or explosives, and, more widely, the breach of any " general order or regulations made by the Army Authorities." In short, the Government wished to abrogate its own powers and to give to the Army the task of restoring order. These courts had power to inflict the death penalty. In supporting the measures, General Mulcahy quoted from captured correspondence between Liam Lynch, who was now the Army Chief of the Irregulars, and de Valera, who represented the political wing. De Valera, continuing to write as though he was still in the Dáil, complained that : " Even if we had the allegiance we have not the military strength to make our will effective, and we cannot, as in the time of the war with the British, point to authority derived from the vote of the majority of the people. We will be turned down definitely by the electorate in a few months' time in any case."[2] De Valera then suggested that " the Army " should take control and assume responsibility, and, if it was so desired, some of the Party could join the Army executive. De Valera's colleagues afterwards met and agreed to give control to the Army and to work with them.

"You have," said Mulcahy, "to look to the leaders for hope, for some kind of sanity ; and you have the leaders saying that they have absolutely no right to talk as public representatives. You have them telling the Army that they can get on, as they will not be expected to justify themselves in the eyes of the people in the same way as an honest political person would."[3] In a speech of great candour, Mulcahy admitted that in one case, where a bomb had blown up eight soldiers at Macroom, their companions refused to accept the surrender of a man who offered himself as a prisoner and killed him. In another case, when Irregular prisoners laughed at the spectacle of a dead soldier sitting by the roadside, the troops who had captured them were with difficulty restrained by their officer from shooting the prisoners.

The power asked for by the Army was, in fact, the power to execute prisoners. It was a declaration that the Civil War was not a war. It was an issue of supreme moment. When the powers were granted, they achieved two results—the end of the Civil War and the political destruction of those who granted them. "The grass soon grows over a battlefield but never over a scaffold" are words which Churchill has quoted with approval. The history of Ireland had forced a patriot to be a man in conflict with the law. Hanging, a death of shame, was not so regarded in Ireland after the rebels of 1798 and Robert Emmet had died by the rope. The courts and the police, to which people should look for justice and protection, had become symbolical of oppression and force. Some of the people could not rid themselves quickly of these associations, nor comprehend that these instruments were just as necessary for maintaining a native government as a usurping one. Their initiation would, in any event, have had to be gradual. Now, by executing those, who, however insincerely—and there were many who were perfectly sincere—professed to uphold the doctrine of untainted Republicanism against a Constitution dictated by the British, the Government were inheriting the odium of the suppressors of all Irish revolutions in the past. In vain, O'Higgins argued : "The life of this nation is menaced. It is menaced politically, it is menaced economically, it is menaced morally. . . . There is a time limit. This thing cannot go on indefinitely and to a large extent the task of the Government is a task against time."

In the previous December, there were 130,000 people out of employment ; the number had swollen, "the threads and ties which bind society are strained to snapping point." The very means which destroyed their rebellion ensured the eventual political triumph of the Irregulars. They were now free to tap the sentimental reservoirs of nearly a thousand years. But, even if he had realized that the Government could not do this thing and retain the title deeds of the national struggle, O'Higgins for one would not have hesitated. "I do not think that any of us hold human life cheap ; but when, and if, a situation arises in the country when you must balance the human life against the life of the nation, that presents a very different problem, and we, at least, do seriously consider that such a situation has come to pass in Ireland and that we are presented with a spectacle of a country steering straight for anarchy, futility and chaos. . . . If this country fails to get through, if this country fails to win out to democratic government, that will be unfortunate. But if this country fails to win out to democratic government because of any lack of clear thinking on the part of those who had the primary responsibility, that would be criminal—criminal for us. It would be putting a certain mawkish sentimentality before the thing that the people look to us to do, and we will not do that."[4]

O'Higgins was dead before the pendulum of power swung over to his opponents, but if he had known what political capital would be made of the Government's decision, and its consequences, he would have regarded it as a greater crime not to do what, in the circumstances, seemed to be right. It was not O'Higgins's way to speak softly in public of what he disapproved, and he never suppressed his feelings about the Irregulars. "I venture to say that since last December this country has more heroes to the square mile than any other country in the world," was his remark on one occasion, and now he reviewed the claims of the Irregulars to the sympathy of their countrymen. "It would perhaps be a generous estimate to say that 20 per cent. of the militant opposition to the Government is idealism. I know that there is a percentage, whatever that percentage is. It would be, perhaps, a generous estimate also to say that only 20 per cent. of it is crime. And between those 20 per cents. there flows 60 per cent. of sheer futility, that is neither one thing nor the other, but that will go on until some very definite reason is put up to it why it should not go on. We hope to put up such a reason . . ."[5]

The hostility to Childers, which Griffith took no trouble to hide, had been transmitted to O'Higgins. He now spoke of him as " the able Englishman who is leading those who are opposed to this Government," and described him as without a programme, " steadily, callously and ghoulishly on his career of striking at the heart of this nation, striking deadly, or what he hopes are deadly, blows at the economic life of the nation."[6]

This was, surely, as much a distortion of Childers's motives as it was of his position on the Irregular side. He was in charge of their propaganda, and did at times take part in fighting, which he had not done against the British. It was believed that he and his wife had very strong personal influence on de Valera, but beyond that there is no evidence that he had any predominating influence in the counsels of the Irregulars.

Childers was destined to be one of the first to suffer from the Dail's decision, by a large majority, to grant special powers to the Army. The first executions under these powers were carried out on the 17th November, when four youths, captured with revolvers in a Dublin street, were shot. O'Higgins supported Mulcahy, who was called to account for the act by Thomas Johnson, and on every subsequent occasion of the same kind he defended the acts of the Army. His manner of doing so, his air of solemnity and weight, won him the reputation of being the responsible Minister. He had already earned the reputation of being the strong man in the Cabinet. As the Minister for Defence, in charge of the Army, General Mulcahy attracted a large share of the odium which these stern measures invoked, but it was O'Higgins who was popularly believed to be the instigator of the proposals and the most vigilant for their exercise. He defended the killing of these four youths who were found carrying loaded guns and before they had shown any disposition to use them. The carrying of loaded guns had become almost a national pastime, and Johnson voiced the shock it gave a great many people to hear that anyone could be shot for indulging in it. General Mulcahy explained that the men were lying in wait to take the lives of other men, and Johnson, in replying, said: "The object which I had has been achieved. . . . I have the utmost detestation of street ambushes above everything that is happening in this country, and I have not the slightest sympathy, nor do I want to utter one word which would seem to condone in any way whatever the action of any man or woman who is engaged in the organization of ambushes in the city streets. The protest, or, at least, the question that I raised was because of the uninformative announcement, and I think the reputation of the Government will have been saved by the statement that that query has educed. Recent statements that have appeared, recent developments, conclusively prove to me that there is not going to be any life for this nation unless by the taking of stringent measures." [7] As Johnson was a persistent critic of the Government and insisted on maintaining in every crisis a sometimes pedantic liberalism, his agreement with these executions of four unknown young men has considerable significance.

"The nation's life is worth the life of many individuals," said O'Higgins. "The whole question as to whether it is to be a Nation in the future governed by constitutional principles, or whether it is to be a mob dictated to by an armed minority was at stake. There is a point beyond which we could not coax or compromise. The point came at which it became necessary to strike to save the life of the nation. And only then we struck. Only when it was clear that there could be no peace ; only when it was clear that when the political leader had gained his political advantage his military associates were free to dishonour him by denying the price. Then we struck." [8]

At the time O'Higgins was speaking, Childers, having been captured by the military in Robert Barton's house in Wicklow, had been sentenced to death. He came out of his room carrying a revolver, meaning to defend himself, and, under the Army regulations, was thereby liable to the death penalty.

Whatever the public reaction to those executions, the reports show that the Dáil, as a whole, irrespective of Party, seemed prepared to accept the first shootings as something drastic which the circumstances justified. The case of Childers, who was shot a few days later, met with quite a different reception. The atmosphere was tense, and Gavan Duffy, in a very emotional speech, made a strong attack on the Government. Having praised Childers's qualities, he denounced the secrecy of the trial and the propaganda of which he had been a victim. The application to the Master of the Rolls for a Habeas Corpus Order on Childers's behalf had been refused on the ground that a war was on. If that was so, Duffy argued, Childers was a prisoner of war. While other men had been sentenced to imprisonment for having revolvers, Childers was shot for the offence. Were other matters allowed to influence the court's judgment ? If they were, they should have been stated, and he should have had an opportunity of answering them.

President Cosgrave was the first to reply to the attack on the

Government, and he had a good case inasmuch as, if anyone were to be executed, it should be the leaders rather than their followers ; and if there was to be a discretion exercised, it would be quite unfair to execute the friendless and spare the influential. O'Higgins joined in the debate. Having repeated that Childers was an Englishman, he spoke of those who came into the national struggle " on the last emotional wave." The country was entitled " to act on its own intuitions of self-preservation," and " will see that any people coming in here for adventure will get it." The ownership of the country by the plain men and women who inhabited it was something that must be asserted and indicated. The country was not a stage on which neurotic women and megalomaniacal men " may cut their capers."[9]

It was a very ruthless speech, one which revealed the tigerish streak in O'Higgins's character, a streak which would only become apparent when he felt that the community was being injured by the individual.

*   *   *

By giving these powers of execution to the Army, members of the Government were inviting assassination. It became a point of honour among them to make no reservations in their speeches which would make it appear that anyone was less responsible than the others. The gentle and scholarly Eoin MacNeill supported the policy of the executions, and while he agreed that Childers had been the victim of prejudice, he and his colleagues were themselves the victims of " deliberate propaganda that is creating and intended to create deep-down feelings of bloodiness and vengeance between one set of Irishmen and the other. . . . We have to meet here now carefully planned and studied fanaticism calling to its aid the lowest and grossest passions."

Nevertheless, the shooting of Childers caused intense dismay in England as well as in Ireland. It was generally believed that there were not many men of his calibre left in the public life of the country, and that whatever mischief he had done, was done with noble, if cranky, intentions. He faced death bravely, comforted his executioners and displayed no resentment at his fate, which was one of the tragedies of a time when fanaticism had burst the bounds of reason and swept away all simple, human values.

O'Higgins, speaking on the case of the first four men to be

executed, used, what Miss Macardle described as, " ominous
and cynical words." He was endeavouring to explain that the
fact that the men who were the first to be executed had been
selected because they were ordinary and average examples, and,
as such, more likely to prove a deterrent than if the victim had
been someone " outstandingly wicked in his activities " ; then
the people might think " he was killed because he was a leader,
because he was an Englishman or because he combined with
others to commit rape."* The word Englishman was a reference
to Childers, who had been sentenced to death, although the sentence
had still to be confirmed. The reference at such a time was
unfortunate. Winston Churchill, after Childers was captured,
referred to him in a speech at Dundee as " this strange being,
actuated by a deadly and malignant hatred for the land of his
birth. Such as he is may all who hate us be." Childers did arouse
deadly hatred, but one can only regret that a great Englishman
and a great Irishman did not give him the benefit of that reticence
which the common law demands for the most wretched criminal
before his trial.

Eoin MacNeill made the best speech from the Government
benches on this terrible occasion. He put the case that the destruction of the material life of the country must be stopped, and " the
right amount of force to be employed is the right amount of
force to put that thing down and to put it down as quickly as
possible." No one denies that the stern measures now being taken
had this effect. Miss Macardle writes : " The Provisional Government had devised a war measure better calculated than any used
by the British Government to break down the resistance of those
opposed to them."

Nevertheless, there were further efforts made by the Republicans
to break the spirit of the Government. On the 26th October,
1922, the Irregulars united themselves once more with their political
representatives, who, calling themselves " the faithful deputies
of Dáil Eireann," elected de Valera " President of the Republic
and Chief Executive of State," and on the 30th November the

* Inherent modesty or defective hearing made a newspaper reporter write
" raids " for " rape." This made the whole sentence seem to apply to Childers
when, in fact, it instances three kinds of men. Miss Macardle, in
The History of the Irish Republic, quotes the passage from the *Independent* newspaper
report and not Hansard. Hence, the mistaken over-significance she gives to
O'Higgins's words.

Chief of Staff (Liam Lynch) signed an order, which was afterwards captured, for the shooting "at sight" of all members of the Provisional Parliament who had voted for the emergency powers that had been given to the Army, certain Senators, High Court Judges, those associated with the hostile Press, and "aggressive Free State supporters." The residences of these people were to be burned and the residences of all Senators. Many mansions were burnt to the ground with their contents ; when the house of one Deputy was set on fire, a child died of burns, and there were many other outrages in obedience to this order. On the 7th December, 1922, two Deputies, Seán Hales and Pádraic O'Maille, leaving their hotel on the Dublin Quays to attend Parliament, were fired upon. Hales was shot dead, O'Maille wounded. A last desperate effort was being made to make the task of the Government impossible. "But these men," in Churchill's words, "although deeply troubled in their souls, were courageous and hot-blooded, and driven as they had been into a corner with their lives at stake—and far more than their lives, the cause they had conducted so far—they hit back with primordial freedom."

The Cabinet was called, and General Mulcahy, as Minister for Defence and the Army representative in the Government, asked that four Republicans who were in custody should be taken out and shot without trial as a deterrent to further assassination of Deputies. When he had given his reasons, the majority of the Executive Council agreed. At length, after discussion, all consented. It was absolutely essential that the Cabinet should be unanimous in sanctioning so awful and unorthodox a proposal. The men selected for execution were four leaders from the four provinces, who had been in prison since the capture of the Four Courts—Liam Mellowes, a disciple of Pearse and a man of considerable ability, from Connaught ; Joseph McKelvey and Richard Barrett from Ulster and Munster. The Leinster victim was Rory O'Connor, who, a year before, had been best man at O'Higgins's wedding, who, in other circumstances, would have been the godfather of his first-born child. These men were wakened from sleep in their cells, given until dawn to prepare themselves, and then shot in the yard of Mountjoy Prison.

The only excuse for this decision was its value as a deterrent. As such, and only as such, O'Higgins agreed to it. If the parliamentary representatives of the people were only to do their duty at the risk of their lives, there would not be a Parliament for long. Something had to be done to preserve democratic government. But O'Higgins was chagrined to see, on the day of the shooting, an Army announcement that the act was a reprisal. He would not for a moment have sanctioned the act for a Corsican motive of that kind.

" A murder," this act of the Executive Council has been described as by those who gave no such description to the shooting of the Deputy Hales. And the men who ordered the executions in Mountjoy did not hide under the cloak of anonymity. They faced the public after their act. " The deed," said Gavan Duffy, " is a dishonour to any civilized government," and he could only explain it by assuming that the men who perpetrated it were " not in their normal frame of mind." From the Labour benches, Johnson, in a speech redolent of Shakespearian quotations, which gave an air of artificiality to his protest, accused the Government of having murdered the four prisoners. A more convincing criticism of the Government's action came from Gerald FitzGibbon, member for Trinity College, who spoke with calmness and courage. " I confess," he said, " that it seems to me that the men who suffered this morning were treated with extraordinary leniency in being allowed to live so long." But he appealed to the Government " not to let what happened this morning occur again." He was prepared to support them in stronger measures, if necessary, on condition that they came and asked Parliament for extra powers. As a lawyer, and the son of one of the most eminent barristers of the previous century, he was shocked by the cavalier disregard for all procedure, by the primitive ruthlessness of the Government's act.

Upon O'Higgins fell the task of defending this terrible decision, and it was noticeable that he spoke under stress of great emotion although he had at first complete command of himself. " What has happened this morning," he began, " was very sad ; it was very terrible. The times are very sad and very terrible ; and all events that happen now must be judged and considered in perspective." It was not an act of revenge. " I think that somehow we must have gone long past anger and past the mere emotional wave of temptation." When Collins was killed, no one ran amok ; this thing was not done in any wave of anger. " Such as it is, it was done coldly. . . . It was at once punitive and deterrent. The members of the Parliament of Ireland must be kept free and safe to perform their duties. . . . When one strikes at a representative man the crime is particularly horrid." He reminded the House of the protest which Griffith made when Sir Henry Wilson was murdered. "His instinct was right and sound. When one strikes at a man of representative character, one strikes at the people who gave him his mandate and who invested him with his representative character; and therein lies the most criminal aspect of the wretched crime that was committed yesterday."

Unlike his speech on Childers, of whom he did not approve and whose death left him unmoved, this occasion obviously caused him an intense pain as he repeated the thoughts which had been burning in his brain. Only once did he depart from the impersonal when his growing antipathy to Gavan Duffy expressed itself in a few blasting sentences. "There was talk here of the rules of war and the laws of war. There was more talk of the rules of war, if such there be, than of the practices of war; and the Deputy who, with a kind of doll's house mind, comes here and talks to us of the rules of war is careful to say very little of the practices of war. . . . So let us not proceed just on those lines. And if not the rules of war or the laws of war, what law holds good?" While the life of the nation was being threatened, there was, he thought, but one answer to that question, "but one code—though it sounds a grim code—*Salus populi suprema lex*." The Army Council would have to look to Parliament in due course for an Act of Indemnity. When it did so, the members of the Executive Council would take their places with them. A state of war or "armed crime" existed, and it was necessary to delegate far-reaching powers to the Army, but O'Higgins did not seek to shift the odium of this deed to the Army. "We do not disclaim responsibility for this act this morning. It was taken after the fullest discussion with us. . . . Ultimately all government is based on force, must meet force with greater force if it is to survive. . . . We may be lacking in judgment, we may be lacking in wisdom; undoubtedly we have not the long tradition of government that families in certain other countries have—families from which members have been selected for generations—but I do say that from the day the Provisional Government was set up, and from the time we functioned below there in the City Hall, there was not an act done that was inspired by any other motive than the securing of the welfare and the safety and the freedom of the Irish people. There was never an act done through personal vengeance and never an act done through hot blood. We have no higher aim than to place the people of Ireland in the saddle of Ireland, and let them do their will, but we will not acquiesce in gun-bullying, and we will take very stern and drastic measures to stop it. Personal spite, great heavens ! Vindictiveness ! One of these men was a friend of mine." [10]

With the last words, O'Higgins, for the only time in his public life, broke down and was unable to continue his speech. For the rest of his career he was pursued by calumny for his part in the shooting of O'Connor. The relationship between the two men was regarded as an aggravation of the cruelty. Had he exerted his influence to have had another put in O'Connor's place, would that have silenced his critics ? He was a man who would not have lifted a finger to save his brother in the same circumstances. The type is not common. O'Higgins belonged spiritually to another age. " The youthful Kevin O'Higgins," wrote Winston Churchill, " a figure out of the antique cast in bronze "—as such he was destined to the loneliness of all men who transcend human weaknesses, for we do not love those who are stronger than ourselves. On this occasion the screen fell for a moment, and it was visible to all how terribly this killing afflicted him.

The next speaker apologized for referring to O'Higgins, " realizing his emotion in this question." And yet myths grew that " O'Higgins signed the death-warrant of the best man at his own wedding " ; that O'Higgins, having signed the death-warrant, said in a matter-of-fact tone : " What is the next item on the agenda ? " These are myths. There was no signing of the death-warrant. The Cabinet was merely consulted by the Army in the matter. Perhaps because of the legend which had now grown that O'Higgins was " the strong man," he attracted to himself, to a greater extent than Mulcahy, the hatred of Republicans. " One of the most blood-guilty Irishmen in our generation," was the comment of their paper, *An Phoblacht*, shortly after his murder. A stream of propaganda against him poured from this paper and from Republican speakers for the rest of O'Higgins's life. They fostered hatred of him, and so filled the minds of their young followers so with it that in some places, when the news of his murder was read, people cheered in the streets.

No Irishman can read of these happenings without misery. They deprived the members of the Government responsible for them of a place in the hearts of the people. But it is wrong to judge the men responsible without putting them against the background of the times. The derailing of trains, raiding of banks, smashing of printing-presses, burning of houses, not having proved effective, the newly-reconstituted Republican Party decided to kill everyone in a position of responsibility in the Provisional Government. The evidence of Liam Lynch's order is still preserved. The secret service informed the Army that the Republicans, before putting the order into full force, decided to make a modest start in the campaign and to feel their way at first. The shooting of Deputy Hales was the result of this restraint. Had there been no drastic reply by the Government, the experiment would have so far succeeded and a more drastic purge might have resulted. So the Army Council believed ; so it informed the Cabinet. The result was the shooting without trial of the four prisoners. They had conspired to destroy the Government elected by the people ; they had made war on it ; they were captured in arms. It is not, therefore, reasonable to argue as though they were innocent men. They were men who had defied the expressed will of the majority of the people. But after long imprisonment without trial, for a specific offence for which they could not have been responsible, their shooting was an act of ghastly severity. Fortunately, the act justified itself to the extent that it served its purpose. No more attacks were made on public representatives ; their homes and, in some cases, their relations became the new victims of the defenders of the national ideal. The shootings of the 8th December may well, like Napoleon's " whiff of grape-shot," have determined the destiny of a political regime. Had the terrorizing of public men developed successfully, anarchy would have set in.

In due course, the country was free to decide whether it wanted to change the Government that had done such drastic things. The Republicans had created the happy position for themselves that a majority at the polls gave them a mandate to take over the government, while defeat at a General Election enabled them to form a non-representative Republican executive not responsible to Parliament or the people. The people showed their will by returning the same Party to power, and if further evidence was wanted, Gavan Duffy, who had become the leading critic of the Government in the Dáil, suffered a heavy defeat at the polls.

CHAPTER IX

MAKING A STATE

THE life of O'Higgins, like that of his colleagues, for the year after the Treaty, was one of unrelieved work. The background of a home which, when it is happy, gives to the statesman, as well as the navvy, solace and relaxation, was taken away from these men, who, locked up in Government Buildings, could not venture further than the roof for air and that only at night. Lighting a cigarette, as O'Higgins discovered, attracted an immediate bullet. There was no rest. " I have not read a book for the last four or five years. I have had no time," [1] he snapped in reply to Professor Magennis, who, in the Dáil, at the end of a speech, distended by miscellaneous information on inappropriate themes, inquired whether the Irish Ministry accepted the view of Sir Robert Borden on a point of constitutional law.

The imprisoned life was made tolerable by having his wife with him, and the close friendship of Patrick Hogan, who had agreed to live in the O'Higgins's household as soon as it was possible to lead a normal life again.

The name of Patrick Hogan will live in Ireland in connection with the Land Act of 1923, the first by which the State compulsorily acquired land from owners, who were paid in $4\frac{1}{2}$ per cent. Bonds, and divided the acquired holdings either among tenants or landless men. The social policy behind the Act was to create a peasant proprietary and to relieve congested districts. The Bonds, which the Free State Government issued to the owners, were backed by the British as well as the Irish Government, and this gave a sense of security to the enterprise from the start. The land purchase scheme played an important part in the negotiations between the two countries, and concessions were made on the Irish side to secure the backing of the British Treasury.

But the success of the Act owed a great deal to Hogan. He was a practical farmer himself as well as a lawyer, and landlords found him not unsympathetic, while his candour and ability won him both trust and respect.

O'Higgins was attracted by his friend's intellectual qualities and his sincerity of mind, for it was a time when there was very little clear thinking and a great deal of emotional dishonesty. Hogan was ruthlessly clear-sighted. It was very important for O'Higgins to have at his side a comrade so able and so loyal. With all his appearance of indifference, he was a sensitive man and, for his position, a very young man. "You see," he said on one occasion, "we have had to outrage in the execution of our responsibilities certain of our feelings. Deputies know that. They know that we have had to arrest and imprison and even execute people who were our friends and who were our comrades, and Deputies do know, even though at times they talk as if they did not, that that was not a pleasant task for us."[2]

The extraordinary achievement of the next few months was the formation by O'Higgins of the machinery for civil government. He reorganized the improvised police force on the model which serves the country to this day. He remodelled the judicial system. He sent out the new district justices, who were to take the place of the magistrates of the previous generation. There was a twofold problem—to gain public confidence for new institutions and to create a civil administration in a time of comparative anarchy. His success was due to his faith and his fearlessness. He believed in the ultimate sanity of the people. It gave him the conviction that inspired his work ; believing that he served the people, he was inflexible with those who opposed the people's will.

Of himself he was absolutely unsparing. On one occasion a soldier in the Army was condemned to death for murder. The parents of the condemned man asked for an interview with O'Higgins. He granted it. A colleague asked him whether he intended to grant a reprieve, and when he said that he was determined not to, asked him why he went through the ordeal of interviewing the man's family. "I do it," said O'Higgins, "so that afterwards they may feel assured that they had taken every step to secure their son's pardon. If I had refused to see them they might think afterwards that if they had seen me their son would have got off."

The Irish police had been divided into two forces. In the country the Royal Irish Constabulary operated ; in Dublin the Metropolitan Police Force. At first it was decided to keep on the latter as a temporary measure and to disband the R.I.C., which was more repugnant to popular feeling. In this matter, however, O'Higgins refused to subscribe to the orthodox view about the constabulary. Not so long before throughout the country, he said, " let us not forget that it was the height of the ambition of most young fellows who happened to be 5 feet 9 or thereabouts."[3]

Insubordination broke out in the hastily-recruited police force, but in September a new force, consisting of 1,500 men, under the Chief Commissioner, Eoin O'Duffy, was organized, and a recruitment up to 4,300 was proposed. At first, these Guards were only effective in a limited area ; an unarmed police force in an armed country was at a marked disadvantage, but in spite of this, the new force was a success from the beginning. A greater problem was the Criminal Investigation Department, who, though extremely efficient, contained many members who were brutal and violent in their methods.

O'Higgins, impatient at the failure of the Army to end the Civil War, was more distressed by the occasional lawlessness of the Government forces. He approved of a motion whereby the local authorities, instead of the State, had to bear responsibility for damage done in their area, and instanced a conversation between a friend of his in Cork and a pro-Treaty farmer, who told him, " with a certain complacency, and a certain smug pride, that his son had been in charge of a party who had blown up a bridge about a mile and a half from his house. He said he was pro-Treaty but he believed in giving a young fellow his head." When that farmer found his rates going up to pay for his son's wild oats he would not " be so inclined to pride himself upon his broad-mindedness and the latitude he is prepared to give to a young fellow."

Early in September, in answer to a question, O'Higgins outlined his plans for the civil government of the country. The new police force, which was called the Civic Guard (until a member of the Senate suggested that the Irish equivalent, Garda Síochána, be adopted), were to follow the Army into the areas where the Army had restored order. " The history of that force," O'Higgins confessed, " it is right to say, has not been a happy one."[4] But he believed, under the new Commissioner, O'Duffy, it would become " efficient and self-respecting." The old constabulary had been an armed force, the new police would not bear arms. This was an experiment, and its eventual success is an answer to those who,

because the Irish were so often in revolt against the British
Government, gave them the reputation for being a lawless
people.

Following the Guards would come the new stipendiary
magistrates, who would replace the resident magistrates appointed
by the British Government in former days. It was then proposed
to set up a Judicial Committee to review the entire judicial system.
O'Higgins hoped by October that the Civic Guards would be
out through large areas of the country, and when the magistrates
followed, they would help in restoring law and order. "I could
not send out men who would be, so to speak, figures of fun in
their area," who would only have theoretical jurisdiction without
the necessary machinery to ensure that their decrees would be
enforced.

For a while, during the Black and Tan period, when the
administration of justice in the countryside had become almost
impossible, the arbitration courts formed by the Dáil had been,
in many cases, the only method of settling disputes. Although
served by many who afterwards became distinguished lawyers,
these courts had to make use of the services of inexperienced men
who sometimes had no legal qualifications. It became a form of
cant to profess that the Dáil Courts were highly satisfactory, and
that the regular courts were prejudiced and entirely subservient
to Dublin Castle. It was assumed that the judges appointed in
the previous regime would not act fairly under the new system.
Some fancifully-minded people even suggested that the Brehon
Laws should be re-enacted, as the existing law was unsuitable for
Ireland. O'Higgins would have none of this. The Dáil Courts,
he insisted, were intended "to exhibit to the world the spectacle
of a whole people turning from an alien administration to even
the rough and hasty administration set up by Parliament and
by the Government that was holding its own in the teeth of an
armed terror." He did not consider that these courts, "hastily
devised," were adequate to the needs of the time. "We are standing amidst the ruins of one administration with the foundations
of the other scarcely set."

The old County Courts were for the present to continue. He
was not prepared to join in the prejudiced criticism of British
Courts. "There are no British Courts in Ireland at present. . . .
The authority for making, altering and rescinding of law in this
country is now in the hands of the Irish people. . . . When we

are building we must build on a sure foundation and we must not build in a hasty, ill-considered way."[5]

Upon the success of this new police force, the new magistrates, and the adapted machinery of the previous civil administration depended the future of the country. Within six months, O'Higgins thought, it would be decided whether the test which the country was undergoing had been met, " or whether it is simply going in a fractious, futile way to throw away these opportunities and allow the harvest of the last few years' sowing to perish ungarnered in the field." Had the present position not arisen, had a unanimous Dáil stood for the settlement with England, there would have been a grave problem for a transitional government. It would have had to face the reaction from the conditions of the last few years, as well as the world-wide reactions from the war of 1914–1918, but that problem " had been multiplied a thousand-fold " by one man, " no doubt an honest man who loves his country well and not wisely, [who] came with his torch to that barrel of gunpowder and multiplied that problem a thousandfold. That is the situation with which we have to deal . . . a rather general breaking of bands, a disintegration of the moral fibre of the country, a lack of civic sense, a lack of responsibility, a lack of appreciation for the fact that one cannot do things and escape the consequences. . . . There are standing in the path to-day armed men saying to the massed men of this nation : You must not take a certain course. That is a position which has never been conceded here, which never has been conceded in any democratic country. It will not be conceded here. No small section have a right to say : You must go back to war with England. You must, if needs be, make another Thermopylæ of it and go down to the last man. That is not sanity, that is not patriotism. They can keep their high principles, they can keep their own political convictions, but some men must be allowed to work that Treaty settlement for the benefit of the Irish nation ; and they must drop back and they will drop back sooner or later into the position of con-stitutional opposition in the attempt to convert the majority of the country to their political creed. But they have not the right to kill this nation, as the nation will be killed if the democratic will of the people is not allowed to prevail."[6]

It was O'Higgins's habit on all occasions to bring every question back to fundamentals and first principles, and to discuss it in its setting rather than as an isolated matter. The effect of this was

to make his speeches somewhat repetitious, the same phrases occur
again and again, and those responsible for the Civil War were
never given a holiday. But this was not from any mental or
imaginative limitation. It was very deliberate. He was clear in
his own convictions, and he was determined to hammer them
home. An experienced barrister, addressing a jury, never flatters
their intelligence by touching lightly on important points. He
returns to these and makes certain that the jury understands them.
O'Higgins was determined that the people should understand
that self-government did not mean a release from government.
It meant an increase in responsibility. More, not less, had to be
done, and obedience, which had been a submission, was now a
duty. So long as there were men out on the hills, the chimera of a
romantic existence in which nobody worked and everyone was
a hero, where banks could be raided for money, shops for food,
where there was no rent to pay and one grazed one's beast on
the fields of one's neighbour, danced before the eyes of the young.
What schoolboy has not prayed for a fire in the school, or an
outbreak of measles which will relieve him of the thraldom of
discipline and study ? How popular with the boys would be the
schoolmaster who organized disturbances of the daily round.
But the discipline of life has to be faced at last. O'Higgins confessed the seeming irrelevancy of his remarks to the question of
the Civic Guard or the Dáil Courts, but " it is relevant to the
entire question of the attitude of the people towards the administration that is set up by the Government. . . . It is the people's
own machinery and the man who sets his face against it is sinning
against the people . . ."[7]

There was not sufficient time, between September, when the
Dáil met, and December, to forward the legislation necessary
for the setting up of the machinery of the new State.
Once the Constitution became law, the duty of the assembly was
done, and it fell upon the Governor-General to summon the first
Parliament under the Constitution. At the same time, the Parliament at Westminster passed two Acts—the Free State Constitution
Act and the Consequential Provisions Act—approving the Constitution and confirming the Treaty.

During the debates on the Constitution Bill, O'Higgins had
insisted that the articles concerning the King should not be too
fiercely contested, because, in his view, the personality of the
King's representative in Ireland was far more important than the

definition of his functions. The more the Irish proved recalcitrant about the theory, the less the English would be inclined to consult them on the fact. Viceroys and King's representatives were usually selected from the peerage ; a new departure for Ireland was the selection of Timothy Healy as Governor-General.

The memory of the Parnell split was still sufficiently green to prevent the choice from being widely popular in Ireland ; but John Dillon, the alternative choice if the representative was to be selected from veteran Nationalists, had been violently opposed to Sinn Fein and the policy of assassination : to many, the existence of the office was a symbol of the death of Republican hopes ; ex-Unionists, who had sighed at Lord Aberdeen, thought of the Cadogan and Dudley reigns, and sighed again. But, from the point of view of the Irish Government, Healy as Governor-General meant that they had acting for the King an Irishman of Nationalist views, and not a representative imposed by the British Government. His acquaintance with many of the older Members of Parliament was a great help. He had personally visited Churchill when the police threatened to strike soon after the Treaty. He also visited de Valera in an effort to divert him from the path to Civil War.

On the 6th December the Governor-General was sworn in to office by Chief Justice Molony and took up residence in the Viceregal Lodge in Phoenix Park. He was married to an aunt of Kevin O'Higgins. This connection was not lost on some, who used to taunt O'Higgins with interested motives ; in fact, the relationship was an embarrassment to him, as his position in the Government was such that he had more opportunity of coming into conflict with the Governor-General than had any of his colleagues. People who favour the promotion of their relatives usually see to it that they are not placed over themselves.

On one point O'Higgins was very definite. It had been the contention of Erskine Childers and others that England would only keep the Treaty so long as it suited her to do so. This was not the opinion of O'Higgins. " It is right to say that we are satisfied that whatever Government emerges from the present break-up in English politics that the Treaty and all honourable implications of the Treaty will be observed and adhered to. . . . If we are asked to suppose the unthinkable . . . that attempts would be made by a future Government in England to tamper with the Treaty . . . then our attitude in such a condition of things would be quite simple. There will be nothing complex about it ; and certain little fishes who have been straining themselves to talk like whales since last December might have an opportunity of showing their form." [8]

*   *   *   *   *

On the 6th of December, Cosgrave was re-elected President and Kevin O'Higgins Vice-President of the new Dáil, and the other holders of office were re-elected also. The shooting of one of the Deputies, Hales, and then the execution of O'Connor and his companions, cast a shadow over the new Parliament. As when in wartime, people accustom themselves to terrible happenings (any one of which would create panic in times of peace) so, those engaged in the politics of the time had supped too full of horrors to be long dismayed by additional experiences, however terrible. In this as in all civil wars families found themselves on opposite sides and in October, one of Eoin MacNeill's sons, who had joined the Irregulars, was, with his companions, shot in an encounter with the military. Death had become a matter of daily experience, and there was for every member of the Government and, to a lesser extent, for every member of Parliament, the imminent prospect of assassination.

O'Higgins had the plain man's dislike of people who did not pay their debts, and a marked contempt for those who, under cover of the Civil War, never went into the line of fire but were " always ready to pick up the garbage of war." " The bailiff as a factor in our civilization has not been particularly active or particularly effective in recent years,"[9] he said when introducing The Enforcement of Law (Occasional Powers) Bill, 1923, a Bill designed to give greatly-increased powers to sheriffs and to award them armed protection when fulfilling their duties.

As well as people who refused to pay on judgments given against them, there were many who flouted decrees for possession of lands into which they had illegally entered. " In acknowledging the supremacy of these courts the people are asked to do no other thing than to bow their heads to the collective majority of the people of this country," he said. For it was clear that if the country was going to live, it was necessary not only to restore peaceful conditions but to ensure that people who embarked on business or gave credit were not to do so without the effective protection of the law. Over a year after the Bill was enacted, there were still 7,000 decrees, representing £170,000 of debts, outstanding, but by degrees the position was improved. It was clear, however, that the old procedure was not sufficiently drastic for the roughness of the times. Deputies raised hypothetical cases where injustice might be done under the new Act. "I have never yet," O'Higgins replied, "heard a man who is withholding payment of his debt to say 'I am withholding, but I could pay very well if I liked.' I never met that rare individual, and if I do meet a man honest enough to say that, I hope he will allow me to shake his hand." [10]

Judges, when administering the law of the land, are regarded as instruments and do not invite hatred or excite feelings of vengeance. It is very different when laws are in the making. Then those who see that the law is made to curb their particular activities, regard the legislator, if not the judge, as a personal enemy. It fell on O'Higgins to introduce measures against debtors, drinkers, gamblers, as well as political terrorists, and he was singled out for especial hatred. The reorganization of the courts meant that many posts had to be filled, and the responsibility of selecting the most suitable candidates fell on him. There was always an objection raised if the selected man was connected in the past with either the old police or the British Army, although, as the Minister said, "at one time three-fourths of the country favoured and backed the people who were preaching the policy of recruiting for the British Army." [11] Moreover, as he explained, there was no method of exercising patronage which gave satisfaction to all. "When you have ten men applying for a position, each believing absolutely that he is the one and only man for the position—that, in fact, he has a kind of vocation for it, you can only give it to one of the ten. The other nine are going to be dissatisfied, and the people will hear about it." It was a stock grievance that the clerks employed in the Dáil Courts were not always thought fit for employment in the new system, and part of the cant against which O'Higgins had to fight was that these men were being thrown out after suffering incredible hardships in the past. "Let us not allow mists to intervene between ourselves and that period," he urged. "What are the facts, as a matter of historical accuracy? Those courts had a hectic few months in the summer of 1920. They were on all lips; they were in all the papers. . . . And there were May, June, July, August and September not quite so hectic. After that, when the business started in hammer and tongs style, it became practically impossible to hold those courts. . . . I am talking not in heightened fiction nor in blank verse. I am talking dead, rock-bottom, stone-cold truth." [12]

There had been sufficient damage done by the system of two governments after the Treaty. The attempts to keep going two different sets of courts promised to lead to equal confusion. Applicants, refused relief in one, made appeals to the other. The Dáil Courts were suppressed. For this, Gavan Duffy had left the Government, and as he failed to secure re-election to the Dáil, it would appear that his constituents did not agree with his view that the Government was wrong in preferring to retain the old-established courts which they took over from the British.

One of the things which O'Higgins fought was the desire to make outlaws of some people and privileged persons of others. An apocryphal story of the "troubled times" is that of the domestic servant who said to her mistress : "Soon youse will be us and us will be youse." O'Higgins very quickly disappointed such hopes, if they existed. The Army had been called in to preserve the property of a Mr. Lewin in the West of Ireland, and when the matter came before the Dáil, O'Higgins declared : "Some little stress was laid on the fact that Mr. Lewin was a landlord. For many a long day we have been seeking in this country a time when one man would be as good as another, and we have it now ; and Mr. Lewin's home and property will be defended as sternly and as rigidly as the home of any poor man, or tenant, or labourer in the country." [13]

He was irritated profoundly by the growing tendency to call old unpleasant things by new-fashioned names. "I think," he said, "that we were probably the most conservative-minded revolutionaries that ever put through a successful revolution." [14]

No more Deputies and Senators were shot after the execution of Rory O'Connor and his companions, but the other items on the Republican programme were carried out. Mansions in every county went up with flames, railworkers were threatened if they did not obey orders from the Irregulars. The position became so serious that the Army asked the Dáil to sanction further powers, and O'Higgins grimly defended the motion : "We have got past the threat of death stage and there is nothing left but the actuality of death." [15] He quoted words once used by Liam Lynch, who was now leading the Irregulars : "The people are a flock of sheep to be driven anywhere at will." Less than a fortnight after these powers were granted, Senator Bagwell, whose mansion had been burnt down not long before, was kidnapped. A threat of reprisal by the Army, if he were not released, was followed by his escape, and it is an open question whether the threat was not responsible for the apparent carelessness of his captors. Almost every day a Senator's house was burnt. In February, the gasworks at Tralee were smashed with sledges, the waterworks at Athlone and Maryborough were destroyed, and an engine-driver in Kerry was shot dead for not obeying orders which would have involved the destruction of his employers' property. Donal O'Sullivan has given a very comprehensive list of these outrages by Irregulars in his book, *The Irish Free State and Its Senate*, a work in which there are not many references to reprisals or acts of lawlessness by Government troops. Miss Macardle gives a detailed account of the sufferings of Irregulars in her *History of the Irish Republic*, but never mentions the death and destruction they caused in the country. Certainly, the Volunteers never fought the British as the Irregulars fought their countrymen, nor did the British Government punish with such Draconian severity as did the rulers of the Irish Free State.

A feeling of national shame and frustration oppressed O'Higgins, and he gave vent to it in no uncertain terms when, on the 7th February, 1923, an announcement was made in the Dáil that two days previously a force of fifty Irregulars, fully-armed and with three machine-guns, entered the small town of Ballyconnell in Co. Cavan, at seven o'clock in the morning, broke into a grocer's shop, and pulling his assistant out of bed, shot him dead, at the same time wounding another man in the thigh ; then, entering a neighbouring house, they mortally wounded another man. Goods were taken from the shops, two Ford cars were stolen, the Post Office was raided, and a garage blown up. All this was done to the accompaniment of casual shootings through windows in the town, and before departing, the attackers held up a train and fired at it. They then departed for the Arigna Mountains, where they had their lair. The raid was discussed in the Dáil, not only "on its merits," but because it revealed the patent inability of the Army to protect the country. General Mulcahy, to whom a question was addressed, waited to reply until he was in possession of the facts, but O'Higgins was, as usual, only too ready to enter the lists. He gave as his reason for speaking, a desire "to combat the view that it was a natural thing to expect that a body of Irishmen would descend upon this little town and proceed to murder their fellow-citizens. It was not a natural thing. It is perhaps the most unnatural thing that has happened since this unnatural strife began."[16]

After this introduction, O'Higgins let himself go in a fierce denunciation of the raid. It was one of the most vigorous of all the speeches that he had made since the Civil War began. " We can all sympathize with the relatives of the men who have been murdered, and we can sympathize with the townspeople as a whole . . . these are the things that have to be faced. There are individual tragedies and there is the national tragedy. Anarchy was loosed in this country—wantonly loosed, callously loosed, deliberately loosed—and the men that loosed this saw it coming and knew it was coming, and had ample opportunity to measure the guilt of him who would press the button to set it loose. But the button was pressed and hundreds of young men through the country, young fellows in their teens, are being made the dupes of one man's vanity. He calls them out in the name of the Republic. Some of us know the irony of that. Some of us know that he taught us the necessity for compromise and taught us the immorality, so to speak, of persisting when there was no hope of success and of keeping the country under the horror of British oppression simply for a formula. There is only one way to deal with anarchy and that is the way of force. . . . Those who will not pause and think now can expect nothing from the hands of those who have a mandate to safeguard the lives and property and the interests of the people of Ireland—of the people of Ireland living to-day and of the people who will be born into Ireland in the future—they can expect nothing at their hands but the treatment that one would mete out to so many wild beasts if they were loosed within your territory."

Two days after this speech was made, Liam Deasy, an Irregular, who had been sentenced to death, started peace parleyings with the Government. On the same day, the 9th of February, O'Higgins moved the adjournment of the Dáil to permit the Ministry to pay attention to departmental work.

It was not possible, with a small Army and a new unarmed police force, to give protection to all who were threatened or to every inhabited area of the country. That was the answer given by General Mulcahy to the charge of inefficiency in protecting the people. O'Higgins was destined to get a rude demonstration of this truth. His father, who was still practising at Stradbally, and acting as the Coroner for the county, had received threats that his house would be burnt down. It was part of the policy which had so successfully laid in ruins the mansions of the Moores, Horace Plunkett and so many others ; the architectural insignificance of Woodlands lent it no immunity from destruction. The influence of a priest had helped to keep raiders away on a few occasions. He came very often and sat with the threatened family, convinced that no harm would be done to the house while he was there. A paper was captured by the military in the locality which purported to notify all Irregular commandants that " the sins of Ministers are not to be visited on their families." Doctor Higgins had not been afraid to speak his mind when the British were in pursuit of his sons, and his courage cost him his liberty. His courage had not left him yet, and when a party of Irregulars, having ambushed a military patrol and then put up a white flag, shot upon the soldiers who came forward to accept their surrender, killing two of them, the doctor had only one word for that. He found it very difficult to find a jury in Maryborough to say that word. He dismissed them one after another until finally a verdict of " murder " was brought in. As he left the courthouse, people in the street were heard to shout : " It will be your own inquest next."

On Sunday evening, the 11th February, the day upon which Christians usually refrain from their workaday employments, seven Irregulars, armed with guns, called at Woodlands. Doctor Higgins, his wife and two children were at home. Three of the Irregulars came up to the house and explained that they had orders to burn it. Doctor Higgins expostulated with them, and mentioned the paper which gave immunity to the families of Ministers. He stood at the door, with his foot in it, trying to keep the raiders out, and thinking that he recognized one of them, he remonstrated with him and called him by name. After some parley, he agreed to let the men in while he went in search of the paper. Two of the Irregulars took up their stand in the hall and a third followed Doctor Higgins into the dining-room. What happened then is not quite clear, but it appears that the doctor seized a revolver from the man he was talking to in the dining-room and tried to shake the ammunition out of it. The raider ran out of the room, shouting " Fire," an order which his companions promptly obeyed. The doctor fell, and as he did so one of his daughters, who had come into the hall, cried out : " He is killed ; you need not fire again." "He is not killed yet," said the raider, taking aim ; as he fired, the girl struck up the gun and the bullet went through the ceiling ; but by this time Doctor Higgins was dead. The Irregulars waited until the revolver which he had seized was given to them, and then two of them accompanied one of the children to the gate, and as they walked along, one man asked her who fired the shot. " You did," she replied, " and one other." After they had killed the doctor, some of the raiding party went round to the back of the house and set fire to the hay-rick before going away.

The news was broken to O'Higgins late that night. He had returned from a family party at the Governor-General's residence in Phoenix Park, and was chatting with his colleagues in Government Buildings before going to bed. A telephone message came from the Adjutant-General to his room. Mrs. O'Higgins took the message.

A quiver of the lip as he uttered the name of his father's house, his old home, was the only indication of emotion that O'Higgins gave. As he waited for the armoured-car, which was to drive him to the funeral, he called for his secretary, and in a flat, lifeless voice, dictated instructions. On the evening of the funeral, Patrick Hogan and Desmond Fitz Gerald, the two Ministers with whom O'Higgins was most intimate, came back early and waited in his room for his arrival. As a rule, he had a brisk walk, very different from the slow and heavy footsteps they heard coming down the long stone corridor late that evening—dragging steps like those of an old man or one who is carrying a heavy load. He stood in the doorway for a moment before entering the room, and when they looked at his face, his friends went silently away. By the anxious tenderness which he displayed towards his mother and sisters, who left Woodlands and came to live in Dublin, he revealed some of the torture of mind that he had undergone on the long lonely drive back from the funeral as he dwelt upon the horrors which his family had suffered and wondered what more was to come. The offence which Doctor Higgins had committed was to procreate a son who did what he believed to be his duty.

The death of Collins had confirmed O'Higgins in his resolution to dedicate his life to the nation. The murder of his father was a foretaste of the sacrifices which that dedication involved. His resolution was only strengthened, and he tried in so far as he could to lessen the sorrow which his destiny had brought upon his family.

" Last time I saw him," wrote a journalist in a Methodist paper, when Kevin O'Higgins died, " was on the sands at Greystones on a Sunday afternoon a couple of years ago. He had tended his mother most lovingly down the uneven path that slopes to the shore, his tall stooping figure bending over her almost affectionately. They were both dressed in black. . . . He sat beside his mother on the shingle talking to her, then took his little girl down to the water and skipped some stones into the sea. He returned again and sat by his mother, soon after helping her tenderly up the slope to their waiting car. These things are all now of the past and to-day the country is left mourning."

CHAPTER X

UNEASY PEACE

W H E N the I.R.A. leader, Liam Deasy, who was under sentence of death, asked for a respite and undertook to help negotiations for peace, his life was spared, and on the 8th February, 1923, an amnesty was proclaimed by the Government for all those who, within ten days, surrendered with their arms. It was of no avail. The Civil War dragged on, and the Army Command received information which led to an attack on an I.R.A. post in the Knock-mealdown Mountains in Tipperary. In this engagement, Liam Lynch, the leader of the Republicans in arms, was wounded and died. Shortly afterwards, Austin Stack, another leader, was captured. It was clear that the end was in sight.

O'Higgins reviewed the position in the Dáil in a financial debate. By the end of that year the people would have paid £18,000,000 for the Army, more than a tenth of the national income. In fact, although the Republicans may not have known it, the Irish Free State very nearly came to an end from lack of funds, but a large contribution from the Bank of Ireland to the Exchequer, at a crucial time, staved off bankruptcy. The success of the revolution had not blinded O'Higgins to the fact that it was made by a small section of the population. Analyzing political opinion in the country, he pointed out that at least 1,000,000 people in the North-East of Ireland had been opposed to the Sinn Fein movement, as were about 500,000 in various parts of the South, and there were " close on another 1,000,000 utterly apathetic who looked on at the whole thing with their hands in their pockets and their straw in their mouths with as much enthusiasm as—probably infinitely less enthusiasm than—they would display at a cock fight." The country was paying a heavy bill for their recent experiences. But what were they going to pay in moral degradation ? It was, he thought, a bad atmosphere for children to be growing up in. " It will be strange, it will be providential if they grow up decent citizens with a proper idea of their responsibility." The Civil War was "fizzling out in the sordid and squalid way one would expect. There is very little ennobling in it and very few outstanding acts of personal courage or gallantry, if we except one in the first week in Dublin."[1]

When the Free State was founded, it was probably the only country in the world without a National Debt, and now it was on the verge of bankruptcy. Papers had been found in which Irregular leaders had prayed for the return of the British as a means of uniting the nation once again. This, O'Higgins described as blasphemy. The British would return to a country "with its morale bludgeoned out—a country thoroughly loathing the standards and the shibboleths to which it used to respond."[2] In the West and in the South of Ireland, where the Army had been called in to settle civil disputes, a condition reigned which O'Higgins described in the irreverent way that made him particularly obnoxious to those whose political existence depended on a humourless and uncritical following : "In these two provinces," he explained, "people have gone in in a most light-hearted way and burned their neighbour's property to the ground, and for the most part they are people who . . . would lie awake for a week fretting if a hen laid out on them. . . . There are houses in the South and West crammed full of loot, one house like Tutankhamen's tomb. . . . There were hens roosting on valuable oil paintings, there were silver candlesticks and valuable *prie-dieus* plundered out of the house of a neighbour that had been burned."[3]

De Valera's biographers have never thrown much light on his movements during these months. M. J. MacManus describes him wandering, bearded and distraught, round the South.[4] In his *Letters and Leaders of My Day*, T. M. Healy writes that he was driven out of Cork, and went to Mallow, where he quartered himself on the house of the Assistant County Surveyor, Richard O'Connor, who implored him not to allow the railway viaduct there to be blown up—a suggestion of Childers. De Valera answered : "It will save thousands of lives." "An attempt to destroy the Mallow road bridge across the Blackwater was foiled by the pluck of the clergy, Catholic and Protestant. They assembled the people, who held it *en masse*, defying threats. Then de Valera, hunted towards Tipperary, occupied at Cahir the house of Colonel Charteris. He stayed there a fortnight, and on leaving, inscribed his name in the Visitors' Book."[5]

The Army Intelligence Section reported that de Valera was

at Mount Argus, and that a plot was on foot to capture him there
and to shoot him. When this information came to the Cabinet,
O'Higgins was insistent that all necessary steps should be taken
to see that this plan miscarried. "We are not going to set a
precedent for tyrannicide," he declared.

Under the new Army regulations, de Valera would, if captured
in arms, have been liable to suffer death, but the general opinion
at the time was that he was not in a real sense a leader. De Valera
was always underestimated by his opponents. Nevertheless, when
political action was required, de Valera's prestige was availed of,
and it was he, on behalf of the Republican Government, who, with
Frank Aiken, who had succeeded Liam Lynch as "Chief of Staff,"
signed a proclamation on the 27th April, 1923, ordering a suspension of all aggressive action by the I.R.A. At the same time,
de Valera's peace proposals were made known. They were based
on six unimpeachable declarations of democratic truisms. Miss
Macardle, describing the meeting of the Irregular Army chiefs
at which the decision was taken, writes : "All present with one
exception agreed that if the Free State Party accepted these
principles they would themselves, as a principle of order, accept
majority rule."

Four Army chiefs then proceeded to Dublin and authorized
de Valera to make his declaration, which contained, among other
clauses, one : "That the military forces of the Nation are the
servants of the Nation"—the irony of which may not have escaped
him. "The Republican Army," writes Miss Macardle, "was
not ready to surrender its arms. De Valera's proposals for peace
did not include such surrender ; they constituted an effort to
divert the unsolved conflict between pro-Treaty and anti-Treaty
Parties into the non-violent and democratic channel of parliamentary procedure, leaving the central problem to be settled
eventually by the people's votes."

The attempt at rape having failed, an honourable courtship was
suggested as the alternative, and if that failed, facilities for further
violence were to be afforded. It was not a very tempting proposal.
O'Higgins dismissed it with a phrase : "This is not going to be
a draw with a replay in the autumn."

The two points of difficulty in de Valera's terms were the refusal
to surrender arms and a stipulation that no person should be
excluded from Parliament by reason of any oath or test. As this
was the rock upon which the Treaty had split, de Valera's offer

of peace was a request for a surrender to him. No one wanted the oath, but the fact was that the British had proved obdurate over the Constitution only when Collins entered into his pact with de Valera ; any sign of a further pact to alter the Treaty would have—quite logically—been regarded as a breach of the Treaty. The Free State Government were not prepared to risk a war with England, which they knew the people did not want, after a Civil War which cost over £30,000,000, in order to satisfy the suscepti-bilities of the extremists. De Valera also required that individual Republicans should not be asked to give undertakings for their good conduct, as he spoke on behalf of the Republican Govern-ment and Army Command, and would personally assure himself that prisoners when released would act in the spirit of the agree-ment. In view of the relative positions of de Valera and his army a few days previously, he spoke with faith rather than reason when he undertook to answer for all prisoners.

Johnson, the Labour leader, urged the Government to make an attempt to meet de Valera half-way : " While I think a good deal of that is trifling and quibbling, one has to recognize that the same personality, with the same faults and the same virtues, was looked up to and honoured and regarded and trusted by the people a couple of years ago, and it might not be too much for the Government, having achieved power, having its authority recognized by the mass of the people, having arrived at the position when they can impose their authority, if they so desire, to say : ' We will concede something to your fancies, to your peculiar mentality and to the prejudices and convictions—sincere honest convictions—of many of your followers.' "[6]

Gavan Duffy urged that the negotiations should be further pursued. He reiterated his belief that " the oath shall go," and pointed out that " de Valera accepts the principle that the will of the people is to be the supreme test." (At which a farmer Deputy interjected : " Very good of him ".)   " But," continued Gavan Duffy, " he qualifies his acceptance with a form of words which I find it difficult to understand." President Cosgrave concluded the debate on the peace proposals. They reduced themselves, he thought, to an offer of surrender on receiving a guarantee of a lease of political life ; " they want this lease of political life and it cannot be given them at the price they ask."[7]

On the 24th May, de Valera issued another pronouncement which accompanied an order to " cease fire " and " dump arms."

His message ended : "May God guard every one of you and give to our country in all times of need sons who will love her as dearly and devotedly as you."[8]

De Valera, as Johnson intimated, although excluded from Parliament by his conscientious refusal to take the oath, was still to play a leading part in the politics of this country. Since the deaths of Collins and Griffith, he was the only outstanding or widely-known figure in Irish politics ; a possible rival had arisen in the Minister for Home Affairs. O'Higgins was ten years younger, and the two men differed in every respect as much as any two men could, having but one quality in common—a grim tenacity of purpose. This was not apparent, for de Valera seemed to be far weaker, and O'Higgins more ruthless, than was in fact the case.

If there was a law, O'Higgins's attitude was : "Obey the law or do away with it." And he had no belief in the wisdom of a dispensing power. Once in the Dáil he was expounding a method of collecting tax at the source from wage-earners, and when Johnson, Magennis or Gavan Duffy argued in sympathy with the temptations of tax-payers, O'Higgins was obdurate : "If the Income Tax Act is wrong, it should be amended or repealed. If it is not wrong, it should be observed." Johnson accused him of Prussianism. Gavan Duffy described him as having "an incurably feudal mind ; he might have stepped out of the pages of *Ivanhoe*."[9]

O'Higgins introduced his first Public Safety Bill in 1923 ; it was intended as a deterrent to those who had access to the guns dumped by the Irregulars, the prisoners now about to be released in batches, and the ordinary robber who had taken advantage of prevailing conditions and who might not feel that the surrender was intended to apply to him. Once the Civil War had officially ended, the law prevented such precautions as detaining suspects without trial, the seizing and selling of cattle found wandering unaccountably on neighbours' pastures, and other measures which the Government had employed in the increasing difficulty of their situation. This Act retained for a year the abnormal powers of the Executive. It also prescribed flogging as a punishment for arson and armed robbery. There was a frenzied outcry at this provision. Women, standing outside the Dáil, shouted "Murderers" at members of the Government when they appeared. Johnson, O'Shannon and other Labour members gave detailed descriptions of floggings from literature and life which were very horrifying, but had no effect on O'Higgins. "If the punishment is retrograde," he said, "the offence is retrograde." [10] Flogging is the most repulsive of punishments, but it must be said that the burning of property and violent robbery are not offences which sensitive people are likely to commit in a moment of aberration or weakness. Moreover, in the state of the country, when acts of violence had become daily occurrences, and when petrol and dynamite were almost household words, with a new, small, unarmed and inexperienced police force, something drastic had to be done to give any hope of safety to those who lived in remote places. The measure was suggested by the law officers to O'Higgins, but he, as responsible Minister, had, of course, to bear any odium that attached to it. "Without order," said O'Higgins, "there can be no progress and no security." He was convinced that, unless the armed criminal was met by society "lash in hand," men would try "to live by their guns." He did not believe that order would be restored overnight. "Within the last year arson has become the stock-in-trade of the idealist. Robbery under arms became routine." The end of the Civil War was, he believed, "the calm of exhaustion, not of peace." [11]

One of the charges to O'Higgins's discredit in the popular memory is that he ordered the flogging of Republicans. Whatever opinion one may have of that punishment and its effect on those who administer it, it is an abuse of words and reason to describe its prescription *after the Civil War*, for two of the most anti-social of crimes, as an attack on Republican opponents. The days of revolution were over, and O'Higgins was impatient for the reconstruction of the country. He saw ahead great possibilities in the community of nations to which Ireland had been joined. He wanted peace at home to exploit those possibilities to the full.

As soon as the Civil War was ended, O'Higgins moved out of Government Buildings with his wife and daughter, first, to a rented house. Afterwards, he bought a house in Cross Avenue, Blackrock, which, like his last home, he called Dunamase. Patrick Hogan became a member of the family. Like O'Higgins, he was a lover of the land. Both had been brought up in the country and were accustomed to farm work. O'Higgins longed eventually to become a farmer. He discussed all Hogan's plans, and knew the Land Acts so intimately that he could always deputize for the Minister for Agriculture in Parliament. Once he teased Hogan by complaining that while he was always praising Hogan's work in public speeches, Hogan hardly ever referred to him. "But look here," his friend exclaimed, "how can I go round the country saying : 'That is a fine Flogging Bill of my friend O'Higgins ?' Why don't you do something that people like to hear about ?"

Sympathetic as a friend, O'Higgins was often a difficult colleague in the Cabinet ; he insisted on right being done regardless of considerations of expediency. One of the matters which upset him most was the National Army. A small band of guerillas fought the British. It was natural that the professional Army, which the new State would require, could not depend solely on that nucleus, and the Volunteers were not necessarily men who wanted to lead the life of soldiers. Even had they been, the Civil War put the possibility out of the question. Raw recruits were accepted and rushed into action. Accidental shootings by sentries were not infrequent, nor was Bryan Cooper's case unique. To protect his mansion from the Republicans, Free State troops occupied the building. When they left, he estimated the damage to his property at £10,000.

Bretherton, correspondent for the *Morning Post*, found the die-hard Republicans hardly less to his liking than the Treaty-keepers and his account of these times, if often amusing, is quite reckless : "In 1923 and the early months of 1924 there were hundreds of cases of murder, manslaughter, murderous assault, robbery under arms, burglary and theft and in eighty per cent. of these cases the criminals were members of the Free State Army, a disproportionately large number being officers." For Bretherton had a breezy style, and his references to the Army are probably as accurate as his report that, in Ireland " the priests are not expected to live better lives than anyone else, and the country curate is as likely to have a flask of whiskey, a race card, or a pistol in his pocket as a Bible." [13] As the Catholic priesthood carry breviaries and not Bibles, the remark is strictly true and, at the same time, scandalously misleading. Nevertheless, there was some ground for the accusations against the Army. Particularly was this the case in Cork and Kerry.

Throughout the Civil War, O'Higgins was irritated at the delay in restoring order. The failure to bring his father's murderers to justice galled him, and he displayed an increasing antipathy in the Cabinet to General Mulcahy, the Minister for Defence.

On the 12th April, 1923, Patrick McCartan read extracts from

The Times and *Morning Post* to the Dáil. These described unrest in the Army, a general feeling that the civil power did not exercise sufficient control, and spoke of impending changes. More specifically, the *Morning Post* had published statements involving Cabinet Ministers. Written most probably by Bretherton, these included the allegation that " two things were concentrated upon— the raising of the gunmen stalwarts of the Irish Republican Brotherhood to the superior jobs at Portobello and elsewhere, and the elimination of British officers and others who, it was suspected, might behave inconveniently in case the flower of bright Republicanism should suddenly blossom on General Mulcahy's baton." Elsewhere this article stated : " With Hurley at Portobello a game began to be positively apparent and the Cabinet finally screwed up its courage, or to be more accurate, Kevin O'Higgins screwed up the rest of the Cabinet's courage to do something about it. It has been done, and not, one may believe, without a good deal of opposition."

President Cosgrave expressed surprise, and completely denied the truth of these statements. General Mulcahy referred to the difficulties under which the Army was working. Johnson, as leader of the official opposition, accepted the denials and expressed his confidence in Mulcahy. Bretherton, who had been scurrilous about most of the Irish leaders, was always particularly offensive to Mulcahy, but, as Johnson observed, Bretherton had sometimes " got hold of information."

A month previously, at Ballyseedy in Co. Kerry, a Republican, who escaped, gave an account of how Free State soldiers tied himself and eight comrades to land mines. He was the only survivor. The I.R.A. had laid mines and booby traps, and had blown up several of their opponents. The horrible deed at Ballyseedy was supposed to be a reprisal. After an inquiry was held, a report was made to the Dáil that Republicans who had been ordered to clear barricades blew themselves up in traps which their colleagues had set. The inquiry was made by two high Army officers from the local command and a Major-General from Dublin. General Mulcahy expressed his confidence in the report, but it was noticeable that O'Higgins avowed readiness to inquire into the possibility of holding an inquest on the dead Republicans.

There was no more about that particular incident, but in June an occurrence in another part of Kerry, where the Dublin Brigade was stationed, brought O'Higgins into direct conflict with Mulcahy on the question of the Army.

A local doctor had fallen out with the Army officer in command in the neighbourhood, whom, at first meeting, he had facetiously hailed as " Wellington." The doctor's daughters had also failed to please the Dublin soldiers in occupation of the district. A party was given by the local command to which they were not invited, but late that evening three masked soldiers went to the doctor's house, pulled the girls into the garden in their pyjamas, and while a soldier stood on one of the girls, another beat her with his belt. Having rubbed axle-grease into their hair and kicked them, the soldiers ran away.

An Army inquiry was held, and the findings were that four officers were out of barracks at the time of the raid. The President of the Court found that one of these had been identified at the inquiry as having taken part in it. The other members of the court were in agreement that three of the four officers knew of the raid and were in the vicinity of the doctor's house when it took place. That is to say, the whole court was satisfied as to the guilt of one, and two as to the guilt of three, differing only in degree of guilt.[14]

The inquiry was held in June, and a General Election was to take place in August. O'Higgins complained to President Cosgrave that he could not get information about the matter, and at last insisted that if it was not cleared up, he would not join the next Government. After some delay, at which O'Higgins bitterly complained, a Cabinet meeting was held to discuss the incident. O'Higgins attacked Mulcahy with extreme bitterness, and demanded a court-martial of the officers concerned. The Cabinet overruled this, and agreed that there should be criminal proceedings instead, and the matter was referred to the Attorney-General, Hugh Kennedy. His report was not ready until after the election, and the matter came up for discussion at two Cabinet meetings, which were held on the Tuesday before the new Dáil was due to assemble.

The advice which the Attorney-General gave the Cabinet did not satisfy O'Higgins, and, in a rage, he left the meeting, stating that he would retire from the Government, for it was clear that the report did not encourage any action over the Kerry affair. O'Higgins's friends urged him to reconsider his decision. However humiliating to submit, the issue involved was not as important as the future of the Government. Eventually, he agreed to remain in office, but his relations with President Cosgrave were very strained for some time afterwards.

Cosgrave's difficulty was manifest. General Mulcahy had been Chief of Staff in the Volunteers, and his adherence to the Treaty Party had been of importance. After Collins and MacEoin, he was perhaps the most influential member of the fighting arm. As the Minister in the Cabinet responsible for the Army, he was in a key position if there was a renewal of fighting. Even now, that the Civil War was over, the danger of a sudden rising had by no means passed, for arms were dumped over the country. O'Higgins had asked in the Dáil some months previously—speaking on the Governor-General's address—against whom were the arms to be used ? " If Mr. de Valera or Mr. Aiken or Mr. Ruttledge and their friends can secure a mandate from their fellow-citizens, they will be entitled to all the military and financial resources of this country ; the man who attempts to oppose them will be a rebel against lawful authority here, and I have no doubt these people would know how to deal with him." It was a speech made in his most provocative mood, and he had prefaced his remarks by describing himself as " one of the dictators who answer daily here to the representatives of the people."

The end of the Civil War, and the amnesty issued by the Government, had not meant the end of lawlessness, as one dreadful occurrence made manifest. While the Dáil was discussing the Army mutiny, President Cosgrave asked for an adjournment, as a mark of national regret at an outrage, the particulars of which he outlined to the House.

On Friday evening, the 21st March, 1924, some British soldiers, who, by the terms of the Treaty, were in occupation of Spike Island in Cork, landed at Cobh for shore leave. They were unarmed and accompanied by civilian friends, some of whom were women. Just before their launch drew in, a motor-car, containing four men dressed in the uniform of Irish soldiers, stopped at the landing-stage and opened fire with machine-guns as the party was coming ashore. One soldier was killed, seventeen dangerously wounded, and among five minor casualties were some women. The soldiers were on the friendliest terms with the neighbourhood, and the only explanation which President Cosgrave was able to give for the action of " the four murderous ruffians " was a desire to embroil the country once more in war with Great

Britain.   The perpetrators of this crime were never captured, and no Government, which was aware that such citizens were at large in its territory, could feel at ease.   It was not possible, as O'Higgins had observed, to "talk vague sentimentality about our bravest and best and about letting them go home to their peaceful avocations."

O'Higgins had come to be regarded as the strong man of the Cabinet, but he had been always on the political side, and, whatever his influence with the general public, in the event of another armed outbreak, guns would be the deciding factor.   Mulcahy had made it plain that he did not want any drastic step to be taken over the Kerry affair, while O'Higgins had pressed for disciplinary action. O'Higgins complained of Mulcahy to Cosgrave, who was doing his best to avoid bringing matters to a crisis.   At the first Cabinet meeting, O'Higgins had attacked Mulcahy openly, thanked him for his condescension in attending the Executive Council as the representative of the Army, and complained that he did not seem to know what collective responsibility meant.

Mulcahy, for his part, considered that O'Higgins did not understand the mentality of the Army, and was too rigid and doctrinaire, too unsympathetic to its history and the sentiment that inspired it. The familiar and homely ejaculation with which he dismissed O'Higgins's remarks seemed to convey that the phrase "collective responsibility," which meant so much to O'Higgins, was caviare to the General.   O'Higgins refused to consider that, in a civilized country, the Army should not be directly and fully under the control of the Government.

The Army had taken in several professional British soldiers in place of former I.R.A. men, who were demobilized, and this fact was made a cause of complaint by a group, who, although in arms against Republicans in the Civil War, professed that Collins's plan had been to move away from the Treaty as rapidly as circumstances permitted.   These men regarded the Free State Government as static in its national policy, and in the subsequent crisis designated themselves the *Old* I.R.A., as distinct from the I.R.A., which was what the Irregulars called themselves.   In fact, a great many of these men had taken sides at the time of the Civil War on grounds of personal loyalty to Collins or others.   Temperamentally, they would have been happier in the other camp.   The Irish Republican Brotherhood, which had its origin in America, and its roots in the Fenian period, and which was always regarded as the most extreme and belligerent group in the national movement, had after 1916 come gradually under Collins's control. Owing to his influence, the I.R.B. had supported the Treaty. This secret society had been revivified within the Army. Mulcahy, who had been on the Supreme Council at the time of Collins's death, was believed to be sympathetic,[15] while the Army Council, consisting of the Adjutant-General, Gearoid O'Sullivan, Seán MacMahon the Chief-of-Staff, and Seán Hurley the Quartermaster-General, to whom the *Morning Post* correspondent had referred, were active in the reorganization. One of the complaints of the Old I.R.A. Army group was that the I.R.B. now dominated the Army, and all control was passing into its hands.

Complaints were made to President Cosgrave by the " Old I.R.A.," and it was well known that trouble was brewing. O'Higgins was adamant that a soldier could only know one allegiance, but the Cabinet was divided. Mulcahy was in touch with the I.R.B., and the protagonist of the " Old I.R.A. " was Joseph McGrath, the Minister for Industry and Commerce.

On the 6th of March, 1924, President Cosgrave received an ultimatum in the following terms :

Dublin, *6th March*, 1924.

To President Liam Cosgrave.

Sir,

On behalf of the I.R.A. Organization we have been instructed to present the following ultimatum to the Government of Saorstát Eireann :

Briefly, our position is this :

The I.R.A. only accepted the Treaty as a means of achieving its objects, namely, to secure and maintain a republican form of Government in this country. After many months of discussion with your Government it is our considered opinion that your Government has not these objects in view, and that their policy is not reconcilable with the Irish people's acceptance of the Treaty.

Furthermore, our interpretation of the Treaty was that expressed by the late Commander-in-Chief, General Michael Collins, when he stated : " I have taken an oath of allegiance to the Irish Republic and that oath I will keep, Treaty or no

Treaty." We claim Michael Collins as our leader, and again remind you that even after the Treaty was signed, that drastic action was taken against enemies of the unity and complete independence of our country. Both in oath and in honour bound, it is our duty to continue his policy, and therefore present this Ultimatum to which we require a reply by 12 noon, 12th March, 1924.

We demand a conference with representatives of your Government to discuss our interpretations of the Treaty on the following conditions :

(a) The removal of the Army Council ;

(b) The immediate suspension of Army demobilizations and reorganization.

In the event of your Government rejecting these proposals we will take such action that will make clear to the Irish people that we are not renegades or traitors to the ideals that induced them to accept the Treaty. Our organization fully realizes the seriousness of the action that we are compelled to take, but we can no longer be party to the treachery that threatens to destroy the aspirations of the Nation.

> LIAM TOBIN, Major-General, President of the Executive Council.
> C. F. DALTON, Col., Secretary to Executive Council.

On receipt of this communication, orders were given for the arrest of the signatories, and Eoin O'Duffy, Chief of Police, was appointed General Officer commanding the Defence Forces. McGrath, while expressing his disapproval of the ultimatum, resigned from the Government as a protest against the " absolute muddling, mishandling and incompetency on the part of a Department of the State." The revolt was, for the most part, confined to officers. In various parts of the country they absconded with arms. In Gorey, Co. Wexford, the soldiers prevented an officer from taking away arms, but he left the post, followed by some sergeants of the garrison. Other officers handed in their resignations. It was clear that a crisis of first-class importance had occurred.

These events had followed one another with rapidity. President

Cosgrave's statement to the Dáil was made on the 11th March, and the signatories to the ultimatum withdrew their threat on the following day, and explained that their object was achieved. President Cosgrave announced that an inquiry would be held. Meanwhile, Joseph McGrath had come to be regarded as the spokesman for the " Old I.R.A." His house was raided and searched by the police, and it was to him that President Cosgrave addressed notice of the terms under which the mutineers would be released. A committee of inquiry was then announced, consisting of Eoin MacNeill, Judge Meredith and Patrick McGilligan. But before that committee could meet, a group of mutinous officers took over premises in Parnell Square. Without consulting General O'Duffy, whose status and functions had now been clarified by appointing him Inspector-General of the Forces, and whose powers had been defined in writing that day, the Adjutant-General having consulted General Mulcahy as Minister for Defence, ordered military action to be taken against the premises in which the mutineers were stationed. Troops moved into position, but, except for a few shots by sentries, no other shooting took place and the occupants of the building surrendered.

These events took place on the night of the 18th March and on the following morning, O'Higgins related the progress of events to the Dáil. President Cosgrave was confined to bed, under doctor's orders to refrain from public duties, and O'Higgins as Vice-President was in control of the Executive Council. He explained to the Dáil that when he heard that Mulcahy had acted without consulting O'Duffy, he sent a message by two Ministers to President Cosgrave suggesting that the resignation of Mulcahy be asked for. Meanwhile the Chief-of-Staff, the Adjutant-General and the Quartermaster-General were called on to resign. Mulcahy, when O'Higgins sent for him and told him the decision of the Executive Council to ask for the resignation of the officers, announced his own intention of resigning. O'Higgins did not disclose that it had already been decided to ask for this and that he was only waiting for the President's agreement.

The split which Cosgrave had been so solicitous to avoid had now taken place. No longer could he hold the scales between Mulcahy and O'Higgins. The position was one of extreme embarrassment. His illness had come at a most fortunate time from his own point of view and it left O'Higgins to deal with the situation on his own.

It would be untrue to suggest that O'Higgins regarded this responsibility with any resentment. Difficulties and dangers were the breath of his nostrils and he welcomed an opportunity for acting decisively and promptly. He was faced with a formidable crisis—the President was away, two Ministers had resigned, and several members of the Dáil were announcing their intention of leaving the Government Party in sympathy with McGrath. O'Higgins did not take sides, he cut right through the two Army groups. The officers who absconded were treated as having retired from the Army and the three Army Generals who were members of the I.R.B.—MacMahon, O'Sullivan and O Murthuile—were dismissed from their posts. In June, General Mulcahy moved a vote of censure on the Executive Council for these " ill-considered " dismissals and for not acting on the report of the Army Inquiry Committee, and used the opportunity to give his own version of the Army events. As the Executive Council had in fact done the will of O'Higgins, he was the real target for the General's attack. " I labour," said Mulcahy, " under the disability that I have worn the uniform of my country and that to many persons young in the feeling of being democrats, that is a very great blemish nowadays . . . and I labour under the disability that I sat on the Executive Council in uniform also, with the result that a colleague in the Executive Council could be so affected by that sight that he could state to the Chairman of the Army Inquiry Committee these words : ' I could not get away from the impression that the Minister for Defence came to the Executive Council, not so much as a colleague, to do business with colleagues, as in the capacity of a delegate—almost as a man coming to the Executive Council who held a watching brief for a particular organization, a watching brief for the Army in the Executive Council.' "[16]

The General, speaking now as an ordinary Deputy, revealed curious information about the I.R.B. It appeared that during the Civil War, Barry, an Irregular leader in the South, suggested that the Republican forces should release themselves from their allegiance to de Valera, publicly destroy their arms and ask for the " formation of a National Organization into which the best elements of both sides could come and co-operate." The medium through whom these representations were made was Lieutenant-General O Murthuile (Hurley), the Quartermaster-General whom O'Higgins had afterwards dismissed. General Mulcahy had thought well of these proposals as the policy of the I.R.B. " was fully controlled by us," and he had interviewed Cosgrave, O'Higgins and MacNeill. O'Higgins interrupted Mulcahy's speech to ask him whether they had not given to these suggestions " the strongest and most emphatic dissent."[17] This, General Mulcahy denied.

When it came to O'Higgins's turn to reply to Mulcahy, he began by claiming : " I had in a sense primary responsibility for the action that was taken which Deputy Mulcahy asks the Dáil now to repudiate and condemn. I was acting in the illness of the President and I had in my hand a letter from the President's physician stating that he was not to be worried about public matters and that interviews, correspondence or even telephone messages were to be avoided as far as possible. And I owe it not merely to myself but to those members of the Executive Council who were acting with me during that week or ten or twelve days of very high tension to tell plainly to the Dáil, so far as it is possible, and to analyze the reasons and motives that caused this decision that was announced to the Dáil on the 19th of March last."[18] He went on to explain that the reason why the three officers had been dismissed was because the Executive Council had lost confidence in them ; the responsibility of the Cabinet " transcends personalities, transcends any question of personal equations . . . there is no question of personal venom or personal vindictiveness. One of those men I used to regard, and would hope still to regard, as one of my closest and most intimate friends, but the substantial broad fact is that the Executive Council had lost confidence in these men as a group." O'Higgins proceeded to make public the dissatisfaction which he so long nursed against the control of the Army. " Two groups, or factions, or secret, or semi-secret societies " had been " lining up " within the Army and the Cabinet had refused to allow " the national position to be bedevilled by a faction fight between two letters of the alphabet . . . in the proper place and in the proper way I charged to Deputy Mulcahy in February, 1923, that officers were being summoned up from the country to sit in uniform in Portobello under the chairmanship of Lieutenant-General O Murthuile, who was then Assistant Adjutant-General, for the purpose of reorganizing the Irish Republican Brotherhood within the Army, resurrecting and reorganizing it. I charged that the Staff of the Army were, for all practical purposes, an inner circle or upper circle of that secret society, and these two allegations were blandly denied by the ex-Minister for Defence." And when O'Higgins came to the portion of his evidence at the Army Inquiry which Mulcahy had read out in his speech, he acknowledged it and repeated it. "There was no candour, no frankness, no straight dealing, and one cannot do the business of a nation in the darkness or even in the dusk. There was a cloud-bank between the Executive Council and the Army, and that cloud-bank was the Minister for Defence."[19]

Equally drastic was the language in which he described the attack on the mutineers in Parnell Street. "There a faction struck venomously and bitterly at a faction behind the back of the Government and behind the back of the people, and we had to act and act promptly to show to the people and anyone concerned that we were not willing to allow this country's interests to go back into the melting pot so that there might be an interesting dog fight between any two groups. If we were to strike out and hunt down the men who had joined themselves into a quasi-secret political group within the Army, well, then, we ought to do that otherwise than through the medium and the agency of men who had done the same, and not through the medium and the agency of men who were out of court with regard to action of that kind. I cannot understand how men assented to the shelling of the Four Courts on the grounds that there were those within who challenged the right of the people to decide their policy freely and openly in the light of day . . . and then subsequently took a course which, at any rate, can be interpreted as a denial of that right, and as an intent to question or challenge it at some time in the future. Any man who has a political message, any man who has a creed to preach, can go out and preach it to the people openly, but men ought not to take the pay of the State and to wear the uniform of the State and then proceed to form themselves into what I have heard euphemistically described as an influential organization. An influential organization may mean much or mean little. The tendency is, when it is armed men who form themselves into such an organization, that it will mean very much indeed."[20]

O'Higgins was speaking two years after the march on Rome and nearly ten years before the world had come to hear of the speech that Hitler delivered over and over again with ever-increasing effect on the neurotic German masses. At the conclusion of his address O'Higgins referred to rumours that had been in circulation about him. He had read his " notice to quit" in one paper. There were a few issues on which he was prepared " to quit at short notice, and one of them is this, that those who take the pay and wear the uniform of the State, be they soldiers or police, must be non-political servants of the State."

The Army mutiny was the proof that the reputation which O'Higgins had earned as the strong man of the Government was his of right. A weak man may, if he cannot avoid it, take a course which makes enemies in one camp ; only a very strong man will do what he thinks right and make enemies in two.

It seems to have been clear before long that the action of the mutineers, although outrageous, was meant as a signal rather than a threat. It is by no means clear what the I.R.B. faction intended. It was unfortunate that Mulcahy did not consult O'Duffy or the Executive Council when he heard the troops were about to attack the house in Parnell Street. From the time of his resignation until he returned to the Government as Minister for Local Government, Mulcahy was a loyal supporter of Cosgrave and has proved himself since to be a most disinterested servant of the State, but O'Higgins did not respect his judgment and he was convinced that, if it were allowed to proceed, this penetration of the Army by the I.R.B. would lead eventually to the Balkanization of Irish politics.*

By his firm action O'Higgins saved the country from such a possibility and it revealed the essential soundness, both of the Army and the country, that they withstood this second blow within two years so well.

But O'Higgins trampled on many toes and there can be no doubt that a man who was not brave would have hesitated to cut across such formidable combinations as the " Old I.R.A. " who evoked the name of Collins and the new I.R.B. leaders who were synonymous with the Army Council. The first body had threatened to mutiny, had in fact deserted and taken away arms, giving as one of their reasons dismissals and demobilizations of which they did not approve. O'Higgins not only dismissed the

---

* " It was henceforward understood," writes Miss Macardle in *The History of the Irish Republic*, " that the inclusion of Mulcahy and of several other Army officers in the Cabinet at any time would involve the resignation of Kevin O'Higgins." This pronouncement is misleading in view of the fact that Mulcahy returned to the Cabinet before O'Higgins died.

mutineers, he dismissed their more important rivals as well. Viewing the scene from this distance, it seems that there was nothing else a responsible statesman would have done ; but those were not normal times, nor was O'Higgins dealing with an ordinary army. The greatness of O'Higgins exhibited itself in that he refused to set a precedent by acting as though times were not normal. He insisted on the dignity of the State. He insisted on treating the Irish people as civilized human beings, and not as an immature political community.

So ended the Army crisis. There were further dismissals subsequently, but stability was assured by the firm and drastic handling of the situation by O'Higgins. It is, perhaps, worth recording that when he first heard of a mutiny he immediately demanded five hundred men to challenge the mutineers, if necessary, in arms. The situation did not, however, lend itself to so simple and vigorous a solution.

From the revelations in the Dáil the outsider is given a glimpse of the complexities of the Irish political scene and it is clear that anyone who believed the Civil War was fought between ardent Republicans and loyal subjects of King George is making a great mistake. The relatively small proportion of the population engaged in the conflict with Great Britain acted in concert up to December, 1921. The split which then occurred involved more than a mere political difference. Personal loyalties and, perhaps, personal jealousies played their part. There were many who took sides against the Treaty who had their spiritual home on the constitutional side and there were those who followed Collins who would have been equally happy on the hillsides. And thousands took arms against the Government who had taken no part in the fight against the British. Revolutions throw to the surface fierce and dangerous men as well as pure-souled idealists. There were men who shot down policemen and British soldiers to order but who were quite incapable of enunciating any political theory. They took to violence as a duck to water and revelled in a revolutionary period. These are the men who are misfits in normal times, who clutch at Nazism, Fascism, Mosleyism and, in Ireland, at the I.R.A. as an outlet for their anti-social impulses. Without labouring the point, the fact remains that in 1924 the Army, which had fought the men who claimed to represent the Irish Republic, itself nursed two factions, one calling itself the Irish Republican Army, the other the Irish

Republican Brotherhood. When in time de Valera, the political leader of the Republican Party, came to power, he found himself confronted by an Irish Republican Army which was composed of yet another group of enthusiasts. Against them he used military courts and, eventually and reluctantly, the firing squad.

CHAPTER XI

THE MAN

O'HIGGINS was not immediately attractive in the way that his friend Hogan was. He lacked the capacity for easy friendship and even with many of his colleagues he remained always on almost formal terms. Small talk he rejected and he would not encourage fatuity for the sake of passing the time. As a result he was sometimes an uncomfortable neighbour in society. One lady who sat beside him at dinner, failing to catch his interest, became so uneasy that in the desperation of nervousness she asked him why he brushed his hair back instead of parting it in the centre. On that, as on many occasions, his penetrating and slightly quizzical glance petrified any further innocent garrulity. His sense of humour was never dormant but he rarely, except in sarcasm, exercised it for those to whom he was not attracted. An intelligent and attractive woman who met him for the first time at a garden party was relieved to find how he belied his reputation for being difficult to talk to. They went into a greenhouse together and had helped themselves to some grapes when they saw a notice: THESE GRAPES ARE POISONED. O'Higgins took out a piece of paper and wrote on it: THIS NOTICE WAS NOTICED TOO LATE—and fastened it beside the other on the vine.

Where women were concerned he was almost mediaeval in his attitude. He had excluded women stenographers from the circuit and criminal courts and he wished to keep them off juries for the same reason that they would hear things "one would not wish to discuss with the feminine members of one's family." This protective instinct did not arise from any fanatical puritanism. In matters of the mind he had the liberal outlook of a scholar. The censorship of literature which has been so often discussed did not exist in his time. When the proposition was suggested O'Higgins declared: "Under the existing law there are ample powers to deal with the sale and distribution of obscene literature.

. . . I am afraid there are serious difficulties in the way of the
State interfering to enforce censorship such as the Deputy requests.
. . . This would appear to be a matter for public opinion. . . .
I am not yet satisfied that the State can usefully interfere."[1]   The
topic had been discussed in a debate on film censorship in 1925
and Professor Magennis, who afterwards became the warmest
apologist for the extension of censorship to literature, then
expressed a philosophic approach to the problem. "I fully
recognize," he said, "that to propose a censorship of reading
matter would be very bold and would doubtless create a great
amount of discussion, would produce, perhaps, endless controversy,
and I do not believe that the country is ripe, or, it is possible, would
ever be ripe, for a drastic proposition of this kind to meet with
general approval."[2]

The revival of the Irish language had been knit up with the
whole Sinn Fein movement which had its roots in the founding
of the Gaelic League in 1893, the influence of which was enormous.
To Pearse the language was of paramount importance.   When
the Free State was founded the Cabinet Ministers used the Irish
forms of their names and, in this manner, O'Higgins came to use
the O in his surname as the Irish form of Higgins is O h-Uigín.
Phrases in a speech which he delivered at the starting of some
Gaelic classes in 1922 show that O'Higgins believed in the
principle of the language revival.   "On the mind and soul of
Ireland there are the fetters of a foreign language," he wrote,
and he praised the Gaelic League "with its call to all that was
best, to all that was spiritual in the young manhood and womanhood of the land."   The lecture has a propagandist air.   It may
be doubted whether O'Higgins in the last few years of his life
would have subscribed to such passages as this : "It" (the
Gaelic League) "learned that we had a language, a literature,
a muse of our own, better, purer, sweeter by far than the dreary
tongue of the conqueror—or would-be conqueror."   And in
another place he advocated the use of the language as a means
of breaking the chains that bound Ireland to "a country in the
grip of a moral leprosy."

In further support of the Gaelic revival O'Higgins showed
how "by the insidious propaganda of language England has
forced her outlook upon us," giving as instances such words as
"loyalist," which in Ireland "is used to describe a person who
stands with the foreign invader against his own people."   Those

"who believing in Ireland's right to separate national existence
have the moral courage to demand it and the physical courage
to fight for it are termed 'extremists.'"

There is no evidence in O'Higgins's life that his enthusiasm for
the Irish language was very intense. When, once in the Dáil, a
Deputy demanded that knowledge of Gaelic should be made
essential for a certain post, O'Higgins interposed : "I deprecate
the tendency to use the Irish language as a spearhead for jobbery."[3]

It was not that he became in any way less devoted to his country.
To that service his life was dedicated, but his outlook was greatly
modified by the fact of Ireland's position once she had obtained
the power of self-government. He once asked Joseph McGrath
whether he thought he (O'Higgins) was an Imperialist. McGrath's
answer was not direct, and O'Higgins pressed him for a candid
opinion. "Sometimes I think you are," he replied, " and sometimes I think you are not and honestly I don't know." O'Higgins
then stated his political creed : "I am not an Imperialist. I try
to do what I think The Big Fellow (Collins) would have done.
I try to play them (the English) at their own game." Those who
regarded him as a national renegade must have found it difficult
to make their case after his speech when it was proposed that
Merrion Square should be made into a memorial for those who
fell in the War, 1914–1918.[4]

"I believe," he said, "that to devote Merrion Square to this
purpose would be to give a wrong twist, as it were, a wrong
suggestion to the origins of this State. It would be a falsehood, a
falsehood by suppression of the truth and by a suggestion of
something that is contrary to the truth. I want Deputies to picture
the effect on the minds of strangers coming into this State and
visiting this capital. You have a square here, confronting the
seat of the Government of the country, and it is proposed to devote
that square to this purpose. I say that any intelligent visitor, not
particularly versed in the history of the country, would be entitled
to conclude that the origins of this State were connected with
that park and the memorial in that park was connected with the
lives that were lost in the Great War in France, Belgium, Gallipoli
and so on. That is not the position. This State has other origins,
and because it has other origins I do not wish to see it suggested,
in stone or otherwise, that it has that origin.

"I want it to be understood that I speak in no spirit of hostility
to ex-servicemen, *qua* ex-servicemen. Two members of my family

served throughout that war—one who did not survive, in the British Army, and another who did, in the Navy—and so it will be understood that it is in no feeling of hostility to those who were through that war in the ranks of the British Army that I oppose this scheme ; but this proposal, if it is proceeded with, means that you are to have here, straight in front of the seat of the Government of the country, a park monument dedicated to the memory of those men. I object to that because the fulfilment of such a project suggests that it is on that sacrifice that this State was reared. No one denies the sacrifice, and no one denies the patriotic motives which induced the vast majority of those men to join the British Army to take part in the Great War, and yet it is not on their sacrifice that this State is based, and I have no desire to see it suggested that it is. We have to go back a bit to get our perspective of this proposal. We have to take really the decade leading up to the war to remember the political position of this country from about 1908 or thereabouts, on to 1914. . . .

" Then we narrowed on to the war situation of 1914. We had our talk of political dismemberment ; we had our talk of partition ; we had our conference on the less or more of partition ; we had the shelving of the whole issue, the hanging up of the Bill until after the war, when that whole issue was to be reopened. The horse was to live, and it would get grass after the war. The horse, not unwisely, as I see it, decided that it would have a bid for grass before the end of the war. Someone said, or wrote, that somehow, some time, and by somebody, revolutions must be begun. A revolution was begun in this country in Easter, 1916. That revolution was endorsed by the people in a general election of 1918, and three years afterwards the representatives of the Irish people negotiated a Treaty with the British Government.

" It is on that Treaty, won in that way, that this State and its Constitution are based, and I submit to Deputies it is not wise to suggest that this State has any other origin than those. Let men think what they will of them ; let men criticize them and hold their individual viewpoints, but those are the origins of the State. It would be lacking in a sense of truth, in a sense of historical perspective, a sense of symmetry, to suggest that the State has not those origins, but that it is based in some way on the sacrifice of those who followed the advice of the parliamentary representatives of the day, and recruited in great numbers to the British Army to fight in the European War. Fifty thousand Irishmen died in

France. I hope that the memory of those men and their sacrifice, and the motives of their sacrifice, will always have respect and reverence in Ireland."

In this matter, O'Higgins was no bigot, and when Cosgrave, as one who had taken up arms against England, declined to lay a wreath on the Cenotaph in London, O'Higgins agreed to represent the Irish Government at the ceremony. At the time it required a great moral courage for any active Irish politician to do that. None can have ever acted with such sublime indifference to the passions and prejudices of the electorate. "I am certain," said Bryan Cooper of O'Higgins, "that if he woke up some morning and found that he was popular he would examine his conscience."[5]

With the same indifference to his personal fortunes, O'Higgins attacked what he regarded as the abuses of the liquor trade. The publicans of Ireland, he once confessed, were far harder to deal with than the Republicans. The licensing reforms of O'Higgins were strenuously opposed. One of the chief alterations in the existing regulation, was the introduction of a period in the middle of the day when all public-houses had to shut. This came to be called "Kevin's hour," for he confessed that his own experiences had convinced him of the necessity of trying to "shift the long sitter." If a man had to leave the bar for an hour, there was always a chance he might not return the same day. Although dogged, O'Higgins was by no means humourless on this subject. When Bryan Cooper suggested that on days when drinking was prohibited an exception should be made when drinks were ordered with a meal, O'Higgins took advantage of the suggestion to picture a time when in every hotel in a country town there would be a mouldy sandwich which would go down to history as "Cooper's meal, having done service on successive Christmas Days and Good Fridays for every thirsty soul who dropped in for a drink."[6] He related an imaginary conversation between two topers when one asks the other whether it is possible to get a drink on certain days, and when he hears that he can, if he takes some food, replies : "Then we will risk the meal."

One of the offences to which O'Higgins was most opposed was the poteen traffic in the West of Ireland, "where children going to and coming from school are reeling round the roads drunk," and he hoped to abolish that ubiquitous character, "the bona-fide traveller." He was not fanatical in this. The abuse of drink has been greatly modified since his day, for one reason because it has become so expensive, but also from the legislation which O'Higgins initiated in Ireland. Anyone who remembers the country a quarter of a century ago will agree that it possessed too many publichouses.

A man who fasts for half a year before he marries, as a preparation for the ceremony, is not an ordinary man, according to the ideas of this age, in which ascetical practices are immediately suspect. There was a time when it would have seemed not an abnormal practice for a Christian on the eve of a sacrament. It fits the idealized conception of a dedicated knight. O'Higgins was not a psychopath; he was a Catholic who took his religion seriously, who lived in the light of his religion. It is impossible to interpret his character on any basis other than that of a man to whom religion was the inspiration of life. With his remorselessly clear and logical mind, he found it impossible to make the usual compromise between the claims of this world and the next. It would, however, be quite misleading to leave the impression that O'Higgins made any demonstration of unusual piety. Of his moral strength all were aware, but, just as his family were surprised when he declared his intention of becoming a priest, so were his friends unaware of any unusual religious fervour. He had no pomp, nor did he smear his speech with the oil of sanctity.

Compton Mackenzie, a man of the world with romantic enthusiasms, described O'Higgins, whom he met at this time, as a Savanarola. It was meant, probably, to be more picturesque than accurate. O'Higgins was a convinced democrat, living in a country where the principles of democracy had been challenged and very nearly overthrown. Had he not contributed his strength to the small group of inexperienced men who met that challenge, Ireland might have become like a Balkan province.

A devout Catholic, he had joined a revolutionary movement which took its chief inspiration from a body that had incurred the disapproval of the Church, from a poet who raised the mystique of nationalism to a point where it threatened, if it did not supersede, religious belief as the first loyalty of the heart. "Holier to us even than the place where Patrick sleeps in Down," said Pearse, comparing the grave of the deist Tone with that of the Irish patron saint. Pearse's obsession with the idea of a blood-sacrifice, an atonement, as it were, for the sins of the unpatriotic multitude, had in it something strikingly reminiscent of the Christian doctrine of the Redemption. Nationalism had been exalted in their minds to such a pitch that the Irregular Army Chiefs clearly regarded their submission to majority rule as a great concession of principle.

O'Higgins came into the national movement not emotionally, but after study, argument and thought. He did not act quickly, but when he had made up his mind, it took formidable arguments to deter him from any course he had decided upon. "It is not," he said of his Public Safety Bill in 1923, "a popular Bill, but it is a just Bill, an honest Bill, and some of us did not come into politics for popularity."[7] It was tiresome to have had continually to face "the taunts of irresponsible people," to find that Aiken, after the truce, still styled himself "Chief of the General Staff," to read, when the first National Loan was floated, a solemn warning by P. J. Ruttledge to all members of Sinn Fein to save people "from sinking their savings in such an unauthorized flotation and thereby incurring subsequent loss."[8] He was adamant that the suspension of hostilities should not mean an amnesty for "bank robbers, arsoneers, murderers," while he advocated leniency for "the ordinary poor mug . . . who drifted round the country playing the ass." He had a passion for fair play. When the question of compensating rate collectors who had not sided with Sinn Fein came before the Dáil, O'Higgins took up their cause.

It is the fashion, in books written since 1921, to paint the relations between the people and the I.R.A., during the struggle with Britain, as one of mutual regard. It is pretended that the I.R.A. were obeyed always from love rather than fear. O'Higgins would have none of that. "We brought considerable pressure, amounting almost to compulsion, on those people," he declared, speaking of the recalcitrant rate collectors. "We fulminated against them . . . from a human point of view they were in a serious position." These men had given bonds and enlisted friends to go bail for them. They were ordered to act in a manner contrary to their bonds. "It does not become us, who, after all, won that struggle to try and go back now and in any way victimize or in any way lean against the people with whom we had differences. . . . Not all the country was Sinn Fein, not all the country approved of the course that we were taking . . . those men should be compensated . . . they were the victims of circumstances. We won . . . we should not be ungenerous."[9]

While he professed never to have "believed in the theory of the double dose of original sin for Irishmen," he was merciless in exposing what he considered the weaknesses of the native character.

He had, in particular, a dislike for that relic of conquest—the slave mind, whether it manifested itself by subservience or unnecessary combativeness, an excessive desire to imitate or an unnecessary striving after difference. "We have," he said once, "no real conception of freedom, no real conception of independence. If we had we would be dignified enough to appreciate what democracy means, and to resent more savagely and fiercely than we do the claim of any wretched minority to dictate to their fellow-citizens at the point of the gun. It is the slave drop in us, the slave mind lingering in our midst, which makes us bear that thing with the equanimity and complacency with which we have borne it." [10]

He was never ashamed to acknowledge unpalatable truths. "Crime," he said in the Dáil, "has not been the monopoly of any particular political party." And he had to face an unending campaign of vilification. At times he took it lightly : "Speaking as one of the dictators who answer daily here to the representatives of the people," he began his speech on one occasion in the Dáil. But no human being is so strong as to work happily under a constant rain of venom.

*   *   *

There are many ways of judging a man. His face tells a great deal, his voice something, his walk something, the way he uses his hands, and the words he employs must also be clues to his mind. Words of which O'Higgins was very fond were "reality," "responsibility," and, when assessing men, "gumption." He had the filling of many posts, and going down the list of candidates he struck out immediately many names, saying : "He can't say 'No.'" It was, in Ireland certainly, a stringent test. These favourite words of O'Higgins suggest the kind of man he liked. He had, perhaps, excessive impatience with those who, however brilliant, talked in the air. With the humbug or the charlatan he had no patience whatever. When the Free State began, some enterprising people saw opportunities of making money out of the situation. With this, O'Higgins had very little sympathy. He strenuously opposed sweepstakes, which have since his death become a national institution. On one occasion he attributed a cold that he had contracted to the dampness of his office, caused by people weeping over the condition of medical charities, people whom he had never previously suspected of being philanthropists. "The fruits of labour without labour" were not to be encouraged in a new State, he considered. It was not to be encouraged "amongst the rank and file of the people or in the minds of the types that gravitate round an enterprise of this kind." [11]

President Cosgrave employed methods to gain his point which natural quickness suggested, and which shrewdness and years of local politics had brought to perfection. O'Higgins had no patience with the circuitous approach, and his directness, although attractive to sincere people, was not the most effective way of dealing with the ordinary politician.

Youthful intolerance was O'Higgins's early weakness. It manifested itself in his biting replies to critics in public, and in the Cabinet he was not inclined to be conciliatory, but loyalty to his colleagues was absolute with him. Some who met him in London thought that it irked him to be in a subordinate position in the Cabinet. This was only true in so far as he found that, from time to time, President Cosgrave insisted on conciliation when O'Higgins was impatient to take a strong line regardless of the consequences. He was an authoritarian. A writer in *The New Statesman*, after his death, said : " He knew himself to be a Triton among minnows." It was certainly remarkable how Cosgrave kept together a Cabinet with such contrasting personalities in it, and if, in time, O'Higgins had succeeded to the leadership, he would have appreciated the achievement when faced himself with the problem of chairmanship. However critical of his colleagues when occasion demanded it, he never betrayed these differences of opinion, and once, when an intimate friend joined in a disparaging conversation about a member of the Cabinet, he was amazed when O'Higgins attacked him afterwards. " But I was only saying what I know you believe," he replied. O'Higgins was not mollified. " In my job," he replied, " I have to do hard things and to say hard things about public men. I dislike having to castigate, though most people would doubt the fact. I have to follow the light as I see it, regardless of my personal feelings. I am a representative of the people. But in God's name, why should you behave in this harsh way ? The man whom you criticized so bitterly to-night is a decent man, a sincere man. His main fault is that he is a muddle-headed man. As a public representative I must point out the faults that arise from this woolly thinking. Surely, you are not one of those who believe I take pleasure in building up this wall of hate ? That I get some grim satisfaction out of hurting people ? "

Even when it seemed that life had become easier, when the Civil War and the danger of assassination began to recede,

O'Higgins was not allowed to escape from personal sorrow. He loved his children to the point of adoration, and was overjoyed when a boy was born in November, 1924. Within twelve days, the child developed pneumonia and died. The grim Minister for Justice sat up at night by the side of his little son and insisted on helping to nurse him until the end. " Our little baby has gone to God," he said when the child died. He never afterwards referred to the son that he lost. We affect to despise men who wear their hearts on their sleeves, but, as a rule, we are intimidated by those who don't.

He asserted himself, by force of personality, without effusiveness, bombast or eccentricity. A French journalist attributed the intense gravity of O'Higgins's demeanour to self-consciousness : [12] carrying a greater load of responsibility as Minister for Justice, at thirty, than most statesmen are asked to bear at any stage of their careers, he felt the necessity to dissipate any misgiving which his youthful appearance might arouse. This was half-true. He put aside all personal considerations when he was engaged on public business. He only understood life in terms of dedicated service either to God or to man. When he knew that he was not going to be a priest, he was unable to adjust himself to life until he found another service to which he could devote himself. He did not feel the same sympathy with the professional man whose success was demonstrated by his wealth as he felt for the man with a cause. It was an intense period, the world had rocked on its base, and the eruption in Ireland was symptomatic of universal unrest. It was ·no local phenomenon. When the Civil War period was over—in 1926—Patrick McGilligan, the most brilliant of the new men in the Cabinet, wanted to leave politics and to pursue his career at· the Bar. He sought O'Higgins's advice and received a characteristic reply :

" Your letter of the 24th only reached me to-day. It makes me the more sorry for the passing of J.G.S.M. [Swift MacNeill, whose death left a law professorship open] that you should be up against this particularly racking kind of problem. . . . I do not underestimate its proportions while I sincerely hope that your decision will be to remain on at least till the completion of the big work with which you are primarily associated. I would prefer to have put the Shannon Scheme through than to be Chief Justice. The next five years are going to be pivotal for this country politically and economically. Don't miss them. It is, after all, the bigger and the fuller life, with all its heart-breaks and damnable wear and tear. . . . I know it is a big responsibility to write like this. Even I may have remorse about it some day and have to add it to my list of crimes but I'm just writing as I feel *hic et nunc* and damning all consequences. Stay on and fight. You are one of a few that know how."

O'Higgins disliked the conventional legal careerist who takes up politics as a means of advancing himself in his profession. The Attorney-General, as a rule, is a Member of Parliament, and it is customary for him to have the first refusal of any vacancy that occurs on the Bench. O'Higgins wished to establish the practice of appointing, as law adviser to the Government, a barrister who had no seat in the Dáil to think about and who could give a detached opinion, as though he were advising a private client. When a present of champagne arrived at his house, he refused to have it at his dinner parties as unbecoming the table of a Minister in a new and impoverished State. Punctuality was with him almost a fetish. Once, driving from Dublin to Greystones to lunch with a friend, he insisted that the chauffeur pull up outside the town and wait so that the car would not arrive ten minutes too early. He had, perhaps, overdisciplined himself, and his whole demeanour in public was exceedingly grave or, to use his own words, responsible. In private he still played practical jokes, and, to his family, seemed gentle, humorous and by no means grim.

When the critical days had passed, and the political prisoners had been released, there was no longer the necessity for the temporary and stringent Acts which gave to the Government drastic powers of arrest, imprisonment and punishment. It was pointed out to O'Higgins by his law advisers that there was now no law in the country to deal with offences which did not come under the heading of Treason, so an Act was passed called The Treasonable and Seditious Offences Bill, which, though general in its scope, had certain features of *ad hoc* legislation. This Act made it an offence punishable with heavy fines or imprisonment for individuals to style themselves " Presidents," " Vice-Presidents " or " Army Chiefs." " Up to a stage," said O'Higgins, " pretensions of that kind may be smiled at." And when one of the Labour members asked that the Bill be withdrawn as unnecessary, O'Higgins explained the necessity for it, ending his speech with the phrase : " It seems to be always my rôle to put before Deputies unpleasant facts, but I discharge the duty with a certain zeal."[13]

Although he mellowed with time, O'Higgins preserved a remorseless tongue to the end. Coming late to a debate in which a member had, as O'Higgins phrased it, "handed out bouquets in his absence," he began his speech by throwing them back rather roughly : "Over a crowded and strenuous three years my experience of the Deputy is that every time the ship rocked his one concern and preoccupation was to know what member of the crew he should knife."[14]

He has been falsely described as a potential Irish Fascist, and his opponents often taunted him with mediaevalism, which, in a sense, was true. Too often the expression Fascist is loosely used to describe a successful political opponent who happens to be conservative, just as Communist is a term of abuse employed by Tories out of office. There is no similarity between a Fascist and a mediaeval Christian, but the essential difference between O'Higgins and a theoretical Fascist was this : while both regarded the subordination of the individual to the State as axiomatic, O'Higgins based his belief on the fact that the State was a mere expression of the will of the majority. He had no belief in any mystique of the State. He was no Hegelian. It gave him particular pleasure to quote Kettle : "The State is you and me and the man around the corner." On another occasion he said : "The nation after all is simply a collection of homes." And as in a family, each member has to subordinate his own inclinations to the good of the whole unit, so O'Higgins considered that "the individual should not cheat the State because man does not live for himself alone."

To O'Higgins had fallen the task of refusing to give way when prisoners went on hunger strike. Senator Patrick McCartan in a letter to the biographer states : "Mary MacSwiney, Mrs. Maud Gonne MacBride, Miss Nellie Ryan (sister of Dr. Ryan) and a Miss Costello were on hunger strike. I was approached by Miss Ryan's and Miss Costello's friends to intercede for them. I spoke to Cosgrave, the late Professor MacNeill and others of the Party and I know Dick Mulcahy was anxious for their release but nothing was done. I got Mrs. Green, W. B. Yeats and others to intercede for them but was informed it was futile. I assumed it was useless to approach O'Higgins but as they were fourteen days on hunger strike and reports of their condition conveyed to me were bad, as a final attempt I went to O'Higgins in his seat in the Dáil while business was being transacted. He said : 'What guarantee can you give that all the others will not go on hunger strike if we free these?' I said I could give none. 'That,' he said, 'is our difficulty.' Then I said if he would promise to free these I would propose a resolution that anybody else who went on hunger strike in future would be allowed to die. 'Very well,' said O'Higgins, 'if you do that we will free them.' . . . I approached his colleagues then—also in their seats—and some said I could not expect them to give a decision then, and I replied that O'Higgins did. The four were free that night. Again it was an example of his quick decisions."

Visiting journalists, avid for copy now that Collins was no more, seized on O'Higgins as their most profitable quarry. It became the fashion to call him the "Irish Mussolini." His strength and determination were exaggerated to build up an Irish equivalent to the Italian dictator, the Turk, Kemal Pasha, and other men of force.

His passionate opposition to law-breakers was not tyrannical, it was essentially democratic. "It is of the essence of tyranny," he once remarked, "that it is politically irresponsible."[15] On this, among other grounds, he pressed for a hasty decision by the Senators on a Bill which excluded them from the Executive Council. He did not consider it right that persons should be called into collective responsibility "who have never been elected, persons who are not conscious, and who cannot be conscious, of a feeling of direct political responsibility to the electors." Labour Deputies sometimes complained that O'Higgins acted on suggestions made by Senators while he refused to accept amendments from them. The fact was that O'Higgins was always definitely impatient with the Senate when it delayed or opposed the expression of the will of the popular Assembly but he knew a good argument when he heard one.

He was, what a Fascist is not, an ardent champion of the full expression of ideas. "If people have a creed to preach, a message to expound, they can go before their fellow-citizens and preach and expound it. But let the appeal be to the mind, to reason, rather than to physical fear. They cannot have it both ways. They cannot have the platform and the bomb."[16] During the worst part of the Civil War a colleague, expecting a ruthless reply, asked him what he would do if the Government were defeated in the Dáil. "I would merely bow gracefully and retire," he said, and he meant it. "We will be as gentle as lambs," he promised, if the Opposition would combine to form a government in 1927. He was a democrat who believed in democracy, the very opposite to those spectacular figures of the last half-century who, beginning as socialists, have moved across the political board from the extreme left to the furthest right.

The sincerity of his democratic faith rings through all his speeches and it was no mere lip-service that he paid, for he was fully aware of the difficulties and defects of the democratic system of government. "Democracy," he said, "is no talisman against bad government. . . . The democracy in Ireland, America, or England is what the sum of the masses of the individuals comprising it is." That no alternative to democracy had been evolved, he was quite certain, but he had no illusions about the Irish electorate. "What," he inquired, "are the social principles and convictions behind our Irish democracy ? They are not Catholic in the measure to be expected—but an unquestionable admixture of feudalism and brigandage in one quarter, and a deplorable amount of grabber and gombeen morality generally. . . . I have always understood Catholicity to be a complete doctrine and rule of life, and this divorce of faith from good works is hardly sound Christianity. The civic sense, the community conscience, is feeble in Ireland."[17]

There is no doubt that on every side in Ireland are to be met people completely divorced from the material side of life, people without pride of possession, covetousness or even ordinary prudence. They provide a welcome contrast to the "grabbers" of whom O'Higgins spoke. But if credit is to be taken by the nation for the number of the unworldly in its midst it must allow on the other side that the Irish people notably lack a sense of social justice. A political party which concerned itself solely with the amelioration of living conditions would have inadequate support, because to use O'Higgins's own expression, "a large element of the Catholic laity is more gregarious than social."[18] The proper application of Catholic social doctrine was, he declared, the only remedy but in saying this he was careful to add : "There is little point in opposing other religious denominations. Men like Grattan, Davis, O'Leary, Mitchel, were by no means last in the race as Irish public men with a high and valiant social code. The word catholic signifies, literally, universal and Catholic and Protestant and Presbyterian are alike catholic in so far as they give beneficent public service." He quoted with approval, O'Leary's declaration that " he had but one religion, the old Persian—' to bend the bow and tell the truth.' "[19]

Of two themes O'Higgins never tired, the irresponsibility of the many and the despotism of a few. In these two elements he saw danger to democracy in Ireland. He was determined never to encourage the former by withholding hard words or plain speech and to give as little rope as possible to the latter. The demagogue he thought was " a much more general type than the matter-of-fact worker and statesman in every department of public life." He was convinced that the enemies of democracy who had challenged the right of the people to decide their destiny by the ballot box or, rather, who were prepared to abide by that decision on condition that it was in their favour, represented a phase that would pass away. " We have not yet learned to content ourselves with the doctrine that politically one man is as good as another. We hasten to add that not only is that the case, but, in fact, one man is considerably better than another provided he has the good fortune to belong to a minority." O'Higgins was keenly aware of the fact that dissension could not be eradicated from society until some solution was found to the social inequality which existed. In this he was in advance of most Irish politicians and statesmen for, since the birth of the Free State to the present day, no original thought on social questions has emanated from Ireland, which suffers at once from petty capitalism, old-fashioned trade unionism and rampant bureaucracy. So early as 1923 O'Higgins was groping for a solution, but he realized that the first task was to establish the foundations upon which society could rest before attempting economic experiments. " As soon as we in Ireland have established a regular State," he said, speaking in Trinity College, " when the authority of Parliament and the rule of the majority have been definitely vindicated, we will then be faced with the social and economic problems—the urgent ones."

What way these would be solved, he did not hint, but he indicated the difficulty with which the democrat was faced in the world after the first Great War : "What seems certain about our modern democracy is that it has not realized itself in its third dimension—in the economic and social order, and that until it does democratic States will always be breaking asunder. That is the real problem for believers in democracy. When we have succeeded in applying in some measure equality in the social order as well as in the political and legal order, then will we be in sight of a stable and workable democracy. The alternative is civil war. No State will have entered a stable orbit until political and social forces are balanced in some measure."

Michael Collins was idealized by O'Higgins because he embodied all the qualities for which the Irish people have won praise and he lacked those national defects which O'Higgins was tireless in emphasizing. Courageous and temperamental, Collins was, in matters of business, painstaking, efficient and exacting. Overmasterful in some ways, he was at the same time no doctrinaire who would deny the people the right to decide their own destiny. To defend the principle of majority rule against those who denied it he was prepared, so he told O'Higgins, to sacrifice "the last member of the Government and the last man in the Army." In him rather than in Griffith, who showed no sympathy with the workers in the General Strike of 1913, O'Higgins saw the hope of a new Ireland. In combination Collins and O'Higgins could have been irresistible, O'Higgins possessed an inflexibility which saved him from those lapses to which the mercurial temperament of Collins was prone but, while he could describe Collins as "big and human and lovable" without banality, his own personality did not evoke such warm and simple epithets.

O'Higgins had an epigrammatic turn and many of his opinions, crystallized in this form, dropped out in the course of debates. Explaining the conception of the State, he said : " It shows a lack of a sense of proportion to settle all quarrels with a stone-axe. You have no reserve for a really big thing. You can only use the stone-axe again, and it probably becomes monotonous."[20] On the question of unemployment and of social policy, he confessed that he was in doubt as to the function of the State in the matter whether it should provide a condition of things to give " the freest possible scope to private enterprise or whether the State should go further and attempt to deal with such problems as unemployment itself."[21] In normal circumstances he did not believe there should be any unemployment in Ireland. " But a people that has not been doing its own housekeeping for centuries is inclined to be woefully irresponsible."

" I am not," he said on one occasion, " a profound economist. I can make that admission now. I could not make it when I was Minister for Economic Affairs. When I pass out from the

Ministry of Home Affairs I shall have equally interesting revelations to make." He would have repudiated the description of Tory as applicable to himself, in so far as that term implied the existence of a gulf between the governors and the governed. On one occasion he took pains to deny that the Government represented the interests of the well-to-do. "From our antecedents and traditions our sympathies could not lie with the upper rather than the under dog." He would no doubt have argued that the Irish people were by nature conservative rather than radical and that if he inclined that way he was more representative of the people than if he advocated socialist or what is called "progressive" views.

He had shown, nevertheless, in more than one speech made outside Parliament that he was alive to the need for a revision of the accepted social scheme and in a paper which he read on a later occasion he revealed a keen awareness of the Irish economic problem long after he had been relieved of responsibility for economic affairs. In that paper, which was written in 1926, he contrasted the appearance of comparative luxury in Dublin with the poverty of the farmers and speculated on how long such an artificial situation could exist in an agricultural country. Then, as now, in the cities the workers demanded higher wages because of the price of goods, and the employers explained the high prices by the increased cost of labour. In the country the farmer who produced nearly all the wealth of the nation found that he could hardly live on his reward for his labour, while town dwellers complained of the price that they had to pay for farm produce in the shops. The economic condition of Ireland was described by O'Higgins as "too many people trying to live too well out of too small a production of wealth." He complained of the numbers who were adding themselves to the non-productive element in the community, an element "exacting in return for such services as it renders an undue share of the country's wealth." It did not seem to O'Higgins that the Government could or should do more than to point out the position. The Transport Union, by far the largest in Ireland, could, he suggested, break the ring by eliminating the middleman and bringing the consumer into direct relations with the producer. It is a strange fact that in the twenty years since O'Higgins made this suggestion, no effort to enforce the co-operative principle has been made by Trades Unionism. Internal politics and indifferent recruits have stunted the growth of the Irish Labour movement.

In some matters O'Higgins could be described as old-fashioned but it is not necessarily a reproach in the light of the history of the last quarter of a century. He generated awe. But in this there was no hint of priggishness. He had not so long before been wont to hear the chimes at midnight and a never failing sense of humour would have saved him from priggishness in any case. He could never refuse demands from the Falstaffs of his student days; there were many calls on his purse and no old friend ever went away disappointed. A Senator who regarded O'Higgins as a rather inhuman person was pleasantly surprised when, arriving on affairs of State, he found the Minister on all-fours in his study with his little girl for whose amusement he was pretending to be a bear. Even when moving round Dublin meant a grave risk of arrest, he had visited his favourite sister, Kathleen, in the convent at Rathfarnham, regularly and, when his father's death brought his mother to him in Dublin, he never allowed affairs of State to interfere with his attentions to her. Before leaving his mother's house he used to take leave of all the family so affectionately and sadly that they came to realize he lived under a constant premonition of death. " Of course, I shall be assassinated," he used to say to colleagues as one would speak of an evening engagement. Once to Hazel Lavery he wrote : " I feel a wall of hate closing round me."

Without being habitually gloomy, he was subject to fits of depressed silence which came upon him without apparent cause. With strangers it had the effect of freezing conversation. At home it was accepted as part of the course of nature. Maeve, aged three, was the only person known to take him out of one of these gloomy fits. He was an affable host, neither gushing nor diffident, with no fine gradations of manner to suit the difference of status in his guests. In many ways, said a historian who knew him, he put one in mind of the men who founded the United States of America. He remained a countryman, equally at home on horseback or with a gun in the country ; he might as well have been a lawyer or a student as a politician. He remained independent of popularity, fear, money, party, or any of the circumstances which usually cramp the individuality of men.

Bryan Cooper once asked O'Higgins to explain his amazing

maturity. "I think 1922 and 1923 could count for ten years in the lives of most of us," he replied. "At a glance," wrote J. L. Garvin, "he was someone. His serious intellectual head, with its look of hushed vigilance and incalculable reserves, was so set on a vigorous frame that you might see he was always thinking and thinking to an issue. He seemed heavy with thought yet instinct with action."

Such men are very rare and it is unreasonable to expect in them the breeziness of an auctioneer or the affability of a curate. His was not a back that invited slapping. He was an antidote to heartiness. A man of high purpose, dedicated to the service of his country, his portrait cannot, of necessity, be intimate, for grandeur is an austere and lonely thing. With no desire for money or knack of keeping or increasing it, he had most definite views on the subject of property. "I am not," he said once, "a believer in the theory of a definite social contract . . . but we by experience—sad experience, or otherwise—know there are broad principles of order which form the basis of civilized communities."

Ideas lived for him. He did not use words until the thoughts they expressed had come to life in his imagination ; and of all ideas that of justice meant, perhaps, the most. When he was appointed Minister for Justice, the title of his office gave him particular satisfaction. On one occasion he gave an embarrassing demonstration of this. It was the night of the 25th January, 1927 ; he was waiting with a life-long friend, a priest from his native county, to hear the news of the birth of his second daughter, Una. When the priest let fall a piece of local gossip to pass the anxious time, he noticed with alarm that the face of the Minister had gone white and that he had taken out a note-book. The priest's story was about a countryman who had died of a blow from a spade and had been buried without any excessive pedantry in the official investigation of the circumstances. Most reluctantly the facts were drawn from the unlucky priest who believed that at such a time even a Minister for Justice would be oblivious to the cares of office. As a result of this disclosure there was an autopsy, the coroner was dismissed, a police sergeant moved to another district and the neighbourhood received a sample of the quality of Kevin O'Higgins.

"Nichevo," now Editor of the *Irish Times*, in an article which appeared in that paper ten years after O'Higgins's death, recalls how, when once they had met by arrangement after a banquet

at Buckingham Palace given in connection with the Imperial
Conference of 1926, O'Higgins invited him to come for a walk.
"We left the Cecil and O'Higgins turned down into Villiers
Street through Charing Cross Tube Station and on to the
Embankment. It was a bitterly cold night in October and the
benches were fairly crowded with 'down and outs.' We walked
along for some little time without the exchange of a word.
Kevin was like that at times, and I knew better than to start a
conversation. Up and down we paced for some ten or fifteen
minutes until finally we got back to Charing Cross Station.
Then, for the first time, he spoke. 'We had our dinner off gold
plate to-night.'

"'Did you, indeed? That must have been an interesting
experience.'

"'It was interesting,' he replied. 'Very interesting. But I
thought I would have a look at the other side. Now, maybe,
I'll be able to sleep. Good-night.'"

CHAPTER XII

GENEVA

IN 1922 the Irish Free State took the status of a Dominion from the Treaty and in the following year became a member of the League of Nations. Great Britain was never over-enthusiastic about the participation of Dominions in the League.[1]

It had been the aim of the British representatives at all conferences to ensure that the provisions of treaties were not to be regarded as regulating relations between component parts of the British Commonwealth. At the drawing up of the Barcelona Convention in 1921 a clause was inserted which stated specifically that the agreement did not affect territories forming part of the same sovereign State even though these parts were individually members of the League of Nations. At an Arms Traffic Conference in 1925 the Dutch were anxious to secure a similar proviso in the agreement in order to allow their Government freedom of action in the East Indies. On that occasion the legal committee of the conference decided that the principle underlay all international conventions. Sir Cecil Hurst, the chief British spokesman on the legal aspect of imperial affairs, always insisted that the British Commonwealth was unique and that disputes between members were not within the jurisdiction of any international tribunal.[2] For some time it had been the practice for the King to sign treaties on behalf of the British Empire and to include in brackets the names of the Dominions. The strenuous opposition of the Irish representatives to this practice received the fullest co-operation of the Canadian delegates, with whom the Irish were usually in concord. The procedure was then altered and the King signed on behalf of each Dominion ; in certain cases where treaties only affected one Dominion, the custom arose of providing for the accession to the treaty by any other Dominion which expressed such a wish.

The problem was complex and difficult of any solution satisfactory alike to Great Britain, the Dominions, and other

States. If, at every conference, each member of the Commonwealth had a separate vote, the British bloc had seven votes so
far as the rest of the world was concerned. The British Government was anxious to preserve unity, and by the world at large
it was assumed that in any major political crisis the interests of
all the Dominions would be one. At the Imperial Conference
of 1926 it was agreed that the practice of enumerating the names
of States in the text of international agreements should be dis-
continued and, in its stead, the names of the heads of states
should be substituted. It was laid down at the conference that
the adoption of this practice and the use of the King as a symbol
of the special relationship between the different parts of the
Empire rendered superfluous any statement that the terms of such
documents were not binding between the various territories
on behalf of which it had been signed in the name of the King.

The Imperial Conference of 1926 represented a step forward
in the development of the Dominions, but it did not satisfy the
Irish delegation who held that the implication that the relations
between the various parts of the Commonwealth were not international relations was tantamount to acknowledgment that the
Commonwealth was one sovereign State ; it put before the world
the conception of a single international unit ; it detracted from
the sovereignty of the members of the Commonwealth, and it
was inconsistent with the covenant of the League.[3] To O'Higgins,
the British Commonwealth had infinite possibilities, but his
picture was diametrically opposed to any narrow imperialism.
He saw a group of States absolutely free, each a Kingdom, each
linked with each by virtue of a common King. In such a polity the
individual States would pursue their own interests, but would con-
fer in order to secure co-operation where the interests of all
were involved. It was an imperial conception worthy of Burke.

At first, O'Higgins found that he could gain little support for
his ideas, but, as we shall see, he impressed himself by degrees
upon the Canadian representatives, and at all times he found
among individual British statesmen unexpected sympathy for
his proposals.

In 1926, the Irish Free State decided to put itself forward as
a candidate for the Council of the League. Desmond Fitz Gerald,
the Minister for External Affairs, was summoned to a meeting of
the Commonwealth representatives, and, at the insistence of Austen
Chamberlain, agreed to forgo the claim, but his colleagues on

the Irish delegation refused to agree ; they were determined to
risk the displeasure of the British Foreign Office, and a notice
was served on all the Dominions that the Irish Free State intended
to go forward. At that time, Czechoslovakia, after five years'
retirement, was a candidate for the Council also, and not very
likely to be successful. But when the Irish decision was known,
a hasty agreement was reached between Sir Austen and Briand,
with the result that Czechoslovakia received unexpected and
overwhelming support at the election. The principle had been
established by the Irish persistence, and, on the next occasion,
Canada was elected to the Council. In 1930, Ireland succeeded
Canada.[4]

While to some British representatives it seemed that the Irish
attitude was designed to discredit the authority of the Commonwealth, to the more enlightened, the Irish policy appeared logical,
destined eventually to bring about a more real relationship between
what were so often referred to as equal and sovereign States.

O'Higgins did not have any knowledge of imperial or international matters at the beginning of his ministerial career, but
he found it impossible to take up anything without looking into
it thoroughly, and, once he had grasped the rudiments of a plan,
he found little difficulty in developing it in detail and enlarging
upon it.

In conformity with their policy, the British were opposed to
the idea that the Dominions should have recourse to the International Court of Justice at the Hague. O'Higgins wrote a
considered statement of the necessity for this, once the Dominions
had been admitted to the League. Britain also opposed the registra-
tion of the Treaty at Geneva as an international document.

The British representatives at international conferences were,
as a rule, obsessed with the idea of maintaining the predominance
of Great Britain in the Commonwealth.[5] In this they were rarely
opposed by Australia and never by New Zealand. Canada and
South Africa, however, tended to join forces with the Free State,
in conclave, if not always in public, as advocates of a more
egalitarian association.

In 1925, O'Higgins went to Geneva to attend the Disarmament
Conference. On the way, he spent a few days in London attempting to win support for the forthcoming tussle over the Boundary.
Denis Gwynn introduced him to Garvin, the editor of the *Observer*,
whose articles rarely failed to shatter the Sabbath calm. " The

hostile orchestra," wrote O'Higgins to his wife, " is tuning up here over the Boundary issue, and it was represented to me that nothing should be left undone to keep the *Observer* out of it. Garvin is an amazing fellow—one of the greatest *talkers* I ever struck against. It has to be faced that there is a tremendous prejudice here in favour of the North-East. However, I think the meeting with Garvin did good as I managed to keep my temper and I put in three or four effective shots in the midst of his whirlwind conversation. Gwynn said I did very well with him and that while he could never be brought to the point of actual support for us, he doubts if he will join the *Daily Mail*, *Morning Post* campaign against us."

On his way to Geneva, O'Higgins paid his first visit to Paris, and was more impressed by the sights there than by the solemnity of the League. In a few months the Locarno Pact was to be signed, and he sensed that " the British and French are out to discourage much discussion of the really important things—the Protocol for the Pacific Settlement of International Disputes—because they are engaged in delicate negotiations over that very matter." At Geneva he kept up his old practice and bathed each morning in the lake before breakfast. He was busy but unimpressed by what he heard, except " a wonderfully finished performance last evening by the French Minister, Paul-Boncour. It was French oratory at its highest point . . . " He met a few people who interested him : an Italian Senator, Chippito, was " a very cultured fellow with an acute and fearless mind. On the whole, I am, I fear, inclined to be mildly cynical about this ' League of Nations ' without denying that it has certain advantages. Personal contact between representatives of Governments is good. It breaks down prejudices and insularities. . . . On the other hand, while there is unlimited lip-service to idealism and abundant use of such terms as ' Justice,' ' Truth,' ' Right,' etc., a crafty imperialism can breathe quite freely the atmosphere of the *Salle de la Reformation* and here as elsewhere ' God is on the side of the big battalions.' Lord Robert Cecil is the finest flower of Geneva. He has an episcopal manner, he exudes High Church morality, his eyes look through you into a better world. He is a useful type to the British—the ' sword and Bible ' type. His sanctimonious exterior conceals an utterly cynical, ruthless, cold-hearted imperialism. He is the High Priest of Humbug and Hypocrisy. Amery is here to assert his inalienable and indefensible right to Mosul and to protest his unwillingness (*sic*) to carry

the 'white man's burden' in any corner of the globe,[6] and Austen
—the stage Englishman—monocled, wooden, stupid and successful.
Oh yes ! It is interesting but don't let anyone convince you that
the League—whatever its germs and possibilities—is a temple
of justice where great and small can meet on equal terms and
only right prevails. It simply imposes the necessity for hypocrisy
—vice's tribute to virtue—but once that is paid, then *sicut erat
in principio*, etc."

Geneva got on his nerves, and a cold did nothing to improve
his spirits. The rooms in which the Committees met were "like
Black Holes of Calcutta," and as a result, after a couple of hours
sitting, "every second delegate one meets has the drop pendulous
which is the outward and visible sign of inward trouble." The
Irish took no part in the General Assembly, and he may have felt
that he was wasting time. At home, there was a storm over the
decision of the Government to put the medical profession in the
Free State on a national register. It was said that O'Higgins,
in his first interview with the profession, was brusque and
unsympathetic. An election for the Senate, which was held in
his absence, was run on the issue of the "medical row," but the
small poll displayed how little the general public was interested
in either the Second Chamber or the medical profession. At
Geneva, whenever he could, O'Higgins tried to get publicity
about the Boundary Question, but, on the whole, he was busy
doing nothing of any importance.

"There are a lot of Americans here buzzing round like blue-
bottles. . . . If America is not in the League she is all round it
unofficially and semi-officially." He was unkind to Americans
—"terrible in their crudeness, in their ignorance, in their appalling
self-complacency." But, to tell the truth, he was not pleased to
be abroad. "I've had enough of Geneva and the League—the
shadow of that vegetarian vulture, Lord Robert Cecil, overhangs
it all, and round about, the American blue-bottles fill the air with
their gummy dronings. I want to go home to you and Maeve
Brigid. 'Security, Disarmament, Arbitration' is a wonderful
trilogy, if it didn't mean—security in my ill-gotten gains, disarmament for the other fellow, and arbitration with the court
well packed. But I fear it does mean all these things, my little
one, at present, and that the time is not yet when the Nations,
like the individual, will lay aside the stone-axe and submit themselves to a Code. Still the direction is right and I suppose that

a big idea has to be talked about for a long time, sincerely and insincerely, before it becomes a fact."

Whatever reservations there may have been in the minds of those who signed the Locarno Pact, in London it was hailed as the first step out of the slough of suspicion and hostility created by the War. Austen Chamberlain, then Foreign Secretary, won celebrity, and the Locarno spirit did seem to be a new force in the world. It impressed itself on the English mind, and there is no doubt that Baldwin and the Tory Government approached the Boundary crisis, when it arose a few weeks later, in a spirit of genuine benevolence.

CHAPTER XIII

O'HIGGINS AND THE NORTH

THE unity of Ireland was one of O'Higgins's ambitions. He believed that he could bring it about, and he is the only Irish statesman since the Treaty to propound a plan which attracted the interest of English and Ulster politicians. A mind that is constructive has to be encased in strong armour ; the negative and anarchic instincts are so powerful that they are almost certain to triumph. Had it not been for the Civil War, the first Irish Government had a wonderful opportunity ; they were beginning to build without any National Debt ; they had the sympathy of a numerically powerful section of American opinion ; they were associated with the States that had won the War ; they governed a British Dominion just at the time when the links which bound the Dominions to Great Britain were about to be lengthened and loosened. There was only one real problem and one genuine anxiety. The problem was the partition of the country, once the Six Counties of Northern Ireland exercised the option provided by the Treaty and seceded from the Free State. The anxiety was the anticipated outcome of the final agreement to decide the financial relations between Great Britain and Ireland. The British War Debt was enormous, and it was feared that Ireland might be allotted a heavy share. These two subjects— Finance and Partition—were governed respectively by Articles V and XII of the Treaty.

The history of Partition cannot be told in a few words. It is always regarded as something which England " has done " to Ireland. " But," to use O'Higgins's words, " when it came to do- ing business, when it came to a discussion with the representatives of the British Government, there was nothing to be gained by pretending to be unaware of the fact that a very considerable proportion of our own population, close on one-fourth, grouped for the most part in a particular area in the north-east of the country, did not recognize, and were not likely to recognize in practice or in action, the sovereignty, the supremacy, or the jurisdiction of that native Parliament which, acting on the mandate of the people in the 1918 elections, we had established here. It is all very well for people to vault upon platforms and say that Sir James Craig is a disloyal citizen of the Irish Republic. I doubt if the statement caused serious worry, inconvenience, or loss of sleep to Sir James Craig and I take it that if it gave any particular satisfaction to the persons who enunciated that great truth he would be willing that they would keep on enunciating it for a long time." [1]

In the times of James I, the North-East was planted with men of a different race and of a different religion to the Irish. It is not practical politics to make a grievance of that 300 years later. O'Higgins considered that it was essential to recognize the facts, and not to pretend the difficulty did not exist, or was of recent growth. True, some of the sturdiest rebels came from Ulster, but so long ago as the time when the Duke of Wellington was Under-Secretary in Dublin Castle, he wrote that, in his opinion, it was useless for the British Government to hope for anything but disaffection from Ireland save in the North-East corner. Lord Randolph Churchill, in the 'eighties, realized the full value politically of this North-East corner, and Sir Edward Carson, in 1912, organized it for the Unionist Party. It may be that if Carson had never existed, moderate opinion would have brought this part of Ireland into a unit enjoying a very mild type of self-government; the fact is that 80,000 Ulster Volunteers could be organized to resist it. That is a large proportion of the total Irish population.

When the Irish Home Rule Bill was put on the shelf until after the War, Carson, unlike Redmond—who did all he could to aid the British people in their trouble—made every difficulty until he contrived to extort from the Government an undertaking that " Ulster " would not be coerced into joining a self-governing Ireland. There followed an Act which nobody wanted, the Northern leaders accepted it, as it copper-fastened the agreement to keep them out of any Home Rule scheme.

It was the great object of Arthur Griffith in the Treaty negotiations " to break on Ulster "; that is to say, to create a position whereby it would appear to all the world that the obduracy of the North was the only obstacle to a peaceful solution of the Irish problem. Griffith had been a student of the Austro-Hungarian system, and he desired a dual monarchy for England and Ireland. He was a Separatist but not a Republican—for some reason the words have become synonymous in Ireland. Lord Pakenham has explained in great detail how Griffith was outwitted by the British delegation, and in return for an undertaking that if Ulster refused to come in, a Boundary Commission would be set up which would result in large transfers of land from the existing Northern jurisdiction to the Irish Free State, Griffith gave a promise to support the British in their Ulster policy. Collins, it seems, was also won over by this prospect. Lord Birkenhead described it as " a certain consideration for their signatures."

According to this arrangement, Ireland and Ulster were to appoint representatives to the Commission and England to nominate a chairman. The Article in the Treaty is short and bald, and, in view of the result, it is worth noting the words upon which the Irish hopes were set. Article XII provided that the Commission, which would be called into being if the Northern Government exercised its option to secede from the Free State, should determine the Boundary " in accordance with the wishes of the inhabitants, so far as may be compatible with economic and geographical conditions." No law clerk would leave a decision upon which rested the ownership of a few acres, to the mercy of so vague a phrase as that, but the destinies of human beings have rarely received the same consideration that men give to the sale of a house. The fate of the inhabitants of Northern Ireland was left to rest on the interpretation that a Commission—in which England was expressly empowered to pack the court, if she so desired— would put upon those words. So completely had Birkenhead won the confidence of Collins, so superlatively had Lloyd George exercised his powers to persuade, that the Irish delegation never seems to have considered that the Commission might make a finding which was not to their entire satisfaction.

Very soon it became apparent that Lloyd George had played Craig and the Southern Irish off, one against the other. On the 5th February, 1922, two months after the Treaty was signed, Craig complained that he had been tricked by Lloyd George and the British Ministers, who had all assured him the Commission would only ratify the existing Border. Collins affirmed that " at no time was there any question of being misled by Mr. Lloyd George. I never went on any opinion of his on the subject." The leading article in the *Irish Times* of February 6th, in which these remarks are reported, made what to many seemed to be a true estimate of the situation, that Lloyd George, " a master in the art of superficial compromise," had got his own way, while Collins was led away by his own optimism or " the vague benevolence of the British Ministers." Lord Birkenhead, in a letter to Lord Balfour, which was written on the 3rd March, 1922, and published on the 6th September, 1924, stated that Collins had " committed himself unguardedly to this doctrine, and it has no foundation whatever except in his own over-heated imagination."

General Mulcahy, in the debate which followed the decision of the British Government to appoint a representative for the North,* made a very spirited defence of the reputations of Collins and Griffith, whose ability and integrity, already assailed by the Opposition in their own country, was now in further jeopardy by the utterances of the men on whose good faith they had relied. He reminded the Dáil that Lloyd George had shown Griffith his plan for dealing with the North and bound Griffith to support him on it. Subsequently, Lloyd George showed Collins a map of Ulster, and " pointed to the small spot which is the Glens of Antrim and said to Michael Collins : ' You do not claim that an island like that should be transferred to you ? ' And Collins said : ' No, I suppose we cannot justly claim that.' Lloyd George answered : ' Well then, if that is the case, there will be no difficulty in finding a formula.' " That formula was the qualifying phrase which appeared in the Treaty, limiting the wishes of the inhabitants by *geographic* and *economic* factors. By opening the door to let the cat out, a chance had been given for the wolf to slip in.

But Mulcahy supported the Bill enabling the Boundary Commission to be set up. " I do it in order to clear the way and leave nothing which should be attributed to us in any way as hiding from the British people what the position is, from the point of view of their honour, and letting us see in this Boundary question what their honour is."

The approved national theory is that Birkenhead and Lloyd George cheated the Irish delegates, but no man of business, reducing a contract to writing, relies on his opponents' verbal expressions instead of seeing that the text speaks for itself. After all, as in this case, when it comes to construing the deed, those

* The Government of Northern Ireland refused to appoint a representative to the Boundary Commission.

who signed it may no longer be the parties in the transaction. No sensible man would expect an assurance as to what a commission, to be set up in the future, would do or decide. It was the ordinary talk of a salesman to assure the Irish that the outcome would be favourable, but *caveat emptor* is a very old precept, and neither Collins nor Griffith were children in the ways of the world.

It seems that the "wishes of the inhabitants" was the rock upon which the Free State Government relied. Whoever put in the reference to geographical and economic considerations had clearly the intention of modifying this. The implications of that qualifying phrase are endless, and yet, during the debate on the Treaty, neither de Valera, nor Childers, nor any of the opponents to that settlement, referred to it.

In any event, nothing was done about the Boundary Commission for some time. Collins met Craig on two occasions in an endeavour to reach agreement without resorting to it. At the first meeting, in January, 1922, Collins showed Craig a map on which were marked the areas which he understood the British believed would be ceded to the Free State. After this meeting Craig said he had been tricked by the British. Riots in Belfast then broke out, and in March, Collins and Craig made a pact in an effort to restore peace. They agreed to ignore Article XII of the Treaty, which in itself is evidence that Collins had lost his first enthusiasm for the good bargain which he believed that he had made.

After Collins's death, Cosgrave and other Irish Ministers met British Ministers and Craig in an endeavour to reach a permanent settlement. All these efforts failed, and on April 26th, 1924, the Free State Government asked the British Government to set up a Boundary Commission. Then Craig followed the example of Carson in 1914 and refused to co-operate. The Treaty had assumed that the Northern Government would appoint a delegate, and no provision had been made in the event of it refusing to do so. De Valera, at a meeting in Cork on 15th September, 1924, read a letter that Arthur Griffith had written to him during the Treaty negotiations which contained a promise by Lloyd George that if Ulster refused to allow a Boundary Commission to delimit the area of the Northern Government, "he would fight, summon Parliament, appeal to it against Ulster, dissolve, or pass an Act establishing an All-Ireland Parliament."

In 1924, Lloyd George was no longer in the Government, and

any efforts on his part to implement this promise would have landed him in the Tower; but it is only fair to his somewhat mottled political reputation to point out that Lloyd George's letter reveals that this dramatic threat was to take effect if Ulster refused the proposals made to them on the 12th November, 1921. It was made abundantly clear, before the Treaty was signed, that the Boundary Commission was the only coercion which was being brought to bear on Ulster.

The Free State appointed as their representative Eoin MacNeill, an Ulsterman, a distinguished scholar and the founder of the National Volunteers. The British Parliament, on the advice of the Privy Council, passed an Act enabling Great Britain to appoint the representative for Ulster. The chairman of the Commission selected by the British Government, now under the leadership of Ramsay MacDonald, was Mr. Justice Feetham of the Supreme Court of South Africa.

On the 1st of August, 1924, a question was asked in the Dáil on the position of the matter, and Fitz Gerald, the Minister for External Affairs, referred to the expressed intention of the British Government, as a matter of honour, " to introduce legislation to give effect to what was the undoubted intention of the Treaty." Thomas Johnson, the Labour leader, then proposed that the inability of the British to fulfil this article of the Treaty, owing to the Northern attitude, should be regarded by the Irish as a breach of the Treaty, which became no longer binding on them, and that they should proceed to make a new Constitution. This suggestion met support from a few, but President Cosgrave, in reply, put forward the view that as the British Government were now expressly legislating to enable them to perform their undertaking, it would be difficult to justify such a course. " I am not prepared," he said, " from the information at my disposal to say or to admit that there has been an attempt on the part of the British Government to escape its obligations in this matter." [2]

Professor Magennis, afterwards a bitter critic of the Government, made an elaborate speech in support of Cosgrave, which O'Higgins gratefully acknowledged when his own turn came to speak. O'Higgins emphasized the necessity to face the fact that almost a quarter of the population of Ireland, mostly grouped in that North-East corner, did not recognize the Sinn Fein Parliament set up in 1918. " Speaking as one Deputy, and not so much in my capacity as a member of the Executive Council, I can say that, to my mind, the North-Eastern position was, perhaps, the biggest factor for the acceptance of the Treaty. . . . We have to remember that we are dealing with a nation and that in the lifetime of a nation—a few years—a decade—is but a heart-beat. It is certainly not anything like in the same proportion that it bears to the lifetime of an individual. And if time had to pass until—Deputies may stand appalled at the thought—even the boys and girls would grow up to manhood and womanhood in the North-East in a different atmosphere and with a different outlook from that which their fathers and mothers had acquired, it might be well worth while to let the time pass. I say that without prejudice to the position that the Irish Government takes and must take on the Treaty."[3]

It was noticeable at this stage that O'Higgins took a seemingly detached view about the North. Time disclosed that he had his own plans for the problem.

It was clear that, if the British Government was not disinterested, this Act gave it extraordinary powers. Sections of the English Press pretended that the matter was purely an Irish domestic problem and not one of any concern to England, which was patently untrue, unless the British had lost all consideration for their naval or military strategy. It was not likely that England would choose an Ulster representative less determined to maintain the *status quo* than any representative whom the Northern Government would have itself appointed. It would be libellous to suggest that Mr. Justice Feetham was not strictly fair, but his mentality was known to the British Government ; he had been trained under Lord Milner and—to state the fact—it did not and was not likely to appoint a South African separatist. Austen Chamberlain had stated publicly that the function of the Commission was to make minor boundary adjustments. Lord Birkenhead had written that he had no doubt that " the Tribunal, not being presided over by a lunatic, will take a rational view of the limits of its own jurisdiction." O'Higgins probably believed that Tyrone and Fermanagh, or a large part of these counties, being predominantly Nationalist and having their situation on the Border, would come south. He may have hoped for South Down.

His hopes we do not know, his reaction to the result we do. The Free State Parliament passed an Act to correspond with the English Act altering the Treaty. President Cosgrave made one of the ablest speeches of his life, stating the Free State case in the strongest terms and pointing out that the alleged pact of honour with the North was no argument as by the Act of 1920, which the North unwillingly accepted, they gave to England treaty-making powers without reservation. In pursuance of that power England made a Treaty with the Free State by which the North was bound. Once again, President Cosgrave affirmed his faith in the honour of the British Government.

A transaction that begins badly is inclined to go badly and to end badly. The affair of the Boundary Commission was such a transaction. It is clear that the policy, both of Cosgrave and O'Higgins—they were in complete accord on this—was to be strictly faithful to the British, to honour their bond in the letter and even in the spirit. There were those who advocated a more self-regarding policy, a less pedantic faithfulness, a more suspicious attitude towards British motives and a stiffer approach to the British Government. O'Higgins always adhered to the view that on the Treaty the fate of the Nation rested. That gone, chaos had come again. In honour he was faultless. The world being what it is, was he wise ?

He over-emphasized, as it now seems, the result of a breach. Again and again he spoke of a return to armed conflict as the certain result of a break on the Treaty. Was this good policy ? To have advocated strict adherence to the Treaty on moral grounds was sound—and he did this—but to reinforce the moral argument by instilling fear of force, was only sharpening the weapons of the British for them. To this, O'Higgins would no doubt have answered : " We can gain nothing by force. I am looking ahead. I see great possibilities in the future. Let us not kick against the pricks. Time will remove them. We have wasted too much in fire and bloodshed. Look forward. Stop looking back. Have faith."

In May, 1924, President Cosgrave gave an interview to an American journalist during which he stated that if the North refused to appoint a representative to the Boundary Commission, it had failed to comply with the conditions which enabled the Six Counties to secede from the Free State and so remained in it with a Parliament subordinate to Dublin instead of Westminster. Subsequently, it was urged by Johnson, the Labour leader, that the Free State, by agreeing to pass the Act which enabled Great Britain to appoint a commissioner for the North, was not acting in accordance with Cosgrave's opinion but adopting a new policy of "tolerated secession" for which O'Higgins was responsible. O'Higgins accepted the challenge: "The Deputy has talked of an interview given by the President in May, and has made considerable play with it. But something has happened since May. Since May the predominant Government and Parliament of the Northern area has expressed its willingness to come and make good the default of the subordinate provincial Parliament and we have concurred in that course."

The fact which filled most responsible Irishmen with alarm was that three of the English signatories to the Treaty, Birkenhead, Lloyd George and Austen Chamberlain, had all expressed their opinion that the function of the Boundary Commission was very limited. O'Higgins insisted on believing that the Commission would act honourably. The utterances of two of the Irish signatories could not be "taken up and dealt with as clearly showing the intention of this Government . . . so, approaching this question of the utterances of British politicians who are now not members of the British Government one must approach it in that way . . . these men are now simply free-lance politicians thinking in terms of their own political fortunes and futures, which . . . do bear weight with politicians in England, as elsewhere."

But O'Higgins was no innocent in the matter. "I have never," he said, "been able to reconcile the views embodied, say, in Lord Birkenhead's letters of March, 1922, as we are told, with his own utterances on the very day on which he signed the Treaty. . . . And when Mr. Lloyd George, a week later, on the 14th December, 1921, said that it was quite clear since the Act of 1920, at any rate, that the majority in these two great counties of Tyrone and Fermanagh obviously wished to be with their southern neighbours, I do not know how he could reconcile that statement with the conception which is now advanced, and which apparently has gained some favour amongst politicians of all parties in England. . . . These things have always been a source of some surprise to me, and without attempting to pronounce upon the political integrity of these men, I say that I would be glad to hear from themselves an explanation of those so obvious inconsistencies."[4]

Despite these observations O'Higgins ended his speech by restating his belief that "arbitration will be conducted fairly and honourably, just as we are bound to say that in this whole matter of the Treaty, and in everything that has arisen under it, we have been treated fairly and honourably by four succeeding British Governments."

The Executive Council did not suffer from lack of advice and among the letters O'Higgins received was one from Patrick McCartan who had played a considerable part in Sinn Fein. A northern Catholic and a member of the I.R.B., he had accompanied de Valera to America and was the first and only Irish representative to Soviet Russia. A Republican, he had voted for the Treaty, although he did not like it. "Personally," he had said on that occasion, "I have more respect for Michael Collins and Arthur Griffith than for the quibblers here." McCartan organized the appeal in America which enabled the final years of the poet Yeats to be spent in moderate comfort and in 1946 unsuccessfully contested the Presidency when S. T. O'Kelly was elected.

McCartan advised O'Higgins to send a note to the British Government stating that as it was obvious Article XII was to be explained away by a far-fetched interpretation, the Free State regarded the Treaty as violated and would not take part in further negotiations. James MacNeill, the Irish High Commissioner in London, and a brother of the Free State representative on the Commission, should be ordered to return to Ireland and the Governor-General to vacate the Viceregal Lodge. Joseph McGrath was to be consulted on the formation of a Civil Defence Force, and Stack or some other member of de Valera's Party asked to co-operate. The Dáil was to be summoned as a constituent assembly to draft a new Constitution in view of the situation. These steps—in McCartan's view—would "bring the English scurrying over" and provide the proper setting in which the question of the Boundary could be settled. In the course of his letter, McCartan made the disquieting revelation that as he could get any information he wanted from governmental departments, the British could also, and he warned O'Higgins not to trust the staff in the Government departments.

O'Higgins's letter in reply is worth quoting in full. It sets out his attitude on a controversy which ended disastrously for his Government. His chief purpose and aim up to the time of his death was by an imaginative and daring stroke of statesmanship to regain not only the lost ground but to settle on a permanent basis the question of Irish disunity. It is a letter which gave him pleasure to write for he chuckled while he read it over before posting it.

"I have your note of the 11th instant. You and I so frequently disagree that I feel you will not be surprised when I say that I am in complete disagreement with the proposal embodied in your letter.

"The keystone of your arch is the sentence : 'It is obvious now that the policy of the British Government is to set up the Commission and decide on some fake about parishes.' If I pressed you for reasons for that statement you would, no doubt, point to the Birkenhead-Balfour letter and George's speech in endorsement thereof. Neither Balfour nor Birkenhead are members of the present British Government and Birkenhead's letter must be read with his own addendum or postscript. If you tell me that the fact that these two men were signatories to the Treaty makes all the difference, then how do we stand with regard to Barton and Gavan Duffy ? Would the British people be justified in ordering MacNeill out of London and returning here to-morrow on the grounds that we were unlikely to keep the Treaty in view of the attitude of the two signatories who ratted ?

"The fact is that no member of the British Government has given the slightest justification for the course which you suggest. It is true that certain British politicians and certain British newspapers are taking a line which we here cannot but regard as advocacy of a breach of faith but we are no more entitled to regard that as the official governmental attitude and to write Notes and take action thereon than the British would be justified in seizing on the speeches of Barton, Duffy, Joe McGrath, Seán McGarry or Miss McSwiney and the effusions in *Eire*, *Sinn Fein* and *The Irish Worker* as clearly indicating the intentions of the Free State Government.

"When people in the uniform of the Free State Army shot down unarmed British soldiers at Cobh we disowned and condemned the deed and the British people as a whole accepted the disclaimer. We would, no doubt, have felt very much aggrieved if instead of accepting it the British people had seized upon it as a sufficient pretext for a denunciation by them of the Treaty and attempted reconquest. Yet it was somewhat stronger provocation to them than the *Daily Mail* or the *Morning Post* articles can be to us or the utterances of politicians who are not at present in a position of responsibility for the internal administration of Great Britain or its international relations.

"That is my Whiggish, West-British view of your proposal. Sooner or later—probably later rather than sooner—this country will grow up and realize that it cannot have a set of standards of international conduct peculiar to itself. If, in the event, you prove a true prophet and the findings of the Boundary Commission prove to be the travesty of the Treaty clause which you seem to regard as inevitable, will it occur to you at all to reflect to what extent the antics of the last few weeks contributed to that result ? It seems to me that we cannot have it both ways. We cannot have the luxury of Dolphin* dinners and ' ultimate goal ' speeches and at the same time wax censorious at the other fellow because we suspect that at some time in the future he may depart from the strict intention of the international document which at present forms the basis of our relations.

" The big argument in favour of the acceptance of the Treaty was that it provided a *modus vivendi* with 1,000,000 people, one-fourth of our population, who were hostile to the objectives which the rest of us had written upon our battle-standards. If in January, '22, we had sat down in grave council to consider how best we could destroy the prospect of union with those elements which were standing out in the North-East we could not have devised a better programme to that end than that which we have in fact carried out from January, '22, to date. One by one such inducements to union as might be said to exist were sedulously sought out and smashed, and every pain was taken to ensure that the leverage value of Article XII would be inadequate to effect what all sane people hoped two years ago it would effect. Article XII itself is no great piece of constructive statesmanship, but insistence on its operation is a matter of National self-respect which we cannot afford to waive. Let the findings be as favourable as we have any right to hope and it will still leave out from your State system a smaller and more homogeneous, and a more embittered area than was standing out before.

" We had an opportunity of building up a worthy State that would attract and, in time, absorb and assimilate those elements. We preferred the patriotic way. We preferred to burn our own houses, blow up our own bridges, rob our own banks, saddle ourselves with millions of debt for the maintenance of an Army

* The Dublin restaurant.

and for the payment of compensation for the recreations of our
youth. Generally, we preferred to practise upon ourselves worse
indignities than the British had practised on us since Cromwell and
Mountjoy and now we wonder why the Orangemen are not
hopping like so many fleas across the Border in their anxiety to
come within our fold and jurisdiction.

" Unlike you, I still hope for a straight deal on the proviso to
Article XII. If we get it, I will consider that the British are an
almost superhumanly wise people politically. If we do not get
it, I will think that they have been foolish, but not nearly so foolish
as ourselves. I will think that their folly and ours, and particularly
ours, have brought about a situation that is not likely to prove
fruitful of good for either country."

Eoin MacNeill, the Free State representative on the Boundary
Commission, was a man whose standards of honour were of the
highest by Christian or classical standards, but he was a bookman
who drifted by accident into politics. He entered into an engagement with his fellow-Commissioners not to disclose their deliberations. He also agreed to sign a unanimous report. His vow of
silence was particularly exasperating to the Free State Government,
as he was a member of the Cabinet.

The Commission proceeded to meet and to take evidence.
The findings were not yet published when the Labour Government went out of office and the Conservatives came in, with
Baldwin as Prime Minister, and Churchill, Chancellor of the
Exchequer. Birkenhead was Lord Chancellor ; Austen Chamberlain, Foreign Secretary. Three of the signatories of the Irish Treaty
were in office again in England, while of the Irish delegation,
two were dead. Duggan had no governmental office. Barton
had joined de Valera at the time of the Civil War, and Gavan
Duffy was no longer a member of the pro-Treaty Party or, for
that matter, of the Dáil.

From the Labour Government much had been expected. But,
just as prisoners in English gaols found that the Home Secretary
Clynes was less sympathetic than Churchill, the Tory, so the
Irish found that J. H. Thomas was no kinder friend than his pre-
decessor. In fact, from the Tory administration of Neville
Chamberlain, the Irish extracted more concessions than from any
government devoted to the interests of the under dog. Mr. Justice
Feetham was the choice of Ramsay MacDonald's Cabinet.

A year had passed, and no one in Ireland was the wiser about

the result of the Commission when, in 1925, an apparently inspired
article appeared in the *Morning Post*, predicting that the report
of the Commission confirmed the existing boundary, save that it
added to Northern Ireland a substantial part of Donegal. At the
same time, in Ulster, Craig's lieutenants were assuring their
followers that all would be well. From the South there was no
sound. Cosgrave had stated his Government would abide by the
findings ; in England, Lord Halsbury had suggested that an appeal
to the Courts was available to Sir James Craig's Party if they were
dissatisfied with them.

Suddenly, MacNeill produced a crisis by resigning from the
Commission on Friday, 20th November, and on the following
Tuesday he gave his reasons to the Dáil. With modesty and
dignity he explained the predicament in which he found himself,
when, having agreed in principle to signing a joint report before
he knew what the report was going to be, he realized that his
interpretation of Article XII of the Treaty was entirely different
from that of Judge Feetham, and that a report was now about
to be issued of which he could not possibly approve. Resignation
was the only alternative.[5] MacNeill's view had been that the
Six Counties was a unit which had never been determined by
any franchise, and that the task of the Boundary Commission
was to ascertain what the area would have been at the time of
the passing of the Government of Ireland Act in 1920 if the
inhabitants had been given an opportunity to express their
wishes.

On the day that the news of MacNeill's resignation reached
Dublin by wire, O'Higgins was due to attend a reception in Dublin
given in honour of the Irish High Commissioner, James MacNeill,
who was making a visit from London. O'Higgins sent an excuse
for his absence, and then, thinking better of it, came late. He
looked pale and anxious, nor did his appearance misrepresent his
feelings, for suddenly he fainted. He revived sufficiently to be
brought home and after a day's rest took a leading part in the
business which now became so urgent.

Patrick Hogan had urged O'Higgins to offer himself as the
Free State representative on the Commission, but he refused to
entertain the suggestion. He could not spare the time which the
sittings would take. Moreover, he thought that a Northerner,
such as MacNeill, would be more suitable for the task.

In public, O'Higgins never betrayed the depth of his feelings

on the disastrous result of the Commission. There can be no
doubt that MacNeill proved unequal to the task, but a man of
more cunning and a keener negotiator would have, perhaps,
achieved no more. A more alert representative would have
probably resigned earlier and gained time. There is no reason to
believe that Mr. Justice Feetham could have been argued into a
different state of mind.

To his colleagues, O'Higgins made no secret of the fact that
if the Government did not retrieve the position they were doomed
politically. At any moment the report might issue ; meanwhile,
the country was in consternation, the National Loans drooped,
and de Valera's supporters sprang into new life.

The Government was faced with the greatest crisis since the
outbreak of the Civil War. Prompt action was essential. President
Cosgrave went over to London and interviewed British Ministers ;
after a few days he returned and reported the outcome of these
conversations to the Cabinet, whereupon it was decided that
O'Higgins, John O'Byrne, the Attorney-General, and McGilligan
should go over immediately. They left the same evening, and
arrived in London on Saturday 28th. Baldwin was not at Downing
Street, having retired for the week-end to Chequers, and the
Irish delegation followed him in a taxi. A note of farce was
introduced to these grave proceedings by reason of a decision
given by the Judicial Committee of the Privy Council that the
report of the Boundary Commission became law as soon as it
was published. The Commissioners were in London, and an
attempt was made to serve the report, like a writ, on the Irish
representatives. They avoided service by adopting time-worn
expedients.

Baldwin and the Secretary of the Cabinet, Tom Jones, were at
Chequers when the Irishmen arrived. It was before lunch time, and
O'Higgins began the interview by expounding the Free State
case regarding the Boundary. When he began, Baldwin's legendary
pipe was firmly planted in his mouth, but as O'Higgins developed
his argument, the interest of the Prime Minister increased to such
an extent that he pulled out his pipe and signalled to Jones to put
it away. When O'Higgins finished speaking, Baldwin exclaimed :
" My God, I am between the devil and the deep blue sea ! "

The other members of the Irish delegation were then asked to
speak, but both agreed that nothing they could say could add
to the strength of the case which O'Higgins had made, which both

agreed was the ablest they had ever heard put forward by lawyer or statesman.

It was a cold day, with thick snow lying on the ground, and by the time O'Higgins had finished speaking, the afternoon was well advanced. Suddenly, Baldwin remembered that the Boundary Commissioners, who had arrived during the morning, were incarcerated in a room upstairs without a fire, and without having had a meal since they arrived. It was agreed by everyone that no one should see them or receive the report. The delegation returned to London, and, on the following day, came back to Chequers to meet Sir James Craig, who had come to England to attend the funeral of the Dowager Queen Alexandra.

Craig proved to be a far less intransigent character than the Free State representatives had expected. "I am committed politically," he said. "I cannot alter my ground but anything I can do to help you get what you can off *those fellows*, I will." Craig and O'Higgins talked in private for a long time at Chequers. Other meetings followed in London. In order to avoid the consequences of the Feetham award, legislation was necessary both in Ireland and England to alter the Treaty. Two articles of that agreement had been left in abeyance. No. V, which dealt with finance, and No. XII, which dealt with the Northern question. It was now proposed, in order to remove the possibilities of a further crisis, to endeavour to settle both these questions at once. Over the Free State hung the liability for an unascertained share of the British War debts ; against this, the Irish claimed, as a set-off, the sums paid in overtaxation since the Union, a fact which the Childers Commission had argued in Gladstone's time. The difference between the claim and the set-off was this, that the British were in a better position to enforce their claim, it was more readily ascertained, and in an arbitration court from within the Empire it was unlikely that a claim so involved as the Irish one was likely to receive all the attention that its historical and financial complexities required.

An Agreement was signed on the 3rd of December, which provided for the cancellation of all claims, and the Free State agreed to increase the amount of compensation paid to those whose property had been destroyed in Ireland between July, 1921, and May, 1923—in the main, a concession to Irish Unionists ; compensation for depredations to property before that date were undertaken by the British Government. The Council of Ireland,

a creature of the 1920 Act, the operation of which had been
suspended, was transferred to the Northern Government.   It
was a body upon which North and South had equal representation,
and to which the British Government was to have appointed a
chairman.   Its function was the discussion of topics, such as rail-
ways, of mutual concern to the two parts of Ireland.   In its stead,
the Governments agreed to meet and discuss matters of common
concern on a friendly and co-operative basis.   In fact, North and
South have never met officially since that day in December, 1925.
A more solid gain by Craig was the cancellation of the North's
War debt liability.   One of the threats by which Lloyd George
had promised to drive the Six Counties into the arms of the South
was this heavy price which imperial loyalty was to cost in contrast
with national unity.

Had the Boundary Commission Report, giving a large slice
of Donegal to the North, been published and become law, there
would have been a recrudescence of violence in Ireland—I.R.A.
activity, coupled with spontaneous violence by Ulster Nationalists.
A Belfast pogrom would inevitably have followed.   It was good
statesmanship to avoid this and to produce a treaty of amity.[6]
But there is no denying that the Free State's difficulty was Craig's
opportunity, and that his party triumphed.   It is equally certain
that the life of the Cosgrave regime was shortened by the whole
affair.   It was, perhaps, a situation which could not have been
avoided, but it is the fate of any party which is in power at a time
of calamity to have to take responsibility for the event.   Increased
opposition arose in the Dáil.   The Army Mutiny had created
some malcontents, the distribution of Cabinet seats others.   Now
an opportunity arose to all disappointed politicians to show
themselves as children of the light.   Republicans attended a meeting
of the Labour Party in the Shelbourne Hotel to discuss the position,
but no decision was arrived at.

O'Higgins, as disappointed as any of his fellow-countrymen,
chose the constructive way out of the difficulty.   Once again he
showed—as did his colleagues also—indifference to his political
future.   "I knew," he said, "when I put my name to that Agreement, that to all those whose stock-in-trade is hate and barren
negation, it would be disappointing."   He made no outcry against
the Boundary Commission.   "If I can be told, as I have been told,
that the proviso admits of the interpretation which has been placed
upon it by the Commission, then that is no good or sufficient

reason for taking a course which spells a denunciation of the Treaty and for plunging the fortunes of this State and of this people back once more into the melting pot. And so we negotiated." [7]

He made no defence for having negotiated with the British. " Hate, whether between individuals or between peoples, is a barren thing . . . " On few occasions did the essential nobility of O'Higgins's mind emerge so clearly as in his speech of justification for the new pact with England. When he spoke of the approach that had been made to a new spirit of friendship with the North, Johnson interpolated : " You have great faith." " I have great faith," he replied, " and with the Deputy's permission I will keep it." [8] Another Deputy intervened to ask what he would do if his hopes did not come true. " I shall die of a broken heart," he replied. And he ended his speech with an appeal for a constructive attitude. " It is the easy thing, the obvious thing, to sneer, to suggest that we were cowed, intimidated, or coaxed or cajoled by the statesmen of other countries into signing this Agreement. It is always easier to believe ill of the neighbour's child than to believe good of him. It is always easier to believe that you have been sold, that you have been let down, that people took their price, whether in flattery or in cash, or in some other way ; but, in the end, people have simply, faced with a grave situation, to do what they believe in their inmost heart and soul and mind to be the right thing, and to chance the sneers of spatted hillsiders and armchair patriots and the jibes of those who think that the real statesmanship is the perpetuation of hatred. We stand not for the perpetuation of hatred but for the rooting up and elimination of the old hatreds, old furies, and the quenching of old fires ; we stand for peace and sanity and construction in this country and peace between neighbours." [9]

As to whether a good or bad bargain was made, it is hardly possible to say. De Valera wrote : " I had hoped that no Irishman, North or South, would be found prepared to put his hand to an instrument dismembering his country. . . ." He did not make a suggestion as to what should be done. Had agreement not been reached, there would have been more bloodshed, more civil commotion. Was it good statesmanship to endeavour to prevent this, to endeavour to reach agreement with England and Northern Ireland, to endeavour to remove sources of irritation ? The Boundary Commission, the child of Article XII, the Article which more than any other had persuaded Collins to sign the Treaty, had proved a disaster. Was it good statesmanship to endeavour to settle once and for all the only other matter in the Treaty which awaited arbitration—the financial questions in Article V ?

"You would not," said Deputy Baxter, "handle Article V as badly as you handled Article XII. You would be wiser the next time." Challenged by O'Higgins, the Deputy was unable to suggest a method by which Article XII could have been handled satisfactorily. Nor did de Valera make any constructive suggestions. "What," said O'Higgins in the Dáil, "was the first brief venomous message shot out to the Press when this complexity had arisen ? 'I told you so. You have had the shock of Article XII. Brace yourselves now for the shock of Article V, and it is going to be a big one. I can tell you in advance that the British claim amounts to £19,000,000 a year.'" [10]

If de Valera was correct in November, the cancellation of this enormous claim was a diplomatic triumph for the Irish representatives. But, when the Agreement was made, achieving this only eight days later, he addressed a public meeting with the words : "The gain lay solely in being relieved from the possibility of being cheated further . . . ," and he gave £3,000,000,000 as the approximate sum which England owed Ireland at the time of the Treaty.

The words of a politician at a meeting, like lapidary inscriptions, are not on oath ; they are too often brought up in Irish controversies to charge opponents with inconsistency. De Valera would have been more than human if—so bitterly divided were the Treatyites and anti-Treatyites—he had spared his opponents on an occasion which provided so much political ammunition. O'Higgins had no particular feeling of resentment that the national emergency had not produced a closing of the ranks. Ever since the Civil War, he had been implacable in his hostility to de Valera. He made no effort to disguise it, and he was very angry with anyone whom he suspected of even parleying with him.

Figures were not O'Higgins's strong point, and the financial details of the revised Treaty were not of such interest to him as the possibility he saw of a new era in the relations between England and Ireland. The Civil War had bedevilled any slender hope of Irish unity ; the atmosphere in London made O'Higgins hopeful that there was a possibility of making up lost ground. Craig had proved more agreeable and reasonable than the Free State party had expected. (Only Cosgrave had met him before.) Baldwin, Churchill and Birkenhead had all seemed friendly.

At a reference to the absence of Griffith and Collins from these discussions so soon after the Treaty negotiations, it was observed that tears came for a moment into Churchill's eyes, and Birkenhead proved helpful in every difficulty, appearing to see the Irish case with perfect fairness and sympathy. His parliamentary utterances have been used against him in Ireland to show his hostility to the Irish people. These speeches are usually printed with the phrases, that might modify this impression, omitted. O'Higgins believed that Birkenhead was a friend of Ireland, and said so in public.[11] The regard that the Englishman had for him is illustrated by an incident which took place after O'Higgins died. The news of the murder threw Birkenhead into a state of acute dejection. Shortly afterwards, at a dinner given to him in honour of his birthday, an English statesman—afterwards a Cabinet Minister— was invited to propose his health. In the course of his toast, the speaker said : " It must be a source of great satisfaction to Lord Birkenhead that no one has been murdered in Ireland for two days." Whereupon, Birkenhead, black as thunder, rose to his feet, ripped the orator to pieces in a savage speech and left the room.

Birkenhead could have enormously enhanced his position in the Unionist Party if he had refused to take part in the Irish settlement. Having taken that step, he had, in order to win over the Tories, to make a case that no concessions worth mentioning had been made to Ireland, and endeavour to show that what he did was entirely to the advantage of England. Similarly, the Tory Press, when Baldwin was in power, hailed the new arrange- ment of 1925 as shrewd British diplomacy. Years before, Collins had complained that his opponents preferred to accept facts from an unfriendly English Press than from himself or his colleagues.

If evidence is required that the Agreement contained some concessions to Irish opinion, it can be gleaned from the behaviour of Lord Salisbury, one of the British spokesmen. Inheriting the Cecil dislike for all things Irish, he could not be brought to put his name to the document. Twice, Baldwin sent for him ; twice, an excuse came back. The Prime Minister betrayed annoyance. " Tell Lord Salisbury that I insist on his presence immediately." At length the door opened, and O'Higgins described him, standing immobile in the doorway, " yellow with hate." He came to the table at which the representatives were seated and took his place. When the paper was put before him, he made no effort to sign it. Birkenhead seized a pen, pushed it into his hand, and told him to sign. He begged to be excused, and his signature does not appear on the document.[12]

The defects in this revision of the Treaty were an inheritance from the circumstances in which the original document was signed. It was not a case of trickery or intrigue. No treaty is satisfactory unless it is freely entered into by both sides. There was a large measure of compulsion behind the Irish signatures in 1921. Even had that agreement been voluntary and spontaneous, there would always have remained the question of the northern pocket. A cordial arrangement between England and Ireland in 1921 was, in the light of what had happened in the previous years, impossible and the prospect of the Six Counties willingly sending members to a Dublin Parliament was in the same case. No English Government in 1925 could have dared to alter the position by forcing the North to join the Free State. The charge made against the Agreement by de Valera's Party was that by signing it, the Free State Government sanctioned the partition of their country. It is probable that the concessions made to the Free State in return were chimerical and that no toll would ever have been exacted from her, but it was sound policy to settle that question for ever. Sir James Craig made a concession by signing the Agreement. Had he insisted on the publication of the Boundary Report he would have won an addition to the area under his Government. It would have been diverting to see the Northern Administration insist on adherence to the findings of the Commission to which it had refused to send a representative.

Baldwin and his Government did wish to repair the situation and did so in so far as it was reasonably possible. To the extent that this was achieved, a great deal must be attributed to the impression made upon the English Prime Minister by O'Higgins. O'Higgins set great store on the possibilities that lay in this change in the Tory Party's Irish policy. "The best day's work I ever did," said O'Higgins to Mrs. Baldwin as he left Chequers after the first meeting with her husband, "and the best day for Ireland." He had already conceived what he thought would prove the solution to this Partition question which still prevents Ireland from realizing her full potentialities, leaves her a truncated monument to the prejudices, follies and passions of men. O'Higgins said to an English statesman : "Try and get the King crowned

in Ireland as King of Ireland; that would pacify the Irish."
For that had become his dream. A separate Irish kingdom in
which the Northern Counties could, if they wished, have a local
administration, was to be the groundwork of the plan. The
details he discussed at length with various English representatives.
The King was to come to Ireland and be crowned by both the
Primates of the Catholic Church and the Church of Ireland in
Dublin.

"I want," said O'Higgins during the Boundary talks, "to see
the day when the Lord Mayor of Dublin will be cheered in the
streets of Belfast and the Lord Mayor of Belfast in the streets
of Dublin."

"And when will that be?" inquired a British civil servant.
"In ten years if I live, but they'll get me before that," he replied.[13]
For how long the idea of an Irish Kingdom had been in O'Higgins's
brain, we have no means of knowing, but it was characteristic
of the man to seize upon the facts which any situation presented
and plan an advance from that position. He never wasted time
or thought on repining or protesting.

He had been disappointed by the terms of the Treaty in 1921
but determined to build the nation upon the foundation that it
presented. He was thrown back once more by the failure of
MacNeill's mission, but began without delay to seek a new
solution. Just as he demanded peace in Ireland in order to build
a nation, he now sought a solution to Partition so that Ireland
might play her full part in the world. All the time he was
convinced that death was at his shoulder. He hoped to live to
see the realization of his dream but he was determined to lay
foundations properly even if other men had to complete the
structure.

At the Imperial Conference in 1926 he kept always in view
the possibilities of a united Ireland and one of his stiffest fights
was to secure an alteration in the King's titles which would fit
such a possibility.[14] The idea had been one of Griffith's.
Impressed by the dual monarchy that had existed in Austria and
Hungary, Griffith saw in such a plan a solution of the Irish-
English conflict. O'Higgins regarded the device as the only one
which provided a way in which Ulster's boasted loyalty to the
Crown could be reconciled with the separatist urge of the
South.

The idea of an Irish Republic had no part in the Gaelic past, nor was it the ideal of the luckless men who supported Charles the First, and suffered the penalty for their allegiance at the hands of Cromwell. It was unknown to the generation who took the field for Scottish James against Dutch William when they fought in Ireland for the throne of England. A child of the eighteenth century which Tone adopted in France, it came back to Ireland from America when Stephens returned from exile in 1857. Only in 1916 was it given a mystical character, for the men who were executed then had proclaimed a Republic and to many minds any deviation from that status was treachery and a denial of the aim for which those lives had been sacrificed.

O'Higgins had arrived at his political views, as a convinced Nationalist and Separatist, after much hard thinking and reading. His logical mind would not allow emotion to influence his decisions. He had, in the light of his reason, in the conditions that prevailed, to decide what he thought best to do for the country. A democratic system allowed the country to deprive him of the power to do these things if it did not approve of them. He had not been elected to govern the country according to what Pearse might have done faced with similar circumstances. A great deal of horror had already been let loose by those who affirmed that they were keeping faith with the dead. O'Higgins regarded his function as one which concerned itself with the welfare of the living. And he aspired to build for the future as well.

Each generation has to decide for itself. Its duty is to decide honestly. The past can be an inspiration or a lesson, it should not be a millstone.

To judge the merits of O'Higgins's plan it must be borne in mind that when he conceived it the new State was less than four years old. Its limbs were supple. After nearly a quarter of a century they have become brittle, the bones could not now be easily bent into a different shape.

At the time this book is written the Dual Monarchy plan seems as remote from practical politics as the conversion of the country to Confucianism. Southern Ireland feels the pangs of Partition in the soul only. It does not affect the belly. Indeed some there are who profit by the artificial barrier. It would be interesting to see whether the offer of O'Higgins's scheme now to the South as a means of ending Partition would be received with any enthusiasm. The extraordinary interest which a large section of the Irish public took in the wedding of Princess Elizabeth shows that the idea of monarchy is not in itself repugnant to a great many, but any step such as O'Higgins contemplated would now be regarded as retrograde and would find a determined and united opposition. Ireland may become a monarchy but the choice of a monarch would keep North and South at logger-heads. It is doubtful whether a ruler who was not a Catholic would be acceptable to the Southern Irish, it is unlikely that they would select any member of the House that ruled in the days of the Union.

CHAPTER XIV

IMPERIAL CONFERENCE

THE time spent by O'Higgins at the Disarmament Conference in Geneva was not wasted. He had opportunities of studying foreign politics, of meeting the statesmen of Great Britain and the Dominions and of watching the imperial machine in action in a new sphere. The Irish mind has been rather addicted to monomania where Great Britain is concerned and it was a new experience to meet Dominion representatives who were anxious to discuss Commonwealth matters and relations with Great Britain in the light of existing conditions and their common problems without regard to past injustices or historic grievances.

Desmond Fitz Gerald had been Minister for External Affairs since the formation of the Irish Free State. He was a man of extraordinary physical and moral courage, a loyal colleague. With a remarkable memory and considerable cultivation of mind, he did not possess the dynamic qualities which were required in the position that he held and once O'Higgins began to take an interest in foreign affairs, Fitz Gerald had to play second fiddle to him. At the Imperial Conference which opened in September, 1926, O'Higgins was the leader of the Irish delegation.

In the three years that had elapsed since the previous Conference the Free State had been firmly established and her representatives were more self-confident than they had been on the previous occasion. Moreover they went to the Conference with a plan and an objective. That objective was attained in part only, but O'Higgins was satisfied. Had he lived four years longer he would have seen its full attainment enshrined in the Statute of Westminster which, although fiercely assailed by de Valera's Party in the Dáil, when a resolution to adopt it was proposed, was by de Valera himself hailed as conferring on Ireland the power to do "anything that they can do in Britain as regards relations with the Crown."

Lord Balfour presided over the Committee on Imperial

Relations at the Conference in 1926 and the wording of the report owed something to his mellifluence of phrase. O'Higgins set himself the task of achieving a change in the King's title which remained ever since the establishment· of the Free State as " George V by the grace of God, of the United Kingdom of Great Britain and Ireland and of the British Dominions, etc." At the Conference it was agreed that this should be changed to " Great Britain, Ireland, etc." The exchange of comma for conjunction was not readily conceded and O'Higgins fought with such persistence that the change became known as " O'Higgins's comma." " A very interesting young man," said Balfour, " but rather pedantic, don't you think ? "

There was for O'Higgins greater significance in the altered title than the removal of an inexactitude ; his dream of a Dual Monarchy required just that alteration. If ever that dream became a reality, no alteration would be required in the King's title. Sir James Craig went in some alarm to London to find out the significance of the change, newspapers in Belfast expressed their suspicion that the Northern position was being undermined, but the British Home Secretary was able to satisfy Craig that no plot was afoot. A further development at this Conference was a statement of the alteration in the functions of Governors-General in Dominions. Formerly they represented the British Government in each Dominion. For some time they had represented the Crown and acted on the advice of the Dominion Governments without reference to England. But the Governor-General was still used as the channel for inter-government communication. Henceforth the Governments of Great Britain and the Dominions were to hold direct communication with each other.

A matter in which the Irish did not get their way was that of appeals to the Privy Council. To Dominions, such as Australia, formed on a federal basis, it seemed an advantage to have an outside tribunal to which they could refer. To a unified country like the Free State the machinery was unnecessary, as such cases did not arise, and there could be no rational argument for bringing suits to a court which in the nature of things could not be as well-versed in the Irish law or local circumstances as Irish judges sitting in Dublin.

O'Higgins had, himself, recently introduced legislation of a drastic character to discourage the taking of Irish cases to the Privy Council. In 1922 Lord Haldane, then Lord Chancellor, assured O'Higgins that the appeal was theoretical, having himself laid down the principle that the Privy Council should not interfere in the internal affairs of any Dominion but confine itself to the disputes of the non-unitary Dominions. Nevertheless, when in 1926 an unsuccessful litigant in a small land case, which had been decided by the Irish Supreme Court, appealed to the Privy Council, it was agreed by the Judicial Committee that the appeal should be heard.

O'Higgins promptly introduced a Bill which made the decision of the Supreme Court, in that case, the law of the land. Lynham v. Butler thus became a more celebrated cause than the subject matter warranted. O'Higgins was extremely forceful in his denial of the right of the Privy Council to override the Supreme Court. He quoted Lord Dunedin who, at the hearing, admitted that he was not familiar with the Land Act on which he was adjudicating. "Let us talk about this Judicial Committee of the Privy Council for what it is—a court," O'Higgins declared. "And if we agree that it is a court, we will be able, without a suggestion of irreverence or indelicacy, to ask whether it is a good court, whether it is a useful court, whether it is a necessary court."[1] He regarded the action of the Privy Council in the case of Lynham v. Butler as the first example of intervention by any person outside the Free State with its affairs since it was established.

In the summary of the proceedings at the Imperial Conference the weight of O'Higgins is felt in the phrases that refer to this particular problem. "It was no part of the policy of His Majesty's Government in Great Britain that questions affecting judicial appeals should be determined otherwise than in accordance with the wishes of the part of the Empire primarily affected." The question of appeals from the Irish Free State, the report discloses, was discussed but not pressed, "though it was made clear that the right was reserved to bring the matter up again at the next Imperial Conference."

O'Higgins's letters from London during the Conference are very different in tone from his Geneva correspondence. "We have made substantial headway," he wrote, "and are likely to make more next week. We have shoved around some excellent memoranda." Apart from conference and committee, "every day there is a lunch or dinner to be faced—generally both—and it is all rather a strain on the innards." The Laverys were as hospitable as ever to the Irish delegation and gave an enormous dinner party. All the delegations acted as hosts to one another. There was a dinner at the Irish Club at which Birkenhead's speech " was very good indeed "—" and this child, though very frightened, did pretty well too." At another dinner Carson was encountered and proved friendly, " talked a bit about the Lane pictures." Then there was a garden party at Buckingham Palace and a banquet to wind up the Conference. The last he dreaded but it proved " not over-stiff after all. ' G ' was very gracious and affable—he talked to me very brightly for fully a quarter of an hour." (King George expressed his gratified curiosity at meeting one whom he had read of as " that beast Kevin O'Higgins " —a phrase of Miss MacSwiney's.)

On the business side O'Higgins was satisfied with the impression which his delegation was making. " We are by far the best team in the Conference—bar one—and one would need to have been here in 1923 to realise the vast change in our position. If that change continues progressively, by 1929 things should be ripe for changing the name ' British Empire ' to ' Irish Empire.' "

O'Higgins was never carried away. Neither great names, nor the lavishness of the imperial entertainment affected his judgment which remained as cool as when he was debating in the Dáil. He wrote a full report of the men he was meeting to his wife. There is no indication of awe ; indeed his judgments are some-what iconoclastic.

" Dearest,

" Thanks for your long letter. It is good to know that you are pegging along all right while we are saving the Empire with our mouths (not to go lower) over here. Some of the work is, and some of the men are, interesting. We are seeing a lot of Balfour, who is Chairman of the Com-mittee dealing with inter-imperial relations. He is assisted by Chamberlain and Amery and occasionally Birkenhead. Hertzog, while a very decent and likeable kind of man, has not been a success—he talks a lot and none too clearly. Mackenzie-King has ' disimproved ' since 1923—gone fat and American and self-complacent. The onus of the ' status ' push—' anomalies and anachronisms '—has fallen very largely on ourselves and while it has made some head-way it would be greater if Hertzog was more effective and King a stone or two lighter. Bruce is too much concerned

getting himself into print to have much time to spare in
attempting to keep in touch with the work of the Conference. New Zealand must be rather like Northern Ireland
—it produces the same type of Jingo reactionary. Presiding
over all sits A. J. B. with a smile like 'moonlight on a
tombstone.'

" Still the *direction* is right and they can't change it—and
when we can't go far and fast the appropriate thing to say
is that it is the direction rather than the pace which really
matters. Consider it said. I think that it is likely that some
day Anglo-Irish relations will be represented by a Dual
Monarchy—two quite independent kingdoms with a common
King and, perhaps, a Defence Treaty. One by one, the
things that divide us from that position are being dropped.
They are neither numerous nor important. It presupposes,
of course, a United Ireland, which, you will say, is so remote
that one ought not to be trying to ever look beyond it.
Perhaps you're right—but Maeve, having a good constitution
and appetite, will see it all."

O'Higgins was disappointed with the other Commonwealth
leaders : Hertzog was obsessed with the idea of establishing the
right to secede and could not be persuaded that this was not the
only good to be obtained from membership of a group of nations.
Mackenzie-King came from Canada in the full glow of success
in a tussle with the Governor-General who had held that he had
the right to refuse to dissolve Parliament when the Prime
Minister no longer commanded a majority. On that issue King
fought and won an election. He came to London a satisfied man
without any desire to make further conquests. In Doctor O. D.
Skelton, the Secretary to the Canadian delegation, the Irish found
a real ally. He appreciated the fact that O'Higgins had a wider
vision of the Commonwealth idea than the other delegates, and
with his help it was arranged that Canada should put forward
suggestions at the Conference upon which the two delegations
had previously agreed. The Free State, as the froward child of
the party, was less likely to win an easy assent. Many of the balls
fired at the Conference by the Canadians were, unknown to the
other delegations, manufactured by the Irish. Bruce of Australia
was loud in his protestations of loyalty to the Empire. Amery
confessed to O'Higgins that he would be better pleased if Bruce

would refer to the British Empire rather less in his speeches and O'Higgins rather more in his.

By degrees O'Higgins succeeded in winning the confidence of Hertzog who eventually co-operated with the Irish in their line of approach to the problems of the Conference. When on his return to South Africa, Hertzog was reported to have said: "We have brought home the bacon," O'Higgins's comment was: "Irish bacon."

To a large section of the Irish population imperial relations were anathema, a larger section were indifferent; but to that portion of the population which accepted the status of the Free State for what it was, it was clear that the Irish were proving themselves to be as formidable in the replacing of the Empire by the Commonwealth as they had been in the building of that Empire. In the Dáil, Professor Magennis, Thomas Johnson on behalf of Labour, and Baxter for the Farmers' Party, attacked the report on the Conference which was presented by Desmond Fitz Gerald. "It appears to me," said Johnson, "that so far from having achieved an advance in the constitutional position of the Irish Free State, there has been, in fact, a retrogression." He argued that the appearance of unanimity on Foreign Policy at the Conference could have a bad effect on the League of Nations, which would have reason to fear the representation of the Dominions on the Council if they were pledged to vote together. Professor Magennis spoke at very great length. Deputy Baxter argued that the change in the King's title was a pity for, as it had been, it was unreal, which was appropriate; as it had become, it was an outrage to Nationalists who, like himself, did not care to get "so near the King."

O'Higgins was not very expansive in his reply. He recalled the attention of the House to the fact that he had gone to London to attend an Imperial Conference and not to negotiate a treaty with Great Britain.

"Now, I do not complain over-much of the state of mind revealed in the speeches of Deputy Magennis and Deputy Baxter. One has to remember the antecedents of our whole position; one has to remember that for very many centuries we were an unfree people, and that we have borne the fetters so long, they have eaten so deep that even when they are struck off, there are those amongst us, believing or professing to believe, that they are still there; those amongst us who cannot realize their freedom and are unable to raise their heads and look their fellow-man in the face and say we are a free people. The whine of the slave was in those two speeches."[2]

He read over the Balfourian definition of the Commonwealth which had been inscribed in the summary of the proceedings. THEY ARE AUTONOMOUS COMMUNITIES WITHIN THE BRITISH EMPIRE, EQUAL IN STATUS, IN NO WAY SUBORDINATE ONE TO ANOTHER IN ANY RESPECT OF THEIR DOMESTIC OR EXTERNAL AFFAIRS, THOUGH UNITED BY A COMMON ALLEGIANCE TO THE CROWN, AND FREELY ASSOCIATED AS MEMBERS OF THE BRITISH COMMONWEALTH OF NATIONS.

"Deputy Magennis is not satisfied," said O'Higgins, who had listened for two hours to the Professor's harangue. "I am not surprised. I do not think Deputy Magennis would be satisfied with even an entirely different status, an entirely different form of Government. I think Deputy Magennis would be dissatisfied, profoundly dissatisfied, with a Republic, except on the conditions that he were President of that Republic. In a speech which it might be unkind, perhaps, to describe as lingering sourness long drawn out, he analyzed, or attempted to analyze, this report and by every device, of which he is master, of misrepresentation and distortion, he attempted to show that we have been, so to speak, busily engaged for five weeks in London riveting fetters on the limbs of our unfortunate country, and Deputy Baxter shook his head and said he was afraid that was so."[3]

O'Higgins, as a rule, reserved his more vigorous denunciations for those who had changed their political allegiance. He could not understand fickleness, change of colour, or the breaking of old ties. Hence he was, in spite of himself, a Party man and he could not tolerate a man who, having taken one side when he might have taken another, decided in the course of time to shift his ground. He made his own mind up quickly in matters of administration but, where principle was concerned, he thought deliberately, suspecting intuition, thinking of the end before he started on the course, for he regarded those who changed their course as too unstable or deficient in judgment to take part in the public life of a country.

From this it must not be assumed that O'Higgins was ponderous.

He was very far from that. McCartan was one of the members of the first Dáil who knew the outside world and he was particularly struck by the rapidity with which O'Higgins gave decisions when appealed to in his ministerial capacity. He was, in that respect, like Michael Collins who had administrative ability of the highest order. But when he spoke on matters of moment in public nothing in O'Higgins's manner suggested that he was thinking on his feet. Everything he said was spoken as though he had learnt it by heart.

During the Imperial Conference in London in November, 1926, O'Higgins, acting on impulse and without disclosing his plan to anyone, left his hotel and went to 5 Eaton Place where Lord Carson was then living. He gave his name to the servant who opened the door and asked if Carson was in and whether he could see him. He was shown into the study where the old man was sitting alone. " To what do I owe this honour ? " he inquired. O'Higgins came to the point at once and outlined his plan for a Kingdom of Ireland. Carson listened with interest and then asked him what was Birkenhead's opinion. Birkenhead had agreed to sponsor the idea when the occasion arose. " In that event," said Carson, " I will do nothing to spike it." He was old, he explained, and would take no part in the project but he would do nothing to impede it although he thought it premature. At parting, he said : " Mr. O'Higgins, each of us loves Ireland. We can shake hands on that."[4]

On the day following, O'Higgins told L. S. Amery, who was then Secretary of State for the Dominions, about this conversation. Amery then discussed the details of the plan. Would a United Ireland have the King's head on coins ? Would it restore the Union Jack in any form ? There would be no difficulty about the coins, O'Higgins thought. (The new Irish coinage had only recently been issued, the designs representing birds, fish, and animals of the farmyard.) The flag would, he thought, be a difficulty. A crown on a blue background might be accepted instead of the tricolour. O'Higgins stressed the fact that Ireland was not a Colony that had become a Dominion, her origins and traditions were in the past. In this she differed from all the other Dominions. He wanted a closer economic relationship with England than that which then subsisted between Great Britain and the other members of the Commonwealth. He also asked for a guarantee for Ireland's defence in return for which Ireland would undertake to make a definite military force available for imperial emergencies.

During the following summer it was rumoured that Lord Londonderry had come to Dublin on secret political business. Whatever the truth of this, it was symptomatic of the fact that O'Higgins was still proceeding with his plan. He discussed it with ardour on his return from the Naval Conference in Geneva, in July, 1927. In June Amery met him again, lunching at the Laverys', and noted that he was rather depressed at the ingratitude of public life. "It was not long," Amery wrote, "before he was destined to experience it in its most sinister form."

O'Higgins affirmed his belief on many occasions that he would solve the Boundary Question if he lived. Those who planned his death may not have cared for his solution, but it cannot be said to have failed because that contingency, which he never forgot, released him from his undertaking. No one has made a proposal since that time which bears the least likelihood of being accepted in the North as well as on the South of the Border. Would he have succeeded? For how many years was that union, which the inescapable logic of facts will eventually insist upon, delayed by his death? These are questions which no man can answer.

CHAPTER XV

THE LAST PHASE

" We knew his foes too well to marvel at his death."

—R. N. D. WILSON.

THE Imperial Conference had been a personal success for O'Higgins. The *Irish Times*, always quite as imperial in politics as the London *Times*, was enthusiastic at the part which the Free State had played in Commonwealth affairs. But in Ireland, as a whole, there was no enthusiasm. The Commonwealth was regarded as the business of Great Britain, and a refusal to attend the Conference would perhaps have won the Government a tactical political success, as indeed would any purely negative gesture which could have been interpreted as a blow struck for Irish pride.

That O'Higgins had helped to pave the way which led to the Statute of Westminster, and the full emancipation of the Dominions in 1931, would also, if it could have been known, have been of very little interest. When that Statute was passed it was described by one of de Valera's followers as an act intended " to nail us, to copper-fasten us, for ever to the British Empire and its King."[1]

So far as the internal politics of Ireland were concerned, a more important event was the repudiation of de Valera by the Sinn Fein organization in March, 1926, and the formation by him of a new party in May, known as Fianna Fáil (Warriors of Ireland). The cause of the split was a proposal by de Valera that a drive should be made to remove the Oath of Allegiance taken in the two Irish Parliaments, and, when that had been achieved, Republicans should take their seats in those assemblies. In the previous December, "the Army of the Republic" had withdrawn its allegiance from de Valera, and, in Cosgrave's phrase, " cut itself adrift completely from all control of anybody."

It was clear that de Valera's steps were now turned towards the Dáil. The late Judge O'Donnell asked John Dillon to meet

de Valera to discuss the possibility of an approach by the latter
to Baldwin to see if the Oath could be dropped. Dillon agreed
to see de Valera, and, at O'Donnell's request, sent all the servants
out so that the visit of the Republican to the Home Ruler would
not become the subject of gossip. De Valera arrived at nine and
stayed until the early hours, but discussed only the history of the
past. The Oath was not mentioned.[2]

Cosgrave was the first to suggest that something be done to
force the Republicans into the Dáil and put an end to the absurdity
of any extra-mural opposition. He knew that such a happening
would mean, eventually, his defeat in Parliament, but he argued
that it would be wrong to allow that to weigh against the obvious
advantage to the country of having so large a section of the
electorate constitutionally represented. O'Higgins believed that
de Valera would enter the Dáil, would gain power, would prove
incompetent, and would lose office in a few months. De Valera
became Prime Minister in 1932 and remained in that position
until 1948. But O'Higgins died in 1927.

A General Election was certain to be held in 1927, but the
Government did nothing to woo the electorate. O'Higgins
rushed a stringent Liquor Bill through both Houses, encountering
as he did so the deadliest hatred from publicans—in Ireland an
influential and wealthy class throughout the country. No one
resented this measure so strongly as Governor-General Healy.
He did his best to dissuade O'Higgins from persisting with it,
and when two emissaries from the Cabinet came to him with the
Bill for signature, he kept them for hours while he discussed it
clause by clause. At length one of the messengers exclaimed :
" A Governor-General is not expected to be a lawyer." " But
at least he is expected to be able to read," was Healy's reply.

At the meeting held by the leaders of the Government Party,
then known as Cumann na nGaedheal, to see how funds could
be raised for the election campaign, J. J. Walsh, the Minister for
Posts and Telegraphs, inquired how much it was likely to cost.
The figure suggested was about £20,000. " Let us say £30,000,"
said the Minister. " I can raise that without any trouble. I have
here a list of names of men who will subscribe it." O'Higgins
expressed considerable surprise, and, being no means naïve, inquired
whether these subscribers were enthusiasts for the cause or was
any consideration expected for the promised assistance. No, it
would be given freely, but on the understanding that the Govern-

ment would change its tariff policy. There was at this time a
Tariff Commission sitting, its function being to weigh the case
for giving a protective duty to any industry that sought it.
O'Higgins suggested that these generous subscribers should submit
their applications to the Tariff Commission at once. That brought
matters to a head; the philanthropists demanded immediate
protection for their respective industries, and would hear no
nonsense about a Tariff Commission.

O'Higgins took the list, and his hand trembled as it always did
when he was moved. "I should take these names," he said, speaking
very slowly, "and mark them on a black list but I will not look
at them because I realize some may have been approached and
this suggestion made to them rather than by them. On that
account I will do this instead." He crumpled the paper up and
threw it into the fire.

Help from that source having been treated in the manner which
O'Higgins felt it deserved and the publicans antagonized, there was
yet another trouble facing the Government. On the night of the
14th November, 1926, the Irish Republican Army launched
attacks on twelve police barracks in various parts of the country
and killed two unarmed Guards. In Co. Waterford, the police
went berserk and took their revenge on the backs of some Republican prisoners who had been captured in a raid a few days before.
The recrudescence of I.R.A. outrages was disturbing enough,
but on O'Higgins, as Minister for Justice, fell the ultimate responsibility for the indiscipline of the police. He was in London at the
Imperial Conference at the time of the raid, and wrote to his
wife :—

> "Hotel Cecil,
> Strand, London, W.C.
> Wednesday.

"My dearest,

"Thanks for your little letter. I hope you are not worried
about last Sunday's happenings. I am not. It is unfortunate,
of course, but it is just a kind of stunt flash in the pan and need
not be taken too seriously. Things are drawing to a close here
and I am in hopes that I will be able to get home on Tuesday
or Wednesday of next week. We have done quite well all
round and in Constitutional matters have made quite definite

and important progress.   It is recognized that this is by far
the most important Imperial Conference which has yet been
held and we can claim to have left our mark all over its
proceedings.   Lord, if only people at home had a true sense
of their interests they would seize the opportunity of next
year's Elections to steam-roll the Irregular elements and go
full steam ahead for a United Ireland and a Dual Monarchy.
If only they would be got to realize how injurious to real
progress events like those of last Sunday are !   Given a fair
chance and decent standards among our people the thing
would be practical politics within five years.   If things were
going all right one could talk straight to men like Birkenhead
and Churchill here and Craig and Andrews in the North-
East—and the ' Kingdom of Ireland ' would be within sight—
instead of which we have lousy futile Anglophobia militating
alike against Unity and complete *formal* Independence.   I
shouldn't run on like this talking shop in a little home letter,
pet lamb, but the thing is very much on my mind and I *know*
the thing is perfectly attainable.   I want you to understand
that all this lopping of old forms and abandonment of old
claims which has gone on for the last month has left a clear
open avenue to that solution—if only we had a smaller percentage of bloody fools in our population. . . . I hope I
will see the little garrison in good order next week.   I haven't
had a spare half-hour yet to make the essential purchases but
I won't forget.

" Best love, K."

Immediately after the murders, President Cosgrave introduced
an Emergency Bill to deal with the situation.   He revealed the
fact that for two years the I.R.A. had been very active collecting
arms and ammunition.   Help was coming from sources in America,
and new recruits were joining.   The Bill was intended as a means
of granting the right to detain on suspicion and withhold the
right of Habeas Corpus in times of emergency.   It was to be a
permanent measure, but only enforceable by proclamation at a
time of national crisis.

Returning from the Imperial Conference, O'Higgins found
himself once more in an unpopular rôle.   There was, he explained,
" a new vintage of Republicans, young men, boys of fourteen,
fifteen, sixteen and seventeen years of age, seized on by propagan-

dists, mostly feminine propagandists, and inspired to commit utterly ruthless, desperate, irresponsible actions of this kind."

Fifty persons arrested in connection with the raids were released because "the reaction of the general public to these occurrences was good, quite good, and the action of the Dáil and the Seanad in passing in a very short space of time the legislation which was thought necessary, was simply an index and a reflection of the state of public opinion throughout the country."[3]   He believed that the raids were planned by the I.R.A. as a form of activity "to hold their dwindling numbers together, to enable them to give those foolish young boys whom they are able to draw into the net of their organization the belief that they were heroes and patriots doing wonderful work for the advancement of the country and its prospects."

And then he asked a question to which he was before long to supply the answer. "What do people responsible for endeavouring to maintain this organization in existence hope to gain ? To put it quite crudely, who are they going to shoot and why and to what purpose ?"[4]

O'Higgins then spoke of the attacks made by the Waterford Guards on prisoners who had been captured in a raid on barracks there. "I refer to it with deep regret," he said, "and a feeling of humiliation. . . . This State can be maintained, and this State must be maintained, without resort to methods of that kind . . . I want to say that I apologize through the Dáil to the people as well as to the individuals who suffered injury for this excess and abuse of authority on the part of the servants of the people."

O'Higgins sent for Eoin O'Duffy, Chief of Police, and demanded the dismissal of the men responsible for the beating of prisoners. O'Duffy took up the defence of the men and threatened to resign. "Resign then," said O'Higgins, white with indignation. O'Duffy left him.

In this matter, O'Higgins was prevailed upon, much against his will, to allow an inquiry to be held for the purpose of giving compensation to the injured men, and he urged that part of this should be borne by those found guilty as well as by the State. "Certainly," he promised the Dáil, "it is the last occasion on which any plea of provocation, or extenuating circumstances, or any plea of meritorious past service, will be allowed to stand between any man and the utmost rigour, not merely of the disciplinary code of the Garda, but of the Criminal Law."[5]

A plaque in commemoration of the murdered Guards was erected in the police headquarters at Phoenix Park. O'Higgins was asked to unveil it. Of all his achievements, that which gave him proudest pleasure was the formation of an efficient and unarmed police force. The very early history of the Guards had been unfortunate, but, under O'Duffy, they had been a credit to themselves and the country.

On the way to the unveiling, O'Higgins was anxious. He did not, as a rule, suffer from stage fright, but on this occasion he had not been able to compose a speech in advance ; the right words would not come, and, for once, he would have to speak impromptu. In due course, he unveiled the tablet, and then, speaking with concealed but considerable emotion, he said : " I profoundly hope that there will be no addition to this Roll of Honour, and that these men who died defending and upholding the people's peace have now found peace eternal." They were the last words he was destined to speak in public.

O'Duffy proved so intransigent that the question of his resignation came before the Cabinet, but he was personally devoted to O'Higgins, who was satisfied that he could always keep in check this efficient but absurdly vain individual.

After the murder of O'Higgins, a smoke-screen of rumour was put up ; his morals were questioned, a *crime passionel* was even whispered of ; but the strongest of these rumours was that members of the police had revenged themselves for dismissals or insured against further changes. There is no foundation for this gossip beyond the fact that there had been indiscipline in the Guards and O'Higgins was the Minister who had to deal with it. There is no more ground for this belief than there is for another which was current—that Army mutineers were taking revenge after three years. Assassination in Ireland since the reform of the land laws has been invariably political in motive, and no one who knows the character of the people would credit, without proof, that discontented servants of the State, however disgruntled, would form themselves into a murder gang for no other reason than personal resentment against a Minister. " He had the blood of a freeman in his veins," said Patrick Hogan. " He hated slaves. Centuries of subjection have made a great many slaves in this country, and they hated him as a standing reproach to them. It is they, the slaves, who have killed him, the freeman."[6]   They who slew him knew well what they were doing. " It was as the chief moral architect of the Free State," wrote Æ (George Russell), "that he was recognized by the hundreds of thousands who followed or watched his funeral with a deeper emotion we think than was felt for any Irish leader since the death of Parnell."[7]

Without any desire to dramatize himself—for there was very little of the exhibitionist in his character—O'Higgins used to speak of his inevitable assassination as other men speak of natural death ; when making plans for the future he used sometimes to add : "If they don't get me before that." By "they," he did not intend to refer to dismissed officers or reprimanded policemen any more than he meant the members of the "licensed trade," the medical profession, or other bodies with which he had come in conflict. It was not fear but a stoical acceptance of destiny. He did not brood upon it or take any precautions for his safety. Friends used to meet him walking to Blackrock along the Stillorgan Road on his way home in the evening, often far ahead of his accompanying detective. In the summer he used to rise very early and go down to Blackrock for a swim. He was never maudlin. An extract from a letter to a colleague, written before going to a meeting in London, is almost schoolboyish in its light-heartedness.

"I am only doing half-time, knocking off at two or three every day and swimming and walking industriously (training for the General Election). I am feeling very bucked to-day because I swam ten lengths of a fifty yard bath without a halt this morning. The channel is wider of course. But it's not so dusty for a poor tired politeeshien ! Hogan not back yet, which may account for the unnatural calm. A Chinaman whose wife died described himself as ' velly lonely but velly peaceful.' I must remember that for H. when he returns. Do you read the newspapers ? I hope you appreciate your responsibility for Partition (*vide* Tom O'Donnell) and then the eternal and ubiquitous ' Long Fellow ' forever blowing bubbles. Forgive that—it's the salt water. Good-bye now, get nice and fat. Who was it who hated lean men about him ? "

In preparation for the General Election, the Government party prepared a record of their achievements. It set out the work done in five years, of which one had been dissipated by Civil War, and the others rendered inevitably less fruitful by the blight of the first year on the country's credit and financial resources. Despite that, the Shannon Scheme, which was the first hydroelectric scheme the country had known, was started at a cost of £5,200,000. The Land Act of 1923 had resulted in the acquisition of 157,526 acres of land for division among landless men, while sales of a further 61,236 acres had been agreed, and negotiations for the purchase of 971,000 acres were in progress. This was the work of the brilliant Patrick Hogan, who had also taken radical steps to improve the agricultural trade of the country which, apart from cattle, had been wholly neglected in the past. Income Tax had come down from six shillings to three shillings in the pound in five years. The duties on tea and coffee had been abolished, the duty on sugar reduced, so that if the taunt was true that this was not a poor man's party, it had reduced his cost of living.

No rash promises were made in this manifesto, and it disclosed on all such questions as Protection and the revival of the Irish language a conservative progressiveness rather than a fanatical zeal. It was a sober statement, an adult statement. Nowhere did the tocsin sound.

Holding it in his hand, O'Higgins declared that it was a record any Government might be proud of. He stood for the constituency of South Dublin, where he was living, instead of his birthplace, which, after his father's murder, he determined not to represent again. His opponents contended that this was a flight from anticipated defeat, and that he was contesting a seat in which there was a larger proportion of ex-Unionists than in any other in the Free State. In fact two ex-Unionists, of whom one was Major Bryan Cooper, contested the seat, and between them polled over 13,000 first preference votes, so that there was not much significance in the taunt. Nevertheless, O'Higgins headed the poll. Cosgrave's Party was returned with the largest number of seats 47, de Valera's followers secured 44, Labour 22, Independents 14, Farmers 11, other parties 15 out of a total of 153 seats. This was for the Government Party a loss of 11 seats, while de Valera's remained the same as in 1923. Professor Magennis, Joseph McGrath and others who had seceded from the Government Party, whether on account of the Army mutiny crisis or the Boundary settlement, all failed in their constituencies. It was clear that the Cumann na nGaedheal Party, elected to put through the Treaty, was disintegrating. Now that law and order had been restored, separate groups—the Nationalist League (the old Irish Party under the leadership of William Redmond) for one—came into being. The burden of government for Cosgrave's administration had been so heavy

that all the energies of the leaders went into their task and they
had neglected their interests as a political party. So, while they
governed, de Valera, without any responsibility and free from
the duties of a normal leader of a parliamentary Opposition, was
able to build up his organization and seize on every possible
opportunity presented by the Government to their critics. The
absence of a party newspaper was probably a handicap to de Valera,
but it had the effect of leaving the Government's supporters with
a false feeling of security. Moreover, their preoccupation with
administration produced—as it always does with a party long in
power—a gulf between the Government and the people.

The Cosgrave Administration laid the foundations of the State ;
but they made no appeal to the imagination of the young, no
concessions to the illogical, no gestures to the poor, no corners
for the speculators. They bribed nobody. It was magnificent
but it was not politics. It was a tragedy for the country that the
Civil War had produced an unnatural alignment of forces. A
conservative or bourgeois party, supported by the larger farmers
in the country, opposed by a Labour Party, would have provided
the healthiest form of political division in the nation. The
Treaty, the Oath, and the other questions upon which the two
largest Parties were divided, did harm in taking the mind of the
public off social problems. The slums of Dublin were a far greater
disgrace to the country than any of the national humiliations
which were laid at the door of the Government. Moreover, the
fact that the second largest Party refused to sit in the Dáil, on
account of the Oath, sterilized the country's political life. Cosgrave
was given a majority in the Dáil out of all proportion to that
which he had in the country.

O'Higgins was dissatisfied with the result of the election, and
made no secret of his chagrin. Writing to a friend in the country,
he said : " The general result is not good and I fear that quite
literally the people will have to pay for it. I refer, of course, to
its reactions on credit. Had de Valera got thirty or thirty-five seats
and ourselves sixty we could borrow at 5 per cent. What will the
rate be now ? If our interest rate rises only a point—it is 100,000
in 10,000,000. If we have to find an extra 100,000 per annum,
this spells new taxation (the shilling back on income tax) or the
scrapping of services. There are, of course, other reactions. The
mass-mind of the North-East was beginning to feel envy—and
envy has an element of admiration. Now they will feel justified once

more. They will feel that safety lies in aloofness, in isolation. I do not myself see any real alternative to Cosgrave forming a government, and so long as Fianna Fáil stays out his parliamentary position will be comfortable enough. Out of the hundred odd members in the Dáil he could count on sixty for every-day purposes. When, however, Fianna Fáil find—as they will—that we are not going to break the Treaty to save their faces, they will probably split—by design and agreement or otherwise—and a proportion of them will take the Oath and enter the Dáil. . . . Then farmers, independents *et hoc genus* would probably draw closer to us while Labour would try to play a balance of power game. It is a rotten picture enough and we can only do our best. The root of the trouble is that people seem to believe that cause and effect work out relentlessly in every sphere except politics. They will not see in impaired credit and the long postponement of all prospects of unity the inevitable result of the unwise dissipation of pro-Treaty strength in the country when the second largest party in the State was challenging its foundations. They would saw at the bough they were sitting on. They haven't cut it through but they have weakened it perilously."

In the new Government, O'Higgins was Vice-President of the Executive Council, Minister for Justice and also for External Affairs. Within a few days of attaining office, he set off for Geneva to attend the Conference for limitation of Naval Armaments. As regards a fleet, Ireland was practically in the position of Switzerland, but O'Higgins attached importance to the meeting because by his attendance he emphasized the identity of his country as a separate State which could not be represented by Great Britain, even though she, of all the Commonwealth, was the only one interested in the subject-matter of the Conference.

By appointing a Minister to Washington in 1924, the Free State had been a pioneer, and O'Higgins never let slip an opportunity for breaking through the diplomatic unity of the British Empire.

It was clear at Geneva that America and Japan, who, with Great Britain, were the only three countries at the Conference with navies of any consequence, and who were accordingly vitally interested in any questions of limitation of sea-power, were likely to object when they found that each unit of the British Empire insisted on having an individual vote on each question. For, in matters of policy, it was clear that, however divided in points of detail, ultimately all would hang together, as all were depending on the same Navy. This gave the British Commonwealth an overwhelming superiority at any conference.

Bridgeman, the British First Lord of the Admiralty, suggested that not more than two Dominions should be ever present at the same session. O'Higgins made it clear that the Irish Free State would not feel bound by any decision arrived at when she was not represented, and he urged that the expression " British Empire " be avoided and " the component States of the British Commonwealth " used in its stead.

The South African and Canadian representatives followed the lead given by O'Higgins, who, on this occasion, as at the Imperial Conference, knew best of all the Dominion statesmen what exactly he wanted. The Free State had a very definite point of view and aim where the Commonwealth was concerned. Bridgeman and Lord Cecil, for England, agreed to expunge the description " British Empire " from the minutes.

The Conference broke down, none of the great nations wishing to be the first to emasculate itself, and a Japanese jurist remarked : " The Conference has been a failure for all except the Irish. They have used it to assert their international status, in which they have fully succeeded."

Writing to his wife from Geneva, O'Higgins suggested that " both the British and the U.S.A. will be anxious to sign *something* to give the appearance of some progress in limitation of armaments but how important the something will be is another matter." During the Imperial Conferences he had formed an unflattering judgment of the abilities of the other Dominion statesmen and he found nothing on this occasion to alter his opinion. " Canada and South Africa," he wrote, " will only fight in *support* of us. They have not yet learned to take a stand on their own and in any case they only see things when they are pointed out to them. Their own vision is entirely second-hand and derivative." But a naval conference can never be a major worry to the representative of a country which boasts a navy consisting of one small ship and the trip was more of a holiday than a task.

" I am feeling much less the leavings of an election campaign than I was four days ago. I rout out Walshe and Costello at 6.45 every morning and we swim in the lake before breakfast. . . . One of my anxieties about being delayed here is the fear that my younger daughter will have forgotten me before I get back."

This letter arrived in Dublin only a day before the writer. On Saturday, the ninth of July, he came back to Dublin, and a journalist, anxious for copy, waylaid him walking home as usual with a bulky parcel under his arm, toys for his daughters which, he admitted, he would probably spend the evening playing with himself.   Among these toys was a small gramophone which was seized upon by Patrick Hogan who pursued O'Higgins round the house while it wheezed and crackled away, in an asthmatic rendering of some tune which at the time was loved not wisely but too well.

There had been a rumour in the village that Cosgrave was going to be assassinated, and when Mrs. O'Higgins told her husband he rejected the idea.   Neither of them knew that, on the previous Sunday, a rumour of O'Higgins's assassination had been current in the West of Ireland.   It was now over two years since the police and the Army Intelligence Service had got tidings of a plot to ambush a car in which he was travelling with his wife and the McGilligans, with whom they had been spending an Easter vacation.   On that occasion General O'Duffy met them in the outskirts of Dundalk and refused to let the car go on until Major-General Hogan, in command of the Army in that area, arrived on the scene.   Hogan insisted that the car should proceed under a heavy escort.   The convoy driving fast arrived in Dublin without any incident.

That evening when O'Higgins returned home, while waiting for some colleagues who were coming to dine, he spoke to his wife about his plans for a united Ireland ; he told her of his talk with Carson and his plans for Irish unity.   " The North," he declared, "will be in within five years."   He now enlarged upon the details of the plan, some of which he had discussed with Amery.   Ireland, he thought, was monarchically inclined.   She needed a king.   The King of England should come to Ireland and be crowned in Phoenix Park by the Primates of the two Churches as *King of Ireland*.   He should visit Ireland for at least six weeks each year and leave a Lord Lieutenant in his absence.   The flag and the National Anthem should both be replaced by others more acceptable to the North.   The new flag should be St. Patrick's blue with a harp on it.   (Talking to Amery a year before this a crown had been suggested.)   The Parliament should be in Dublin but the North could have a parliament in Belfast for local business if it was desired.

When the visitors arrived the conversation turned to other topics : he remonstrated with one of his colleagues who suggested that the Party should refuse to form a government when the Dáil reassembled but should leave the task to a coalition of the opposing parties. To do this, so long as they were the largest Party, was a breach of faith with the electorate, O'Higgins contended. Then he left his friends and went up to bed. He came back to the room after some time, half undressed, looking, he explained, for the toy gramophone which he promised to leave beside Maeve's bed and which he had hidden in the piano to protect himself from Hogan. Before going out of the room, he turned to McGilligan and said, in the mock Irish way in which he habitually talked when at home : " It is when I am undressing that I do be thinking over things and I have been turning over in my mind what we were discussing to-night. You know enough about natural history to understand how the coral insects make their beautiful little islands. I do be thinking that the part some of us may have to play is to leave our bones like the coral insects behind us for others to build upon."

After his friends left he went downstairs to look in his shelves for a book containing a poem " The Song of Defeat " by Stephen Gwynn. It was a favourite of his, and when he could not find the book he refused to go to bed until he had searched the house and discovered it eventually in the guest room. Then he sat on his bed and read it aloud before going to sleep ; read of :

" the women of Eire keening
For Brian slain at his tent "—

and on through those heroic verses which tell of Ireland in the ancient, kingly days—

" Of a land, where to fail is more than to triumph,
And victory less than defeat."

In the morning, he was up before breakfast to have his usual swim at Blackrock. It was one of those fine summer days when it seems that nature is entirely genial, that life must be pleasant, and that evil, if it exists, has been shamed into hiding below the ground.

Before breakfast O'Higgins played with the children and inspected all the toys which Maeve laid out for him. Hogan had obtained possession of the gramophone again and was making a nuisance of himself. Everyone felt happy and O'Higgins had completely cast off the mood in which he had gone to bed. Hogan always drew out the best from him and their conversation was very lively this morning, the first they had spent together since O'Higgins had gone to Geneva. There is no diversion so pleasant as the verbal duelling of two friends who have wit and who are mentally in tune with one another. Wit is a dangerous weapon for any man to carry about in the world, it sometimes goes off at inappropriate moments, its mere presence is assumed by the timid to carry a threat to themselves. It can only be produced with safety when the combatants are well matched and trust one another.

A meal seldom passed without a discussion of politics, and when they had laughed enough, O'Higgins put out his idea that there should be some form of honour which the State could award to those who served her without any public recognition. " There are so many fine fellows," he said, " who do such fine things so quietly."

The household had gone to church earlier in the morning, and O'Higgins went off by himself to twelve o'clock Mass at Booterstown. At the corner, where Cross Avenue meets Booterstown Avenue, there was a seat, and Mrs O'Higgins, on her way home from an earlier Mass, noticed, without attaching any significance to the fact, that men were sitting there. When O'Higgins left Dunamase to go to the church he did not bother to call his personal guard, who had accompanied him on the swimming excursion earlier in the morning. His wife was in the hall arranging flowers ; he kissed her, and went to see his daughter, Maeve, who was playing with her toys. The child had first to be kissed, then the dolls in turn, and finally Una, the baby of the family, asleep in her pram. A policeman stood on duty at the side gate of the garden through which O'Higgins passed. A few minutes later a burst of revolver fire was heard coming from the road. Hogan, who was waiting for a friend to take him out to play golf, ran from the house, revolver in hand, in the direction of the shooting.

Dunamase is only a few hundred yards from the corner where Booterstown Avenue joins Cross Avenue, and, as O'Higgins approached the turn in the road, a boy on a bicycle gave a signal to a motor-car which was parked on the side of the road. A man came out and fired at point-blank range. O'Higgins turned and tried to run for cover to the gate of Sans Souci, a house on the other side of the road. His attacker followed, firing as he ran ; O'Higgins had only strength enough to cross the road. On the other side he fell upon the path, whereupon two other men rushed out from behind the car and fired at him as he lay upon the ground. One stood across the body, pouring the contents of his revolver into it. The murder party then drove away, and the first person to arrive on the scene was an old colleague, Eoin MacNeill.

O'Higgins was alive, but in dreadful agony. One bullet had entered the head behind the ear. Six were in his body. But he had not lost consciousness, and when MacNeill bent over him, he murmured : " I forgive my murderers," and then, after a pause while he collected strength to speak, he said : " Tell my wife I love her eternally." The discipline with which he had habitually controlled his mind did not leave him now, and lying weltering in his blood on the dusty road in the torrid midday sun, he dictated a will. A priest came and administered the Last Sacraments, a doctor was summoned and attended him there on the side of the road until an ambulance arrived.

" I couldn't help it," he said to his wife when they carried him into his house and laid him on an improvised bed on the dining-room floor. " I did my best."

He lay pale but fully conscious, speaking slowly and clearly. That he was going to die he was quite certain, but he was gay in the face of death. Of himself, or his pain, he never spoke, but he asked for each of his family in turn, and sent messages to those who were away. Again and again he affirmed that he forgave his murderers. To his wife he said : " You must have no bitterness in your heart for them." Then remembering the problem with which the Government would be faced, he exclaimed : " My colleagues ! My poor colleagues ! " His friend, Surgeon Barniville, who had been summoned from a distance, arrived early, and noticing his pain, lay down to support him with his arm. " Barney hasn't had his lunch," said O'Higgins, looking up at his wife : to each of those who tended him he had a word of thanks and apology for the trouble he was giving. A doctor offered brandy. He refused it. " Every man ought to drink his quota," he said ; " I have drunk mine in my day." His strength must have been abnormal : he lived for five hours, his life oozing gradually away, his mind clear to the last, although, as he neared the end, he had to be told who they were that came to say good-bye. Sometimes he spoke of the affairs that had filled his last years, and, like other dying statesmen, sighed for the future of his country. Of de Valera, he said : " Tell my colleagues that they must beware of him in public life ; he will play down to the weaknesses of the people." He spoke of death. His wife said : " You will be with your father and Michael Collins and your little son." He smiled and pictured himself sitting on a damp cloud with a harp, arguing about politics with " Mick." A blood transfusion was given to him ; he knew there was no prospect of life, but he agreed to have it. " I'll fight, child," he said. " They are so good to me, but they know I was always a bit of a die-hard." " Do you mind dying, Kevin ? " his wife asked. A smile came over his face. " Mind dying ? Why should I ? My hour has come. My job is done." When his friend, Patrick Hogan, knelt beside him, he said : " I loved you, Hogan. Good-bye, Boss. We never had a row." Hogan whispered : " You can die happy, Kevin." The words had a magical effect, and from that moment he became quite tranquil, praying the simple prayers of childhood. Shortly before the end, he murmured : " God help the poor devils," and then he prayed again. Since early in afternoon the room had been full of people. Some stood against the walls, others knelt in prayer. A crucifix had been placed in his right hand, from which a knuckle had been shot away, so that his wife had to keep her hand pressed against the cross to hold it there.

There was silence in the room, save for the whisper of prayers and the quiet summer murmurings that came through the window from the garden. With undefeated fortitude he had looked up at his murderers that morning, as he lay on the side of the road ; and his serenity did not desert him as the hours passed and his strength ebbed away ; it lighted his face when, a few minutes before five o'clock, a doctor, taking his pulse, found that he was dead.

BIBLIOGRAPHY AND NOTES

The Irish Hansard, the Dáil Reports, start in September, 1922. The Treaty Debates are in a separate volume, and there is a report of the Dáil (16th August, 1921–26th August, 1921, and 28th February, 1922–8th June, 1922). These are referred to respectively as *Dáil Reports*, *Treaty Debates* and *Official Report*.

CHAPTER I

[1] *Dáil Reports*, Vol. 2, p. 1113.
[2] See *John Redmond* by Denis Gwynn (Harrap).
[3] *Dáil Reports*, Vol. 19, p. 395.

CHAPTER II

The material for this chapter is largely obtained from *Michael Collins and the Making of a New Ireland* by P. Beaslai (Harrap). Beaslai was in the I.R.B., took part in the Rising, 1916, and was active in the Irish-British fighting later.

[1] The Fenians originated in America, where they were trained as a militia by John O'Mahony; meanwhile, in Ireland, Stephens was organizing The Irish Republican Brotherhood. The I.R.B. and the Fenians were one and the same. The latter word fell gradually into disuse and was reserved for veterans of 1867.

[2] The trial was reported in *The Leinster Times*.

[5] I owe these prison incidents to Mr. Blythe.

CHAPTER III

[1] Sinn Fein was a political, as opposed to a physical force, organization. It attracted large numbers who had lost faith in parliamentary action, and yet did not countenance violence. It sought to restore Grattan's Parliament until 1917, when it became Republican in aim. See *The Evolution of Sinn Fein* by R. M. Henry (Talbot Press).

[2] This and other Churchillian quotations are from the chapter " Aftermath " in *The World Crisis*.

[3] *The History of the Irish Republic* by Dorothy Macardle (Gollancz), p. 271.

[4] These speeches appeared in July and August, 1919, in *The Leinster Times*.

[5] Macardle, p. 453.

CHAPTER IV

[1] *Field-Marshal Sir Henry Wilson* by Sir C. E. Calwell (Cassell), p. 271.

[2] Calwell, p. 265.

[3] Calwell, p. 263.

[4] These quotations from O'Higgins are all in letters to his wife-to-be, p. 102.

[5] *The House of Gregory* by Robert Vere Gregory (Browne & Nolan).

[6] I have this story from many people. It appeared in *The Sunday Independent* on 17th July, 1927.

[7] Macardle, p. 434.

[8] Macardle, p. 448.

[9] *The Big Fellow* by Frank O'Connor (Nelson), p. 185.

[10] Beaslai, Vol. 1, p. 327.

[11] Beaslai, Vol. 2, p. 147.

[12] *Civil War and the Events which Led to It* by Kevin O'Higgins (Talbot Press), p. 36.

CHAPTER V

[1] *Official Report*, p. 12.

[2] *Official Report*, p. 303.

[3] *Official Report*, p. 505.

[4] *Official Report*, p. 507.

[5] O'Higgins related this during the election campaign of 1927. Reported in *The Irish Times*.

[6] *Peace by Ordeal* by Frank Pakenham (Cape), p. 269.

[7] Beaslai, Vol. 2, p. 308.

CHAPTER VI

[1] This interview made a lasting impression on O'Higgins.

[2] Pakenham, p. 333.

[3] Beaslai, Vol. 2, p. 281.

[4] *Official Report*, p. 304.

[5] *Treaty Debates*, p. 7. (See Donal O'Sullivan, *The Irish Free State and its Senate* (Faber & Faber), p. 51.

[6] *Civil War and the Events which Led to It*, p. 36.

[7] *Letters and Leaders of My Day* by T. M. Healy (Thornton Butterworth), Vol 2, p. 646.

[8] *Treaty Debates*, p. 273.

[9] This and all quotations from Garvin are contained in an *Observer* article, 17th July, 1927.

[10] *Treaty Debates*, p. 42.

[11] *Treaty Debates*, p. 36.

[12] *Treaty Debates*, p. 256.

[13] *Treaty Debates*, p. 327.

[14] *Treaty Debates*, p. 334.
[15] Beaslai, Vol. 2, p. 369 ; Macardle, p. 706.
[16] *Official Report*, p. 101.
[17] *Official Report*, p. 96.
[18] *Three Years Hard Labour*, an address to the Irish Society at Oxford University in 1924.
[19] *Irish Independent*, 20th March, 1922.
[20] Darrell Figgis in *Recollections of The Irish War* (Benn), p. 138.
[21] *Irish Times*, 20th February, 1922.
[22] Griffith used similar language in the Dáil when endeavouring to hasten the election on the issue of the Treaty (June, 1922).

CHAPTER VII

[1] *Official Report*, p. 463.
[2] *Dáil Reports*, Vol. 1, p. 357.
[3] Macardle, p. 753.
[4] *Dáil Reports*, Vol. 1, p. 96.
[5] *Dáil Reports*, Vol. 1, p. 94.
[6] *Dáil Reports*, Vol. 1, p. 115.
[7] *Dáil Reports*, Vol. 1, p. 357.
[8] *Dáil Reports*, Vol. 1, p. 361.
[9] *Dáil Reports*, Vol 1, p. 386.
[10] *Dáil Reports*, Vol. 1, p. 478.
[11] *Dáil Reports*, Vol. 1, p. 480.
[12] See Donal O'Sullivan, pp. 193–4, 217–8.
[13] *Treaty Debates*, p. 338.
[14] *Dáil Reports*, Vol. 1, p. 48.
[15] *Dáil Reports*, Vol. 1, p. 571.
[16] *Dáil Reports*, Vol. 1, p. 571.
[17] *Dáil Reports*, Vol. 1, p. 574.
[18] *Dáil Reports*, Vol. 1, p. 1908.

CHAPTER VIII

[1] The words may not, of course, be exact.
[2] *Dáil Reports*, Vol. 1, p. 846.
[3] *Dáil Reports*, Vol. 1, p. 846.
[4] *Dáil Reports*, Vol. 1, p. 857.
[5] *Dáil Reports*, Vol. 1, p. 860.
[6] *Dáil Reports*, Vol. 1, p. 859.
[7] *Dáil Reports*, Vol. 1, p. 2276.
[8] *Dáil Reports*, Vol. 1, p. 2268.
[9] *Dáil Reports*, Vol. 1, p. 2405.
[10] *Dáil Reports*, Vol. 2, p. 67.

CHAPTER IX

1 *Dáil Reports*, Vol. 1, p. 1779.
2 *Dáil Reports*, Vol. 4, p. 740.
3 *Dáil Reports*, Vol. 2, p. 1295.
4 *Dáil Reports*, Vol. 1, p. 206.
5 *Dáil Reports*, Vol. 1, p. 958.
6 *Dáil Reports*, Vol. 1, p. 959.
7 *Dáil Reports*, Vol. 1, p. 961.
8 *Dáil Reports*, Vol. 1, p. 1946.
9 *Dáil Reports*, Vol. 2, p. 972.
10 *Dáil Reports*, Vol. 2, p. 1250.
11 *Dáil Reports*, Vol. 2, p. 1296.
12 *Dáil Reports*, Vol. 2, p. 1295.
13 *Dáil Reports*, Vol. 2, p. 1910.
11 *Dáil Reports*, Vol. 2, p. 11.
15 *Dáil Reports*, Vol. 2, p. 906.
16 *Dáil Reports*, Vol. 2, p. 1358.

CHAPTER X

1 *Dáil Reports*, Vol. 2, p. 2548.
2 *Dáil Reports*, Vol. 2, p. 2550.
3 *Dáil Reports*, Vol. 2, p. 2086.
4 *Eamon de Valera* by M. J. MacManus (Talbot Press), p. 230.
5 *Letters and Leaders of My Day*, Vol. 2, p. 658.
6 *Dáil Reports*, Vol. 3, p. 790.
7 *Dáil Reports*, Vol. 3, p. 818.
8 Macardle, p. 891.
9 *Dáil Reports*, Vol. 3, p. 957.
10 *Dáil Reports*, Vol. 3, p. 1986.
11 *Dáil Reports*, Vol. 3, p. 2501.
12 *Dáil Reports*, Vol. 3, p. 1000.
See a rare pamphlet (in National Library, Dublin), *The Truth About the Army Crisis*, preface by Liam Tobin, published by the I.R.A. Organization.
13 *The Real Ireland* by C. H. Bretherton (Black), p. 6.
14 I have read the findings.
15 *Dáil Reports*, Vol. 7, p. 3121.
15 *Dáil Reports*, Vol. 7, p. 3110.
17 *Dáil Reports*, Vol. 7, p. 3124.
13 *Dáil Reports*, Vol. 7, p. 3155.
19 *Dáil Reports*, Vol. 7, p. 3157.
20 *Dáil Reports*, Vol. 7, p. 3160.

CHAPTER XI

[1] *Dáil Reports*, Vol. 13, p. 5.
[2] *Dáil Reports*, Vol. 11, p. 1635.
[3] *Dáil Reports*, Vol. 4, p. 1454.
[4] *Dáil Reports*, Vol. 19, p. 400.
[5] *Dáil Reports*, Vol. 19, p. 436.
[6] *Dáil Reports*, Vol. 9, p. 148.
[7] *Dáil Reports*, Vol. 5, p. 1945.
[8] *Dáil Reports*, Vol. 5, p. 1945.
[9] *Dáil Reports*, Vol. 5, p. 1212.
[10] *Dáil Reports*, Vol. 5, p. 1980.
[11] *Dáil Reports*, Vol. 3, p. 874.
[12] *En Irlande* by Simone Tery.
[13] *Dáil Reports*, Vol. 10, p. 414.
[14] *Dáil Reports*, Vol. 14, p. 1224.
[15] *Dáil Reports*, Vol. 10, p. 1229.
[16] *Dáil Reports*, Vol. 11, p. 1944.
[17] *The Catholic Layman in Public Life :* An address to the Catholic Truth Society.
[18] *Ibid.*
[19] *Ibid.*
[20] *Dáil Reports*, Vol. 2, p. 506.
[21] *Dáil Reports*, Vol. 1, p. 1878.

CHAPTER XII

This chapter, and most of the succeeding ones, depend on memoranda and reports, conversations with the surviving actors in the events described, including Mr. MacWhite, the doyen of the Irish Diplomatic Corps. Mr. Amery read this part of the book, and, with his permission, I give his comments in the notes.

[1] Amery writes : " I rather think that on the contrary this country welcomed the participation of the Dominions in the League on the ground that their point of view would generally on big issues coincide with its own. By 1922 the recognition of the international status of the Dominions was advancing fast, though there may still have been a little stickiness over diplomatic representation apart from the League. Anyhow all that was cleared up by the Constitutional Committee of the Imperial Conference of 1926. There again I think your subsequent chapters are a little inclined to overstate and to give the impression that the British Government was forced to yield to pressure by certain Dominions, largely due to Kevin O'Higgins's personal influence. Without detracting in any way from the great impression his personality made on all of us, I think I ought to say that there was hardly anything in the outcome of those recommendations which had not been prepared beforehand and largely drafted in the Dominions Office and indeed to a very considerable extent by myself personally. The conception of complete equality of status is one for which I had worked for many years before 1926, and I have always regarded the results of the 1926 Conference,

and other subsequent conferences put into legal shape in the Statute of West-minster, at least as much my own work as that of any Dominion statesman."

[2] Amery writes : " I have no doubt that on the whole disputes between members of the British Commonwealth are best settled *inter se* in view of their fundamental similarity of outlook. But you will no doubt have noted that recently U.N.O. has been applied to by India in connection with Kashmir."

[3] Amery writes : " I do not think that the 1926 Conference regarded the Commonwealth as one sovereign State, but rather as a free association of sovereign States, constituting an association and to co-operate freely with each other. What we did in 1926 really raises a question of fundamental importance to the whole future of the world. Is there to be anything between the completely sovereign State or federation with its common external policy and a world-wide higgledy-piggledy body like U.N.O., or is not the evolution of the future to lie in nation groups whose members maintain their full sovereignty in every respect but co-operate and consult each other to a greater extent than the nations at large in view of a community of ideas, economics, geography or historical association, or constitutional outlook? I have always regarded the 1926 Conference as part of an evolution which applies just as much to Europe or to South America as it does to the British Commonwealth."

[4] Amery writes : " If I remember rightly, the objection to Fitzgerald's claim was more the fear of other nations thinking that we were trying to pack the Council than an objection to the Dominions as such."

[5] Amery writes : " Here again I think you attribute to the British representa-tives an outlook which was not really in their minds, though obviously on most of these occasions, e.g. at the Washington Naval Conference, as you point out yourself, the United Kingdom interests were in the nature of things more important."

[6] Amery writes : " I was there not to defend any British right to Mosul, but only the right of Iraq, which was recognized. It is, of course, Iraq and not the United Kingdom which exercises any authority over Mosul."

CHAPTER XIII

[1] *Dáil Reports*, Vol. 8, p. 2384.
[2] *Dáil Reports*, Vol. 8, p. 2375.
[3] *Dáil Reports*, Vol. 8, p. 2385.
[4] *Dáil Reports*, Vol. 8, p. 2518.
[5] Amery writes : " I wonder whether MacNeill's subsequent explanation really fits the facts. My recollection is that he definitely agreed, not only to the Report, but to the actual boundary, and that the fundamental divergence as to the interpretation of Article 12 was an afterthought which was not raised by him during the deliberations of the Commission. On that point I should have thought that the wording of Article 12, referring, as I think it did, to the Boundary of ' Northern Ireland,' but then already an existing constitutional entity under the Act of 1920 would have obliged an arbitrator, wherever chosen from, to regard the matter as a readjustment of an existing boundary so as to improve it from the geographical and political point of view. Certainly in the discussions which I had with O'Higgins, I do not remember his ever raising that point, i.e.

that it was anything else than the adjustment of an existing boundary, at all. He did take, what seemed to me a very curious point, namely, that while these considerations might involve reductions in Northern Ireland in one place or another, they could not involve corresponding reductions in the territory of the Irish Free State. We argued the matter at great length and in the end, if I remember rightly, he admitted that his position was indefensible, but that public opinion in the Free State would not stand any loss of territory even if it were counterbalanced by correspondingly larger acquisitions. In fact, unless I am mistaken, even with the portion of Donegal assigned for transfer to Northern Ireland, Eire would have been the gainer, both in population and in area under the Boundary Commission's report."

[6] Amery writes : " I quite agree, however, that the situation was so tense that the only alternative was to leave the boundary where it was, however unsatisfactory from many points of view. One can only wish that a similar attitude had governed the rearrangement of provisional boundaries in India."

[7] *Dáil Reports*, Vol. 13, p. 1360.

[8] *Dáil Reports*, Vol. 8, p. 1367.

[9] *Dáil Reports*, Vol. 8, p. 1369.

[10] *Dáil Reports*, Vol. 8, p. 1365.

[11] Amery writes : " You are quite right about Birkenhead. Like myself a strong defender, not only of Ulster, but of the Union, once the 1922 Treaty was signed, we were both all out to interpret it in the fullest sense and we both worked hard in favour of the financial settlement arrived at concurrently with the acceptance of the existing boundary.

" I see from my diary that the subject was discussed among ourselves on both the 2nd and 3rd December, 1925,. both Birkenhead and myself strongly advocating a settlement of the debt question. By some time late on the afternoon of the 3rd, Churchill settled with the representatives of the Free State and I went up with him, Craig and Cosgrave in a taxi from the House of Commons to the Treasury. As we got out, Craig and Cosgrave both rushed forward to pay the fare. Winston started to do the same, but I pulled him back and told him not to interfere with the first occasion in history in which the two sides in Ireland made an offer to pay for England."

[12] Amery writes : " Here again I think O'Higgins entirely failed to understand Salisbury, who was a man almost incapable of hatred, but who felt very deeply and passionately what he considered the tragedy of partition. You must remember that from the Unionists' point of view the setting up of a separate nation in what Carlyle described as ' one of God's ground plans of the Universe' was a partition or vivisection of what they felt was one nation and the partition was made only a shade less distressing when the boundary line was drawn not by the sea but at the frontier of Northern Ireland. Unlike some of us Salisbury could never reconcile himself to that fact any more than de Valera had reconciled himself to the fact that Ireland is partitioned."

[13] Lord Baldwin in a letter.

[14] Amery writes : " I quite well remember O'Higgins's persuasive advocacy of the comma and I agreed with his general outlook. I was entirely prepared to accept the wording which indicated the historical difference between Ireland and the younger members of the Commonwealth, and at the same time left the door open to eventual Irish unity."

CHAPTER XIV

[1] *Dáil Reports*, Vol. 15, p. 332.
[2] *Dáil Reports*, Vol. 17, p. 298.
[3] *Dáil Reports*, Vol. 17, p. 895.
[4] O'Higgins discussed this fully with his wife and intimate colleagues.

CHAPTER XV

[1] *Dáil Reports*, Vol. 39, p. 2310.
[2] I have Mr. James Dillon's authority for this.
[3] *Dáil Reports*, Vol. 17, p. 693.
[4] *Dáil Reports*, Vol. 17, p. 696.
[5] *Dáil Reports*, Vol. 17, p. 701.
[6] *Irish Statesman*, 27th October, 1928.
[7] *Irish Statesman*, 23rd July, 1927.

INDEX OF PERSONS

AFTERWORD

Fifty-nine years have passed since the murder of Kevin O'Higgins, and thirty-eight since this biography was first published. Looking at it now, whatever its defects, I stand over it, but I am grateful for the opportunity to add the names of his murderers, a secret when I was writing the book and a source of refreshment for malicious tongues. For the man himself I find my admiration undiminished. He was a moral force among the men who defended our infant state in conditions approaching anarchy.

What would have happened otherwise than it did, had he lived, is a tempting diversion. I can think of a few significant happenings to which he would not have given his consent had he retained unimpaired that "fearless intellect" which marked him out among his fellows. He died full of hope for his plan to cure the partition of his country. Looking at the northern scene as it is at present, I cannot see him now holding out much hope for his dual-monarchy solution. The concept of royalty has undergone a subtle change in Britain under the influence of television. At one extreme it is a national *Dallas* programme, providing a tourist attraction unmatched in any other country; at the other, it is a secular substitute for the Church.

During the Boundary talks in 1925 Kevin O'Higgins told a British civil servant that he was looking forward to the day when the Lord Mayor of Dublin would be cheered in the streets of Belfast and the Lord Mayor of Belfast in the streets of Dublin. Asked when that would be, he replied: "In ten years if I live, but they will get me before that." They did get him before that, and ten years later when the present constitution was under discussion in the Dáil, Frank McDermot proposed that the Crown be made an integral part of the Constitution in order to make a beginning of reconciliation with Northern Ireland. When put to the vote, the proposal had only three supporters, MacDermot being one of them. Would Kevin O'Higgins have added his vote? "There is no constitutional hybrid between a republic and a monarchy," he once told the Dáil. Erskine Childers had suggested one to de Valera at the time of the Treaty negotiations, and "external association" with the Crown provided him with a precarious foothold which he managed to retain. It was not de Valera who took Ireland out of the Commonwealth, but John Costello.

The names of O'Higgins's murderers have been made public only recently. Harry White, an I.R.A. veteran, has described in his memoirs how "Archie Doyle laughed as he told him how he shot O'Higgins on that warm Sunday, July 10, 1927" (as the *Sunday Press* reported). The happy man's assistants were Tim Murphy and Bill Gannon. All three are now dead. As most people who were interested had expected, the killers were I.R.A. stalwarts, but the execution was not "official" (in practice this did not matter). In part it was prompted by motives of revenge, in part by an impetus to reactivate the parent body. The Civil War was five years away; the country was beginning to enjoy peace. It was time to stir things up again. The O'Higgins murder was only a beginning; there was soon a long train of atrocities, which had reached terrorist proportions by the time war broke out in 1939.

Without the identity of his killers my O'Higgins biography was incomplete. There was one more important omission.

When I was writing the book I received every help in her power from Kevin's widow, Mrs Arthur Cox. She had his papers in exemplary order, and must I think have contemplated writing about him herself, and abandoned the project. (I must stress that the subject was much more fraught when I was writing about it then anybody nowadays could imagine.) The representative of the O'Higgins family in my briefing sessions was Tom, Kevin's brother, who had given up his medical practice and gone into politics when Kevin died. He too was helpful and candid. I came to enjoy our meetings. Then came the day when he said that he wanted me to promise not to mention any of the details he was going to give me about what happened at the Cabinet meeting when it was decided to shoot at dawn, and without trial, four I.R.A. prisoners — including Rory O'Connor, who had been best man at Kevin's wedding and was an intimate friend of the O'Higgins family. These circumstances gave fuel to the legend of Kevin's ruthlessness. He had to answer to the Dáil for the Government's awful deed, and this was the only occasion that he ever showed emotion in public. He broke down during his speech. This was tragedy in the true meaning of that overworked word. He was taking on himself responsibility for the whole Executive Council, with an inner certainty of what the consequences for himself would be.

I have described in the book what had transpired to make them act in this terrifying way, but what I was not allowed to tell was how Kevin O'Higgins reacted to the suggestion of executing the prisoners. He was appalled, and argued against it in Cabinet at great length, only agreeing after Eoin MacNeill, whom he greatly respected, acquiesced. Kevin was second last to agree, followed by Joseph McGrath, who was utterly opposed and gave in for the sake of unanimity.

This account was confirmed for me in every detail by Ernest Blythe, also a member of the Cabinet. He thought O'Higgins had been over-sensitive about the executions; in any case I was precluded from quoting him by the promise I had made to Tom O'Higgins.

The reason for Tom's embargo was that he had only known about Kevin's attitude from Patrick Hogan's diary. Hogan was Minister for Agriculture, but not as such entitled then to be present at Cabinet meetings. To me, and I should think to most people, it would have been extraordinary if Kevin O'Higgins had been able to sit down in the house he shared with Hogan, his friend and colleague, and *not* have told him about the worst day of his life. But Tom O'Higgins felt that his brother's reputation would suffer if it was known that he broke the rule of Cabinet secrecy.

This is now in the public domain; but it ought to have been in O'Higgins's biography. There it might have done something to lighten what Tim Pat Coogan has called "a certain awfulness that hung about his name".

An immediate consequence of the O'Higgins murder was the coming of de Valera and his followers into the Dáil. Emergency legislation made it compulsory that anyone contesting a General Election must pledge himself to take his seat if elected. This involved taking the Oath to the King. De Valera had opposed the ratification of the Treaty in the Dáil and lost; he had led the opposition to the Constitution and lost; he had led Sinn Féin in the General Election after the Civil War and lost; a few weeks before O'Higgins was murdered, he had led Fianna Fail at the General Election and lost. All this time he maintained that the Dáil was an illegal body, and refused to take his seat. Nothing that had happened since 1919 was valid in de Valera's book. But it was obvious — and it must have been obvious to him — that this perfectionism must end. At the time of O'Higgins's death his party was running out of political steam in any case, and de Valera's time had come. The great depression was on its way, and too much of the nation's resources had been expended on merely keeping the ship of state afloat. It was politically suicidal to insist on cuts in public expenditure, as the Cosgrave party did.

Ireland could hardly have escaped the Fascist plague. Prominent Irish Catholics openly expressed admiration for Mussolini, de Valera among them; he also described Salazar, the Portuguese dictator, as a model ruler. Franco had a large Irish following; support for his cause was for some an article of faith. This reached its apotheosis when Eoin O'Duffy, the former Chief of Police, led his legion to Spain. Communism, not Fascism, was what many people, and not only the Church, were afraid of. (After reading a paper entitled "Lenin and Laissez Faire" in Trinity College in 1932 I was called upon by the police who were anxious to know if any approaches had been made to me by suspicious-looking persons.)

While de Valera was running into ever-deepening trouble with the recrudescence of the I.R.A. in the early 1930s, the opposition was busy storing up troubles of its own by aligning itself with Fascism. If Kevin O'Higgins had been alive I believe he would have seen the danger when O'Duffy took charge of the Army Comrades Association. With Tom O'Higgins as its leader, the Association had been formed to guard Cosgrave's party at public meetings when the police were unable, or unwilling, to secure them freedom of speech. Kevin O'Higgins had had problems with General O'Duffy over indiscipline in the police, and always had reservations about him. The I.R.A. disliked him very much, and one of de Valera's gestures to the I.R.A. when he came to office had been to dismiss O'Duffy from the Garda. An all-party amalgama-

tion which attempted to defeat de Valera in July 1933 saw
Cosgrave standing down in O'Duffy's favour as leader of the new
party, United Ireland. The man had no political experience, and
his short subsequent career was a series of public embarrassments;
he disappeared from public life after his expedition to assist Franco
in Spain.

The ludicrous O'Duffy episode was the extent of significant
Irish involvement with Fascism. I cannot see Kevin O'Higgins,
had he lived, serving in a party which was led by General O'Duffy.
He has nevertheless been described as a Fascist. Conor Cruise
O'Brien has accused him of indoctrinating W. B. Yeats with that
creed, the very negation of O'Higgins's passionate devotion to
democracy. Yeats admired O'Higgins's prose style, which he
likened to Burke's. He was also impressed by the *gravitas* of the
man. O'Higgins was long dead at the time of the poet's foolish
flirtation with O'Duffy, for whom — alas — he wrote a marching
song.

Nor can I believe that if, in 1949, O'Higgins had been a member
of the inter-party government, led by his friend John Costello, he
would have agreed to the declaration of the Republic or to the
manner in which it was brought about — but then I cannot see him
as a colleague of Sean MacBride. Perhaps, had he lived, he would
have taken his place on the cross-benches, a lonely voice. De Valera
would have come into the Dáil anyhow; his style suited the people
better than O'Higgins's aloofness. In the circumstances of the
times de Valera can be seen as the leader brewed by Providence for
Irish consumption. Compare his speeches with the speeches of
Kevin O'Higgins: the repetitions, contradictions, and logical
whirlpools of the one with the classical precision of the other.

De Valera has not escaped criticism for admitting that when he
wanted to know what Irish people wanted he had only to look into
his own heart. To a great extent this claim has been justified. His
countrymen blessed him for having kept Ireland out of the war in
1939. I can picture O'Higgins arguing the case for Ireland entering
the war on the side of the Allies, as Bernard Shaw thought she
should have. On that issue, certainly, he would have been defeated
by de Valera.

With almost his last breath O'Higgins warned his colleagues

against de Valera who, he believed, would "play down to the weaknesses of the people". But I cannot see how Kevin O'Higgins, had he lived, could have deprived de Valera of the power he wielded for most of my adult lifetime, though I can see him saving his own colleagues from many far-reaching errors of judgement. He was a man with a passion for telling the truth.

TERENCE de VERE WHITE
London, 1986